On Indian Ground

A volume in
*On Indian Ground: A Return to Indigenous Knowledge:
Generating Hope, Leadership, and Sovereignty Through Education*
Joely Proudfit and Linda Sue Warner, *Series Editors*

On Indian Ground

California

edited by

Joely Proudfit
California State University San Marcos

Nicole Quinderro Myers-Lim
California Indian Museum and Cultural Center

INFORMATION AGE PUBLISHING, INC.
Charlotte, NC • www.infoagepub.com

Library of Congress Cataloging-in-Publication Data

A CIP record for this book is available from the Library of Congress
http://www.loc.gov

ISBN: 978-1-68123-912-5 (Paperback)
       978-1-68123-913-2 (Hardcover)
       978-1-68123-914-9 (ebook)

Printed in the United States of America

CONTENTS

PREFACE

ON INDIAN GROUND

A Return to Indigenous Knowledge

American Indian education has over a 150 years of contentious generalizations that supported parochial, federal, state, private, and tribal involvement in the education of American Indian youth. The formalization of culturally relevant policy, curriculum, and practice by American Indian scholars, educators, elders, and researchers is relatively recent. Currently there are available texts on the history of American Indian education, as well as specific volumes on language revitalization or curriculum development. This series is not intended to duplicate the exceptional materials currently available. Our intent is to begin to narrow the conversation and to create a readable reference that is available to educators, parents, community members, and scholars as they begin to search for answers that are culturally appropriate to the regions and tribes they serve.

We also chose to move beyond the remnants of a past that gave voice to the victimization of American Indian education. In absence of an authentic, comprehensive approach to contemporary issues and with the specific intent to create resource materials that are engaging, thoughtful, and relevant, we propose the following volumes in our series, On Indian Ground: A Return to Indigenous Knowledge—Generating Hope, Leadership and Sovereignty Through Education:

On Indian Ground: California (Proudfit and Lim)
On Indian Ground: The Bureau of Indian Education (Redman and Gipp)
On Indian Ground: The Southwest (Tippeconnic)
On Indian Ground: Hawaii (Wright)
On Indian Ground: Oklahoma (Pahdopony and Hedgewood)
On Indian Ground: Northern Plains (Gipp)
On Indian Ground: The Northwest (Jacob)
On Indian Ground: The South (Faircloth)
On Indian Ground: Northern Woodlands (Wilson)
On Indian Ground: Alaska (Lillie)

With the assistance of nationally and internationally recognized American Indian/Alaska Native/Native Hawaiian scholars, we believe that best practices need a wider dissemination among the educators who are best served by these policies and practices if we are to prepare American Indian students to be college- and workforce-ready in the 21st century.

The format of this series is designed to provide an in-depth look at topics which are relevant to all levels of education, as well as all types of schools.

These topics include the history of the state or region, policy, politics and law, tribal departments of education, early childhood education, K–12 best practices, language revitalization, postsecondary efforts, exceptional education, curriculum, counseling, technology, funding and finance, parental and community involvement, research, and evaluation. We asked our authors to engage in this scholarship with the intention that the text is readable and accessible to all who are interested. We anticipate that parents, community members, tribal educator directors, classroom teachers and administrators, elders, and community advocates will find the text useful and informative in their efforts to improve opportunities for American Indian students.

On Indian Ground: California is the first in our series. We chose to begin with California because the California Indian Culture and Sovereignty Center (CICSC) is located at California State University–San Marcos and serves over 100 tribes in California. The CICSC fosters collaborative research and community service relationships between higher education and members of tribal communities to develop and conduct research and best practices that support the maintenance of sovereignty and tribal culture. Our affiliation with CICSC created a unique vantage point for determining both the extent of the need and identifying scholars who could best address this need. Thank you for joining us in this journey.

—**Joely Proudfit**
Linda Sue Warner

INTRODUCTION

A RETURN TO INDIGENOUS KNOWLEDGE

Generating Hope, Leadership, and Sovereignty Through Education

On Indian Ground: California is the first of ten regional texts designed to narrow the focus of best practices to regional audiences. Each book in this series covers a wide spectrum of issues, policies, and practices that impact American Indian/Alaska Native/Native Hawaiian students. For this first book, we are sharing the perspectives of native scholars, researchers, and practitioners who share our vision to create opportunities for tribal youth.

In Chapter 1, "Protecting the Treasure: A History of Indigenous Education in California," Yurok, Hoopa, and Karuk Kishan Lara-Cooper traces the history of Indigenous education in California through the telling of a traditional Yurok story that includes the basket, elders, river, and villages. The story symbolizes indigenous knowledge and our reaction to socialization systems contact/genocide, relocation, colonial education, and self-determination in California. Lara-Cooper recognizes that in the face of blatant genocide, policies of enslavement and bounties to hunt California Indians, we have persevered.

Nicole Sabine Talaugon, director of programs and evaluation for the California Consortium for Urban Indian Health details the perpetuation

On Indian Ground: California, pages ix–xiii
Copyright © 2017 by Information Age Publishing
All rights of reproduction in any form reserved.

of colonialism through Indian education in Chapter 2, "History of Indian Education in California." Talaugon discusses the critical issues this climate of education creates for Native students and the consequences to their psychological development and educational attainment. This chapter is rounded out by an evaluation of contemporary efforts and challenges facing California Indians in the pursuit of educational self-determination, specifically the mandates of federal laws, creation of college level Indian education centers, and the introduction of tribal community colleges

In Chapter 3, "Navigating the System: Key Elements and Processes," Gerald A. Lieberman, an internationally recognized authority on school improvement by using natural and community surroundings as interdisciplinary contexts and an educational leader for the State of California's Education and the Environment Initiative, provides us with an overview of the roles of the many entities in California charged with developing, adopting, and implementing curriculum in the state. This chapter further goes on to provide guidance regarding how to become actively involved in decision making related to California's K–12 education system.

Nicolasa I. Sandoval, Santa Ynez Chumash education director and State of California Department of Education member, discusses in Chapter 4, "Tokoy: A Circle of Promise for the Santa Ynez Band of Chumash Indians," how her tribe exercises its sovereignty by investing in systems that ensure each community member has a clear access to educational pathways from birth to career. There are 23 American Indian Education Centers in California that are authorized by California Education Code, Article 6, Sections 33380-33383. Center staff assist schools with professional development, counseling, tutorial services, or parent education. They also provide supplemental and extended day instructional. Sandoval maps out how theSanta Ynez Band of Chumash Indians has worked with the business and education committees and education department to ensure fiscal and systematic sustainability for future generations through a well-administered education center.

In Chapter 5, we explore the "Early Learning and Best Practice in a Native American Head Start Program" from Tamara Alexander and Mikela Jones. This chapter represents diverse experiences in working with native students. Alexander demonstrates best practices in early education through creating learning opportunities for the whole family and ensuring that the environment of the classroom fosters cultural growth and enrichment. Jones surveys the needs of middle school and high school students through examining the need to address trauma and establish meaningful and trusting relationships with students and families over time.

Dr. Melissa Leal, Esselen and Ohlone, advises readers about the foundations of "K–12 Best Practices: Creating Successful American Indian Students" in Chapter 6. She reviews her experiences as a tutor and an administrator in creating a practical plan for meeting the needs of Native students. Her recommendations incorporate strategies for cultural con-tinuity, community-wide engagement, positive relationship building, and extracurricular youth empowerment. Several practical considerations are included, such as transportation, as key factors contributing to student and programmatic success.

In Chapter 7, "Teaching Truth: Social Justice for California Native Stu-dents," Joely Proudfit and Nicole Lim expand upon the experiences of In-dian students in the classroom. Lim chronicles her journey raising a daugh-ter who faces adversity from her educators and peers. She introduces the pressures faced by Native students in attempting to correct misrepresenta-tions and stereotypes, including the hardships of being labeled as "overly sensitive" or the so-called "Native American expert" for the class. Proud-fit examines the statewide impact of stereotypes across California public schools in the adoption of Indian mascots and the dominant culture's ac-ceptance of racism against Native Americans as the status quo.

Chapter 8, "Revitalizing Critically Endangered Languages in California: Case Study and Promising Practices," Kumeyaay Theresa Gregor and Stan-ley Rodriguez showcase the work of a variety of California Indian language teachers and community members working in language revitalization throughout the states. Gregor and Rodriguez surveyed members from the Living Language Circle, an annual meeting started by the Yocha de he Win-tun and Santa Ynez Chumash to bring together California Native Language teachers in an annual forum. The authors provide us with case studies from a variety of tribal communities ranging for northern, central and south-ern California. The efforts made by the Hoopa Valley Tribe; Yocha de he Wintun Nation; Tuolumne Me-Wuk Band of Mewuks and the Iipay/Tiipay Language Immersion at Kumeyaay Community College are a testimony to the resilience and persistence of California Indian languages.

In Chapter 9, Warner and Proudfit review the options for higher educa-tion for California native students. This chapter, "Higher Education in Cali-fornia," draws heavily from the recent reports published by the California Indian Culture and Sovereignty Center at California State University–San Marcos. These reports have been integral to the work at the Center and have influenced policy, including the annual Report to Tribal Nations at CSUSM. The reports were funded by the San Manuel Band of Mission In-dians as part of their commitment to tribal youth and are widely acknowl-edged as the standard that other state offices should replicate. Proudfit and Warner note that California, as the state with the largest identified popula-tion of American Indians and the widest system of postsecondary institu-tions available, still has work to do to increase the proportionate number of graduates.

In Chapter 10, "A Multilogical Approach to Giftedness: Creating a Space for Indigenous Knowledge," Yurok, Hoopa, and Karuk Kishan Lara-Cooper explores the community's concepts of giftedness, which are distinct from Western concepts of giftedness. Lara-Cooper writes that schools need to approach education from a community context, incorporating Indigenous knowledge. Lara-Cooper examines the concept of giftedness as defined and practiced by the Hoopa Valley Indian Reservation located in Northern California. The intent of this chapter is to emphasize the significance of acknowledging and validating indigenous knowledge, embracing diversity, and thinking multilogically whereby indigenous knowledge is recognized, endorsed, and considered through its own theoretical lens.

Nicole Lim, Pomo, conducts an analysis of California's existing educational materials in Chapter 11, "Assessing California State Curriculum and Its Impacts on K–12 Students." Lim discusses the creation of educational myths and stereotypes regarding Mission and Gold Rush eras under the framework of genocide. She identifies common themes and relates them to patriotic motivations and romanticized justifications. Lim also provides strategies for revising the curriculum and adopting unified educational goals for teachers.

In Chapter 12, "Counseling: Cultural Components to Counseling and Advising," Andre P. Cramblit highlights counseling and advising in a historical context and showcases successes in working with Native students in California. Cramblit makes a case for the importance of having a culturally competent academic counselor who works closely with tribal needs to meet the needs of their students.

In Chapter 13, "Miromaa: Awakening California Tribal Languages in Digital Spaces," Tomio Endo conveys his experiences working on a community-wide language revitalization project for the California Indian Museum and Cultural Center. Endo illustrates how a partnership between an Aboriginal Language Center in Australia and a statewide Indian museum led to the creation of six mobile applications for introductory language learning. He examines how technology is being re-envisioned to empower language advocates to create new and affordable digital tools that make language learning accessible to broader segments of California of tribal communities.

Chapter 14, "Funding, Finance, and School Accountability," was compiled by Laura Lee George. Our goal for this chapter was to provide some real numbers on what exactly is funded and financed in support of American Indian education from both the state and federal government. It was both a struggle and challenge to find an authoritative voice to address the numbers specifically. The chapter's author, Karuk Laura Lee George, has a long history in education as a retired and former director of the Indian Teacher and Educational Personnel Program, Klamath–Trinity Unified School District superintendent, and business manager for Klamath–Trinity Unified School District that encompasses the Hoopa, part of the Yurok Reservation, and Karuk country. George provides us with an overview of the federal and state legislative changes in funding and financial practices and measurements for accountability for schools in California.

In Chapter 15, "Parents and Tribal Community Efforts," Tishmall and Hunwut Turner review case studies of how California tribal communities are reclaiming educational content and advancement for native students. They explore a diversity of tribal schools, programs, and nonprofits engaged in ensuring that tribal cultures, languages, stories and parents are active participants in their children's classrooms. Case studies include the Pechanga Chámmakilawish School, the All Tribes American Indian Charter School on the Rincon Indian Reservation, the Rincon Indian Education Center, the Southern California Tribal Chairmen's Association graduation program, and the Inter-tribal Young Men's Camp. These authors explore how leadership and community activism contribute to educational success, cultural sensitivity, continuity and enrichment for both students and teachers.

Deborah Morton's Chapter 16, "Educational Research: Using a Health-Based Model," focuses on both the need for culturally relevant research and the use of tribal institutional review boards (IRBs) to create capacity in local communities.

Linda Sue Warner's Chapter 17, "California Urban Indian Education," is noteworthy because the author was unable to find an exemplar at the K–12 level. Other states have American Indian charter schools in urban areas; however, the districts with the largest enrollment of American Indian students do not use this strategy. If urban educators are to incorporate American Indian/Alaska Native culture or language in their curriculum, the only strategy available to them is the incorporation of cultural values and the inclusion of tribal perspectives using native ways of knowing.

In the final chapter, "Addressing 'Anti-Indian' Historical Bias in California Public Schools through Better Practices," Sabine Nicole Talaugon investigates how California Indian education policies can be informed by challenges and successes of other states that have sought reform. She examines the impacts of multicultural educational theory on California public school curriculum and evaluates viable strategies for consideration, such as the adoption of "essential understandings," or a state constitutional amendment. This chapter is offered as a way to leverage existing ideas into new solutions; we hope that it will serve as a catalyst for change.

We are honored that these educators and scholars continue to support promising practices in California and believe you will find valuable resources here to continue the work to improve opportunities for American Indian/Alaska Native/Native Hawaiians in our state. Your feedback is welcome as well. You may contact the series editors at CICSC@csusm.edu.

—Joely Proudfit
Nicole Lim

CHAPTER 1

PROTECTING THE TREASURE

A History of Indigenous Education in California

Kishan Lara-Cooper
Humboldt State University

Many generations ago, along the Klamath River, there lived a wise woman who wove the most beautiful baskets known to humankind. Her baskets were woven so tight that water could not penetrate them. She was aging and had many experiences to share. Through prayer, she began to weave a basket for the people. The wise woman worked day after day, weaving, praying, and singing. As her strong hands moved gracefully over her materials, she shared a story to be retold, a song to be sung again, and a lesson to be learned. When she finished, she had created a large beautiful basket bowl. She placed the basket in the river at Weitspus (a Yurok village), where two rivers join together, and stood silent as the basket began its journey. The basket seemed to tip-toe across the gentle breakers; it moved along more quickly as it hit the swift currents, and swirled ever so purposefully into the eddies. Round and round, the basket turned through the trials and tribulations of the water and then burst free into the swift, shallow flow of the river. All life that swam below watched with great interest. Although the villagers lived within their own unique environments, each village anticipated the basket's presence. The old woman understood the human need for knowledge and contribution.

On Indian Ground: California, pages 1–18

As such, the people picked up the basket, rejoiced in the lessons, and they too added prayers and allowed the basket to continue its journey. After many stops, the basket reached Requa, the mouth of the Klamath River. It made three final spins, reflecting a ceremonial journey, and drifted its way over the rough water of the mouth and into the belly of the Pacific Ocean. All that the basket had to offer made its final journey into the sunset, where it exists eternally. (Lara, 2006, p. 103)

This story has been with the Yurok people of northern California since time immemorial. In one of the many interpretations of this story, the river mirrors time and the villages symbolize different generations and the phases of history that each generation encountered, including Indigenous knowledge and socialization systems, contact/genocide, relocation, colonial education, and self-determination (Lara, 2006).

INDIGENOUS KNOWLEDGE AND SOCIALIZATION SYSTEMS

Indigenous communities have always had their own knowledge, pedagogy, and child-rearing practices. Despite stereotypes of "Indian time" and "Indian summer," Indigenous communities are very orderly, with specific hunting, gathering, and ceremonial calendars. Prior to contact, teaching was provided in a safe and nurturing environment by parents, extended family, and community. Children were taught methods of survival, oral tradition, custom, and how to live in balance with the world. It is important to note that each California tribe has its own homeland, creation stories, and place of origin (where they came into creation) (Kawagley, 1995; McCarty & Lomawaima & McCarty, 2006). In northern California, for example, the Natinixwe (Hoopa Valley Tribe) story of origin describes their creation at *Takimildin* (a village). The Natinixwe believe that they have always been in the valley (*Natinixw*) and oppose the "land bridge theory" or theories of migration. As such, the *xonta nikya:w* at *Takimildin* has been carbon-dated 8,000–12,000 years (Nelson, 1978).

The exact population of Indigenous Californians prior to contact is unknown; however, Juan Cabrillo (a voyager of southern California in 1542 and 1543) frequently noted in his journal the "dense population" of Indigenous Californians (Stannard, 1992). Population estimates range from 300,000 (Stannard, 1992) to 1 million (Norton, 1979). Regardless of the exact number of Indigenous Californians, it is undisputed that these peoples had their own villages, trading systems, agriculture, trails, and forms of land stewardship prior to European contact.

Just as Indigenous peoples have always had their own worldviews and epistemologies to sustain them, the wise woman (from the story) had valuable knowledge to preserve for future generations. "Through prayer, she began to weave a basket for the people . . . her baskets were woven so tight that water could not penetrate them. . . . She placed the basket in the river . . . and stood silent as the basket began its journey" (Lara, 2006, p. 103). The treasures woven into the basket would help the people to survive what was yet to come.

CONTACT/GENOCIDE

Although Columbus arrived in Hispaniola in 1492, he never traveled to the main continent; nor did he ever set foot in the state of California. As a matter of fact, Indigenous peoples of California did not have contact with non-Indigenous peoples until the late 16th century and in some northern areas of California, contact was not made until the mid-19th century. Consequently, California has a unique and diverse history. An Indigenous California elder states, "We were fortunate in that we were not exposed to non-Natives until much later than the rest of the country, however [sic] we were less fortunate in that the government was very good at their tactics by the time they reached us" (Lara, 2009, Interview Participant 12). Norton (1979) adds that by the time settlers reached California, they had confidently developed an attitude of privilege, entitlement, and justification for their genocidal acts.

Cabrillo in 1542, Drake in 1579, Aguilar in 1602, and Vizcaino in 1603 were among the first to voyage to the California coast. According to their journals, Indigenous Californians met them with open arms, provided them food, and cared for them when they were sick (Stannard, 1992). In return, Indigenous peoples were exposed to violence and disease. Stannard (1992) states, "In raping native women and merely breathing on native men, the marching Spanish soldiers spread syphilis and gonorrhea, smallpox and influenza, everywhere they went" (p. 134). These diseases took a devastating toll on the Indigenous population; this decline impacted the Indigenous population for the next century (Stannard, 1992).

Perhaps the most comprehensive contact with non-Indigenous peoples began in southern California in 1769 when the Franciscan missionaries were established and in northern California in 1849 upon the discovery of gold. The interactions with non-Indigenous people during these times were nothing less than genocide. The legal definition of genocide is defined in Article III of the 1948 Convention on the Prevention and Punishment of Genocide as "any of the following acts with intent to destroy, in whole or in part, a national, ethnical, racial, or religious group, as such":

1. Killing members of the group
2. Causing serious bodily or mental harm to members of the group

3. Deliberately inflicting on the group conditions of life calculated to bring about its physical destruction in whole or in part
4. Imposing measures intended to prevent births within the group
5. Forcibly transferring children of the group to another group. (preventgenocide.org)

Each of the aforementioned criteria have been common practice in California history.

For example, in southern California, the Mission San Diego de Alcalá became the first of 21 Franciscan missions established in 1769. Franciscan missions were founded by the Roman Catholic Church and led by Father Junipero Serra (1713–1784) to "create a civilization from wilderness" (Costo & Costo, 1987, p.1). Spanish troops captured and herded Indigenous Californians to the missions to be imprisoned, baptized, and often killed (Stannard, 1992). In a study of more than 11,000 Chumash children who experienced the Santa Barbara, La Purisima, and Santa Ines missions in the late 18th century, data analysis shows that missions were "furnaces of death" (Stannard, 1992, p. 137). Stannard (1992) elaborates:

> Thirty-six percent of those Chumash children who weren't yet two years old when they entered the mission died in less than twelve months. Two-thirds died before reaching the age of five. Three of four died before attaining puberty....In short, the missions were furnaces of death. (Stannard, 1992, p. 137)

California missions continued from 1769–1834. During this period of time, the Indigenous Californian birth rate decreased to 3.5%, the death rate increased to 70–85%, and the overall population of Indigenous Californians decreased by 50% (Shipek, 1987).

In northern California, in 1848, on P. B. Reading's journey through the Hoopa Valley, he discovered gold along the Trinity River. By 1850, the year that California became a U.S. state, hundreds of thousands of miners and land speculators had traveled to the northern coast of California from San Francisco. Norton (1979) states:

> These aggressive invaders of the 1850s saw the valleys and forests as obstructions to their goal of Manifest Destiny. They were instructed by scripture, they said, reinforced by success, and driven by rank individualistic will, to believe they were destined to be civilizers of the earth. They were charged to go forth upon this earth and subdue it; this was their belief and the foundation of their religion. (p. 3)

Consequently, in 1849 there was an estimated population of 1 million California Indians. By 1900, the estimated population of California Indians had decreased to 17,000 (Norton, 1979). Within 50 years of European contact, 983,000 Indigenous men, women, and children were murdered or died due to European-introduced diseases.

Despite treaties that guaranteed Indian safety and protection, the State of California paid $1 million for Indian scalps (Forbes, 1968). In San Francisco in 1852, Governor Peter Burnett stated in his annual message, "A war of extermination will continue to be waged between the races until the Indian race becomes extinct" (Forbes, 1968). This message not only encouraged the military, but also the local settlers to plan their attacks on Indigenous Californians. Likewise, California residents raised $400,000 in bonds to pay for militia expeditions (Forbes, 1968). In many instances, local residents would raid villages during ceremony or late in the night when families were sleeping. The "Indian Island" massacre of the Wiyot people in 1860 occurred during their ceremony to pray for the continuance of mankind and the renewal of the world. On February 29, 1860, the *Northern Californian* wrote:

> Whites had taken their boats again and left the island without being observed by any persons except those in league with them. But the spectacle they left behind them was horrible. Blood stood in pools on all sides; the walls of the huts were stained and the grass colored red. Lying around were dead bodies of both sexes and all ages from the old man to the infant at the breast. Some had their heads split in two by axes, others beaten into jelly with clubs, others pierced or cut to pieces with bowie knives. Some struck down as mired; others had almost reached the water when overtaken and butchered. (Norton, 1979, p. 82)

The "Indian Island" massacre is one of many horrifying genocidal acts within what became the State of California. Regardless of an 1855 law that forbid Indians to possess guns, the attacks of a defenseless people continued for the next 50 years. The *Alta California* newspaper reported, "The attacking party rushed upon them, blowing out their brains, splitting their heads open, little children in baskets [baby carriers] and even babies had their heads smashed to pieces and cut open" (Forbes, 1968).

In addition to murder, nearly 10,000 Indigenous Californians were indentured or sold as slaves between 1850 and 1863 (Norton, 1979). On April 22, 1850, an Act for the Government and Protection of Indians "established within its twenty various sections, the mechanism whereby Indians of all ages could be indentured or apprenticed to any white citizen" (Norton, 1979, p. 44). Although the act was amended to make kidnap, sale of children, and indentured servitude illegal in 1860, the practice continued for several more years (Heizer, 1974). Heizer and Almquist (1971) summarize their findings of indentures from 1860–1863:

> Ages of 110 persons indentured range from two to fifty, with a concentration of 49 persons between the ages of seven and twelve. Seven are listed as "taken in war" or "prisoners of war." ... Four children of ages eight, nine, ten, and eleven are listed as "bought" or "given." Ten married couples were indentured, some of them with children. Three individuals seem almost too young to have been so treated—Perry, indentured in September 1863 at the age of three; George, indentured in January 1861 at the age of four; and Kitty (November 1861), also four years of age. (p. 53)

From 1855 to 1864, there were multiple accounts of kidnapping and selling of Indigenous Californians. Natinixwe (Hoopa) children, for example, were kidnapped and sold in the local town for $25 each (Nelson, 1978). A letter from an Indian Agent to the Superintendent of Indian Affairs says, "I have just learned that a man ... has stolen a woman and two boys ... and intends to sell them or trade them for cattle which has been much practiced as of late." Another letter reads, "The Spanish stole twenty or twenty five young women and killed one" (Heizer, 1974, p. 226).

Despite the multiple attempts by both the government and California residents to "exterminate" Indigenous Californians, it is important to note that their efforts were unsuccessful. The basket (from the opening story) survived European inflicted disease, the Franciscan missions, murder, rape, and slavery, and "it moved along more quickly as it hit the swift currents, and swirled ever so purposeful into the eddies" (Lara, 2006, p. 103).

RELOCATION

The relocation of Indians began with the Indian Removal Act of 1830, where tribes were forcibly removed from their homelands. Between 1832 and 1843, Eastern tribes that had already been relocated to reservations were relocated, once again, further west. In California, settlers wanted the "Indians" relocated as the eastern tribes had been. However, the concept of relocation posed a dilemma in California, since there was nowhere further west to relocate (Nelson, 1978). Despite the dilemma, the government identified two choices:

> It could "exterminate" all of the native peoples, or it could place them on reservations and "domesticate" them. The second, they argued, was far more practical, since it would be "cheaper to feed the whole flock for a year than to fight them for a week." (Norton, 1979, p. 49)

On April 8, 1864, the California Indian Reservation Act mandated the establishment of four reservations throughout the state of California "to organize Indian affairs" and "constitute one Indian superintendency" (California

Indian Reservation Act, 1864). It was declared that each reservation "shall be located as remote from white settlements as may be practicable" and each reservation must be supervised by an appointed Indian agent (California Indian Reservation Act, 1864). Indigenous men, women, children, and elders were violently stripped from their homelands and herded on foot to their designated reservation. A Lassik woman from northern California, Lucy T'tcetsa Young, was a young girl at the time of European contact. In the following oral account, she describes when she and her people were forcibly removed from their homeland and relocated to the Hoopa Valley Indian Reservation. She states:

> You ask 'bout father. He got killed and brother in soldier war, before soldier captured us. Three days fight. Just blood, blood, blood. . . . White people want our land, want destroy us. Break and burn all our basket, break our pounding rock. Destroy our ropes. No snares, no deerskin, flint knife, nothing. . . . It was in August. Soldiers had all Inyan together. Gonta takum to Hoopa. (Smith, 1990, p. 128)

Some elders and children did not survive the hundred-plus-mile journey, while others attempted to run away and were captured. Once arrived to the reservation, individuals were forbidden to bear arms, which kept them from not only protecting themselves but also from self-sufficiency and food subsistence. Consequently, each person had to rely on the rations of salt, sugar, flour, and eventually alcohol, provided to them. In some of the transitional stations, Indigenous families were encased in barbed-wire fencing and fed like animals from troughs.

In addition, reservations were meant to "domesticate" Indigenous people. Consequently, agriculture[1] and Christianity were heavily imposed. During the period of relocation, many Indigenous peoples died of homesickness, malnourishment, disease, and abuse. However, the resiliency of Indigenous Californians persevered. As Costo and Costo (1987) states, "Despite the rapacity of three invasions—Spanish, Mexican, and American, the natives have stubbornly fought to keep their place on this spot of earth" (p. 9). Likewise, the basket (from the opening story) kept afloat and "tiptoed across the breakers" (Lara, 2006, p. 103).

COLONIAL EDUCATION

When settlers from Spain, Great Britain, and France arrived in the United States, they interpreted Indigenous child-rearing practices, beliefs, and customs as heathen, savage, and unhealthy (Swisher, 1999; Szasz, 2003). Thus, following the era of genocide and relocation, colonizers made it their mission to purify Indigenous people by educating them. The purpose of early

education for Indigenous peoples was to "give service to the colonial government" while shifting away from Native worldviews and epistemologies
(Kawagley, 1995). Cajete (2006) adds that "much of what Native people
have to offer has been ignored or trivialized. Western culture, through its
own unique play of history, disconnected itself from the natural world in
order to conquer it" (p. 211).

In 1879, Lieutenant Richard Henry Pratt started the first off-reservation,
government boarding school in Carlisle, Pennsylvania. From 1867–1875,
he commanded the Black Tenth Calvary troops (Reyhner & Eder, 2004),
at which time he transferred to Fort Marion to manage "Indian" prisoners.
He theorized that an "Indian" could be transformed into a civilized human
being, by stripping him of his "Indian" identity. Pratt theorized, "Transfer
the savage-born infant to the surroundings of civilization, and he will grow
to possess a civilized language and habit" (Smith, 2007). Consequently, he
collected Indigenous prisoners from Fort Marion and other areas and took
them to Hampton Institute, a boarding school for African Americans. As
the civilization experiment continued, Lieutenant Pratt contended that it
would be more efficient to civilize children than adults.

To accomplish this task, hundreds of children were separated from their
parents, taken from their homeland, and forced into Carlisle Indian School.
Later, Indigenous Californians were sent to Hoopa Boarding School (which
opened in 1896) and Sherman Institute (which opened in 1902). Upon
arrival, children were stripped of their traditional regalia, given a haircut,
supplied uniforms, administered an English name, and forbidden to speak
their native language (Szasz, 2003). A boarding school survivor recalled
"seeing boys' spirits broken as their braids, literal ties to their Tribal identity
and holding spiritual power, fell to the floor" (Hopkins, 2013).

The boarding schools operated on a military schedule, with exercise
drills, bells, and disciplinary action. Students spent the day learning vocational trades and providing manual labor.

The philosophy of the boarding school experience was to "Kill the Indian, save the man."[2] In other words, in order to create a human being out of
an Indian child, you must strip them of their worldview, Indigenous knowledge, cultural identity, and even their family. Boarding schools operated
under the belief that parents are detrimental to the civilization process.
John Ward, an Indian agent, stated, "The parents of these Indian children
are ignorant, and know nothing of the value of education, and there are no
elevating circumstances in the home circle to arouse the ambition of the
children. Parental authority is hardly known or exercised among the Indians in this agency" (Bear, 2008). Accordingly, children were kidnapped and
taken as far away from their homelands as possible. Although parents knew
where to find them, Indians were recognized as wards of the government in
1896. Therefore, Commissioner Daniel Browning ruled that Indian parents

did not have parental powers over the decision of whether or where their children attended school. Although this ruling was ended by the Secretary of Interior in 1902, the philosophy continued for years to come. A school teacher in 1929 shares her story of an Indian boy who would not attend school. The boy lived with his grandmother, an Indian doctor, along the river. Minerva Salisbury states in Deike (2003):

> Mrs. Sarver decided that she was going to make the boy attend school. She would do this by going to the Grandmother's house and spanking the boy, she had (me) accompany her as a witness. When (we) got to the house, Evelyn grabbed the boy and gave him ten good lashes with a leather belt. He did not resist and his grandmother just sat and watched. Evelyn informed the boy and his grandmother that he was to be at school or she would give him another spanking and bring the police from Eureka. The boy did attend school every day after the spanking. (p. 136)

The above journal entry illustrates the powerlessness of a highly educated (from a community context) grandmother to protect her grandson from the lashings of a stranger in his own home. Even today, there is a notion embedded in the educational system that "teacher knows best." This monological thinking is deeply rooted in the era of the boarding school system (Lomawaima, 2015)

Another driving force to fulfilling the philosophy of "kill the Indian, save the man" was that "all Indians are savages that need to be civilized" and "that civilization requires Christian conversion" (Lomawaima, 1999, p. 2). As a result, children were given biblical names and were expected to convert to Christianity. Hence, Pratt stated, "In Indian civilization, I am a Baptist, because I believe in immersing the Indians in our civilization and when we get them under, holding them there until they are thoroughly soaked" (Native Words Native Warriors, n.d.). In addition, children were forbidden to speak their native tongue. Winnie George, a student at Hoopa Boarding School in the 1920s, shares her experience. Winnie says in Deike (2003):

> They didn't allow any of us kids to speak to one another in Indian.... They didn't allow us to speak Indian at all. We had to speak English at all times. We had to do extra work if we spoke Indian—like iron, or sweep the floor, or scrub the floor.... They actually had a little jail down there on the bottom. Sometimes, if they was real bad, they'd spend two, three days in there—sometimes one week. (p. 54)

Children who attempted to speak their home language in boarding school were punished by having hot needles stuck through their tongue, having their mouths washed out with soap, given extra chores, or being put into the prison. Since many of the boarding schools were remodeled forts, the schools often had a jail or a dungeon where students were punished.

In the summer months, an additional assimilation tool was instituted; children participated in an outing system where they were placed into "White" homes to be assimilated into mainstream society. Students learned to cook, to serve, and to sew. In many circumstances, the outing system led to servitude.

In 1898, Estelle Reele, the Superintendent of Indian Schools (1898–1910), encouraged basket making in the boarding school for the purpose of sale. Likewise, it was permissible for Indigenous Californian women to make basketry for income purposes. Lomawaima and McCarty (2006) refer to this concept as the "safety zone." Indigenous expressions of worldview, such as language, songs, basketry, or weaving are considered "acceptable," when they are classified by people of power as "safe" or nonthreatening. Consequently, if baskets are made for retail value and not cultural value, then the art of basket weaving is safe and allowed in the school system (Lomawaima & McCarty, 2006, p. 116). Although the safety zone fulfilled a need for many students who hungered for the opportunity to connect with Indigenous culture (even it wasn't their own), it also fostered a sense of consumption, appropriation, and entitlement among mainstream society.

In addition to being stripped of their families, culture, identity, and language, perhaps the most vile act that Indigenous children were exposed to was the "inhumane physical brutality, sexual abuse, and child rape that took place in boarding schools...at the hands of the priests, nuns, and other staff" (Hopkins, 2013). Recent studies and survivor testimonies have exposed that:

> There are thousands of Native children in both the United States and Canada who never returned home from boarding and residential schools; their small, bruised, and broken bodies yet unaccounted for. There are even reports of children who were murdered while still newborns, that their families never knew existed. The babies, who died without names, were the product of rape, when priest assaulted girls and impregnated them. (Hopkins, 2013)

During the boarding school era, at least 100,000 Indigenous children passed through the boarding school system, 50% of these children perished (Hopkins, 2013). Children died of disease, homesickness, and abuse. Lakota John Fire wrote in his memoirs of attending boarding school at fourteen years old in 1917:

> [I]n these fine new buildings Indian children still commit suicide, because they are lonely among all the noise and activity. I know a ten-year-old who hanged herself. These schools are just boxes filled with homesick children. The schools leave a scar. We enter them confused and bewildered and we leave them the same way. When we enter school we at least know that we

are Indians. We come out half red and half white, not knowing what we are. (Reyhner & Eder, 2004, p. 190)

The boarding school experience had shattering effects on Indigenous children, families, and communities that resulted in intergenerational trauma, epigenetics, and internalized colonization. Alternatively, Indigenous people survived and the basket's journey continued, "round and round, the basket turned through the trials and tribulations of the water and then burst free into the swift, shallow flow of the river" (Lara, 2006, p. 103).

SHIFT IN POLICY/ SELF-DETERMINATION

In 1928, the Meriam Report, subtitled as "The Problem with American Indian Administration," recognized the grossly inadequate conditions of Indian education; the culture and language of Indigenous peoples was not recognized, the schools were falling apart, they were run by non-Indigenous employees, and they were far away from Indigenous homelands. Castagno and Brayboy (2008) contend that the Meriam Report was "perhaps the first officially recognized call for Culturally Responsive Schooling (CRS)" (p. 944). To improve Indian education, the Meriam Report recommended a humanistic approach to teaching, bilingual and bicultural programs, community day schools, and the recruitment of Native American teachers. "Although the Meriam Report was a clear call for change, little change occurred until more than 30 years later" (Castagno & Brayboy, 2008, p. 945).

In 1934, the Johnson O'Malley (JOM) Act was passed as part of the New Deal to subsidize education. With the passage of the JOM Act, public schools were established on Indian lands. Later, in 1969, the Kennedy report, titled *Indian Education: A National Tragedy—A National Challenge*, exposed public school issues, such as high dropout rates, low achievement, and lack of teacher support toward Indigenous students. As a result of Indigenous activism and Civil Rights reforms, a shift of legislation bloomed in the 1960s and 1970s. In 1967, the California Indian Education Association was founded to address the needs of Indigenous students (Forbes, 1969). The 1972 Indian Education Act established the Office of Indian Education and provided funding to public schools, Indigenous tribes, and adult education programs. Also in 1972, the Havighurst report exposed a need to include Indigenous peoples in defining Indian education. Thus, the 1975 Self-Determination and Educational Assistance Act authorized Indigenous tribes to contract with the federal government to operate their own educational systems. Likewise, the 1978 Tribally Controlled Community College Assistance Act granted funding for tribally controlled higher education programs.

Furthermore, the 1990 Native American Languages Act (NALA) acknowledged the federal government's responsibility to ensure the survival of Native American languages and cultures and declared Native American tribes the right to use their languages as a medium of instruction in the classroom.

A year later, in 1991, Native scholars, educators, and administrators prepared the *Indian Nations at Risk* report. The report called for the recognition of the federal government's legal and moral obligation for American Indian education through its "trust responsibility."[3] Later, in 1992, the Indian Nations at Risk task force, along with other Native delegates, planned and attended the White House Conference on Indian Education. The goal of the conference was to establish a national board of Indian education, as well as to make recommendations to improve Indian education (Reyhner & Eder, 2004). In 1998, the needs of Indian education were further addressed in Executive Order 13096, also referred to as "The Comprehensive Federal Indian Policy Statement." The executive order addressed six goals to improve and expand Indian education, as presented by Reyhner and Eder (2004):

1. Improving reading and mathematics
2. increasing high school completion and postsecondary attendance rates
3. reducing the influence of long-standing factors that impede educational performance, such as poverty and substance abuse
4. creating strong, safe, and drug-free school environments
5. improving school science education
6. expanding the use of educational technology. (p. 318)

The Indian Nations at Risk Task Force, the White House Conference on Indian Education, and the Executive Order 13096 are distinctive in that they were motivated and articulated by Indigenous peoples themselves.

As Wilson (2006) suggests, "American investment in Indian education, when it is substantial, when it is consistent, and done in a manner where Indian families, parents, have to take ownership of their educational destiny, it works" (p. 6). Having an understanding of the legislation that supports the integration of language and culture in the classroom, parent and community involvement, student support services, and the preparation of Indigenous teachers is integral to shifting the paradigm of education from a monological[4] to a multilogical[5] epistemology. "Although the villagers lived within their own unique environment, each village anticipated the basket's presence. . . . As such, the people picked up the basket, rejoiced in the lessons, and they too added prayers and allowed the basket to continue its journey" (Lara, 2006, p. 103).

Why Is History Important?

Although some may argue that "history is in the past," "Natives use history as a crutch," or "it was a long time ago, get over it," it is important to note that educational and developmental research indicates that there is a direct correlation between historical, social, and cultural contexts of the educational system and the astounding statistics of Indigenous populations in contemporary society. Like "the old woman understood the human need for knowledge and contribution," society must understand the dangers of a single narrative. As Trafzer (2013) says:

> As of 2012, the State Department of Education denies the genocide, so do many residents of California. The general public of California is unaware of the genocide of Indian people because the state of California, major publishers of social studies programs for children, and authors of textbooks refuse to write about the murders, kidnappings, rapes, and slavery. (p. 80)

Exposure to multiple narratives of California history (a) acknowledges that Indigenous people have always had their own forms of education and child-rearing practices; (b) exposes political and cultural oppression, genocide, forced assimilation, and religious conversion that undoubtedly had an impact on the current social and emotional state of Indigenous people; (c) recognizes that the government has a moral and legal obligation through its trust responsibility to Indigenous people; and (d) identifies reports and legislation that support the integration of language, culture, and community involvement in education. Since it (e) addresses resiliency and responsibility, and (f) creates a space for healing; exposure to multiple narratives of California history is not only critical for non-Indigenous peoples, it is also imperative for Indigenous peoples. For example: At the end of a semester-long course on the historical, social, and cultural contexts of American Indian education, an Indigenous student commented in his self-reflection:

> My favorite part of this course was that it helped me to understand myself. I learned that genocide, relocation, boarding schools, and intergenerational trauma have all influenced my life's experiences. Now I realize that the hardships and abuse that I experienced as kid was not my fault. I wasn't a bad kid. I didn't deserve it. My grandparents raised me the way that they were raised in the boarding school. I understand that choices that I made in my life only played out the stereotypes. For some reason, I always believed that those stereotypes were my destiny. Most important, I learned that cycles can be broken.

Often, Indigenous peoples do not have an opportunity to heal because they are silenced or their experiences are minimized when they attempt to share. Consequently, individuals may begin to internalize their experiences. Norton (1979) argues that "[i]n the telling and in the listening, humanity meets." In other words, exposure to a multilogical perspective of historical experiences creates a space for healing and rehumanization of both Indigenous and non-Indigenous peoples.

Furthermore, in California, there are 122 federally recognized tribes (U.S. Census Bureau, 2000). In accordance with "trust relationship," in exchange for the land, the federal government is responsible for (a) protecting Indigenous lands, including water, fishing, and hunting rights; (b) providing beneficial services, including medical and dental care, educational assistance, and emergency food and housing; and (c) preserving tribal autonomy, including enhancing self-determination and protecting tribal cultures (Harvey, Harjo, & Welborn, 1995, p. 173). Consequently, it is important to note that, although education is generally a state responsibility, through its trust responsibility, the federal government accepts responsibility for Indian education through the Bureau of Indian Affairs (Warner, 1999). Wilson (2006) states:

> The United States has a sacred trust responsibility to educate the Native American. And this trust grew out of contractual agreements between Indian nations and the United States, in which sovereign Indian nations gave up millions of acres of the richest land in the world in exchange for continued self-rule, continued inherent sovereignty, health, housing, and yes indeed, education.... Will America's legacy in Indian education be meaningless chaos or will it be one of direct action with coherent vision for what Indian country needs? Only through empowering and involving Indian country can we overcome the great challenges of our time.... This is the birthright of Native children, and we will accept nothing less. (p. 20)

CLOSING REMARKS

Indigenous students consistently rank below average in high school completion, standardized test scores, grade point average, college admittance, school attendance, college completion, and representation in gifted and talented programs (Castagno & Brayboy, 2008). In addition, the Indigenous population has a higher alcoholism rate (514%), suicide rate (1000%), diabetes incidence (177%), tuberculosis incidence (500%), drop-out rate (51%), and youth arrest rate (300%) than the national norm. Furthermore, violence accounts for 75% of deaths for Indigenous youth ages 12–20; 79% of youth in the Federal Bureau of Prison's custody are Indigenous; and Indigenous youth attain the lowest level of education of any racial or ethnic group in the United States.

From an educational perspective, these statistics are due to the lack of culturally specific academic and student support services, the fact that education doesn't reflect the philosophies and worldview of indigenous communities, and the fact that the historical foundation of education is not acknowledged (Brayboy, 2005; Cajete, 2006; Kawagley, 1995; Manuelito, 2005; McCarty, 2002). Furthermore, the pathway to healing involves confronting the pain. Consequently, multiple historical narratives are critical to the healing process. Unresolved grief has everlasting effects that can be connected to intergenerational trauma, epigenetics, and internalized colonization.

Although Indigenous Californians may have some of the most alarming statistics in the world, they are resilient. In the face of blatant genocide, bounties to hunt them, policies to enslave them, authority to kidnap them, and the entitlement to physically and sexually abuse them, Indigenous Californians persevered.

The basket that the old woman wove (in the opening story) contained the treasures of the people, including the songs, language, history, stories, and lessons. Throughout each phase of education, Indigenous Californians fought to survive. During the phase of genocide, the population of Indigenous Californians decreased from 1 million to 17,000 in a 50-year period. Ten thousand of those survivors were committed to slavery. During the phase of relocation, Indigenous peoples were torn from their homelands to become "domesticated." During the phase of colonial education, children were traumatically taken from their families and stripped of everything that they loved. With the strength of the treasure, also referred to as genetic memory, the people persisted. It is critical to acknowledge that every living Indigenous Californian is a direct descendant of one of the 17,000 survivors of genocide. Like the basket that flowed down the river, the treasures of their people flow through their veins.

In the current phase of self-determination, Indigenous Californians strive to pick up the basket, rejoice in the lessons, and make a contribution for future generations to come. Language revitalization programs; restoration of ceremony; revival of basket-making and regalia-making; and preservation of culture, homeland, and Indigenous knowledge are all efforts to protect the treasure.

As the basket's journey continued, "it made three final spins, reflecting a ceremonial journey, and drifted its way over the rough water of the mouth and into the belly of the Pacific Ocean. All that the basket had to offer made its final journey into the sunset, where it exists eternally" (Lara, 2006, p. 103).

NOTES

1. Many Indigenous communities already had their own forms of land stewardship and "agriculture."

2. Colonel Richard Henry Pratt's motto of boarding schools
3. In the late 18th century, Indigenous tribes were considered independent nations. Hence, the 1787 Northwest Ordinance Act declared that "the utmost good faith shall always be observed toward Indians; their lands and property shall never be taken from them without their consent; and in their property rights, and liberty they never shall be invaded or disturbed" (Pevar, 1992, p. 3). Nevertheless, in 1871, the government put an end to treaty making and initiated statutes, laws passed and enforced without the consent of Indigenous tribes. However, between 1787 and 1871, the United States government entered into hundreds of treaties with various Indigenous tribes. The Supreme Court has ruled that these agreements have established a "trust relationship" or responsibility between Indigenous tribes and the federal government. This "trust responsibility" is a legal obligation under which the U.S. accepts responsibility to preserve, provide, and protect.
4. Perpetuates the "kill the Indian, save the man" mentality.
5. Embraces diversity, validates Indigenous knowledge, and creates a space for Indigenous students to make a connection between their home and school teachings.

REFERENCES

Bear, C. (2008, May 12). American Indian boarding schools haunt many. Retrieved from http://www.npr.org/templates/story/story.php?storyId=16516865

Brayboy, B. M. (2005). Toward a tribal critical race theory in education. *The Urban Review, 37*(5), 425–446.

California Indian Reservation Act. (1864, April 8). Retrieved from http://www.standupca.org/gaming-law/unique-federal-indian-law-california-specific/1864 Four Reservations Act.pdf

Castagno, A. E., & Brayboy, B. M. (2008). Culturally responsive schooling for Indigenous youth: A review of literature. *Review of Educational Research, 78*(4), 941–993.

Cajete, G. (2006). It is time for Indian people to define Indigenous education on our own terms. *Tribal College Journal, 18*(2), 56–57.

Costo, R., & Costo, J. H. (Eds.). (1987). *The missions of California: A legacy of genocide.* San Francisco, CA: Indian Historian Press.

Deike, E. (2003). *History of Humboldt County schools.* Eureka, CA: Pacific Lumber Company.

Forbes, J. (1968). *Handbook of Native Americans of California and Nevada.* Sacramento, CA: Naturegraph.

Forbes, J. (1969). *Native Americans of California and Nevada.* Sacramento, CA: Naturegraph.

Harvey, K., Harjo, L., & Welborn, L. (1995) *How to teach about American Indians: A guide for the school library media specialist.* Westport, CT: Greenwood Press.

Heizer, R. F. (1974). *The Destruction of California Indians.* Lincoln, NE: University of Nebraska Press.

Heizer, R. F., & Almquist, A. F. (1971). *The other Californians: Prejudice and discrimination under Spain, Mexico and the United States to 1920.* Berkeley, CA: University of California Press.

Hopkins, R. (2013, March 25). *Sexual trauma: One legacy of the boarding school era— Ruth Hopkins.* Retrieved from http://lastrealindians.com/sexual-trauma-one -legacy-of-the-boarding-school-era-ruth-hopkins/

Johnston-Dodds, K. (2002). *Early California laws and policies related to California Indians.* Sacramento, CA: California Research Bureau.

Kawagley, A. (1995). *Yupiaq worldview.* Prospect Heights, IL: Waveland Press.

Lara, K. (2006). American Indian Studies Association—Student Association. *Wicazo Sa Review, 23*(2), 103–104.

Lara, K. (2009). *Conceptions of giftedness on the Hoopa Valley Indian Reservation* (Unpublished doctoral dissertation). Arizona State University, Tempe, AZ.

Lomawaima, K. T. (1999). The unnatural history of American Indian education. In K. Swisher & J. Tippeconnic (Eds.), *Next steps: Research and practice to advance Indian Education* (pp. 1–32). Charleston, WV: Clearinghouse on Rural Education and Small Schools.

Lomawaima, K. (2015). Education. In R. Warrior (Ed.), *The world of Indigenous North America* (pp. 365–387). New York, NY: Routledge.

Lomawaima, K. T., & McCarty, T. L. (2006). *To remain an Indian: Lessons in democracy from a century of Native American education.* New York, NY: Teacher's College Press.

Manuelito, K. (2005). The role of education in American Indian self-determination: Lessons from the Ramah Navajo community school. *Anthropology and Education Quarterly, 36*(1), 73–87.

McCarty, T. L. (2002). *A place to be Navajo: Rough Rock and the struggle for self-determination in Indigenous schooling.* Mahwah, NJ: Erlbaum.

Native Words Native Warriors. (n.d.). Boarding schools: Struggling with cultural repression. Retrieved from http://americanindian.si.edu/education/code-talkers/html/chapter3.html

Nelson, B. (1978). *Our home forever: The Hupa Indians of Northern California.* Hoopa, CA: Hupa Tribe.

Norton, J. (1979). *Genocide in northwest California: When our worlds cried.* San Francisco, CA: Indian Historian Press.

Pevar, S. L. (1992). *The rights of Indians and tribes: The basic ACLU guide to Indian and tribal rights* (2nd ed.). Carbondale, IL: Southern Illinois University Press.

Reyhner, J., & Eder, J. (2004). *American Indian Education: A history.* Norman: University of Oklahoma Press.

Shipek, F. C. (1987). Saints or oppressors: The Franciscan missionaries of California. In R. Costo & J. H. Costo (Eds.), *The Missions of California: A legacy of genocide* (pp. 29–47). San Francisco, CA: Indian Historian Press.

Smith, A. (2007, March 26). Soul wound: The legacy of Native American schools. Retrieved from http://www.amnestyusa.org/node/87342

Smith, E. (1990). *Lucy Young: Indian/White relations in northwest California, 1846– 1944* (Unpublished master's thesis). University of California–Santa Cruz.

Stannard, D. E. (1992). *American Holocaust.* New York, NY: Oxford University Press.

Swisher, K. (1999). *Next steps: Research and practice to advance Indian education.* Charleston, WV: Clearinghouse on Rural Education and Small Schools.

Szasz, M. C. (2003). *Education and the American Indian: The road to self-determination since 1928.* Albuquerque, NM: University of New Mexico Press.

Trafzer, C. (2013). Silencing California Indian genocide in social studies texts. *American Behavioral Scientist, 58*(1), 64–82.

Warner, L. S. (1999), Education and the Law: Implications for American Indian/ Alaska Native Students. In K. G. Swisher & J. W. Tippeconnic (Eds.), *Next Steps: Research and Practice to Advance Indian Education* (pp. 53–80). Charleston, West Virginia: Clearinghouse on Rural Education and Small Schools.

Wilson, R. (2006). National Association of Indian Education: State of Indian Education Address. Paper presented at the State of Indian Education Address, Washington, DC.

The White House: Office of the Press Secretary. (1998, August). Executive Order 13096: American Indian and Alaska Native education. Retrieved from http:// www.pub.whitehouse.gov

CHAPTER 2

HISTORY OF INDIAN EDUCATION IN CALIFORNIA

Sabine Nicole Talaugon
Iwex Consulting

American Indian education is tainted by a history of cultural genocide and assimilation. While American Indians have, in many ways, regained their power to educate future generations, what is often taught in conventional schooling remains antithetical to our sovereignty and truth. This chapter explores the history of American Indian education in California, from the times of blatant assimilation tactics through decades of increased American Indian involvement in education, as well as the persistent problem of mis-representation of American Indian history and contemporary existence in the current public school system.

As the vast majority of American Indian students are taught at conventional public schools in California, our representation in this education system matters. This chapter discusses points in history that continue to be grossly misrepresented in contemporary conventional schooling, such as the mission era, Manifest Destiny, and the gold rush. This is in order to demonstrate how education is used to hide the faults of colonization and the power in traditional ways of living. Stereotypes promoted through

On Indian Ground: California, pages 19–31
Copyright © 2017 by Information Age Publishing
19

education can alienate Indian students, leading to psychological withdrawal from their education, cultural dislocation, and lowered ability to perform to their best capacity and negatively affecting overall Indian educational attainment (Locke & Lindley, 2007).

Prior to colonization, education occurred as an informal community effort where each community member played a role in teaching information, discipline, morals, manners, and generosity (DeJong, 1993). Among California tribes, similar to other indigenous people of North America, knowledge is considered a virtue and ignorance a vice because respect requires wisdom (Blackburn, 1975). California Indian youth traditionally learned their tribal history, physical science, athletic abilities, etiquette, their roles in taking care of their families, religion, and healthcare by imitating and doing (DeJong, 1993). This way of learning contrasts dramatically with Western modalities.

This chapter focuses on the education of Indians by non-Indians, in an attempt to document the efforts of colonial education to end self-determination and self-education and to celebrate the ways that we as Indian people have resisted their efforts and continue to fight.

MISSIONS

> Here are aborigines whom we are teaching to be men, people of vicious and ferocious habits who know no law but force.... [T]hey are a people without education, without government, religion or respect for authority, and they shamelessly pursue without restraint whatever their brutal appetites suggest to them. Their inclination to lewdness and theft is on a par with their love for the mountains. Such is the character of the men we are required to correct, and whose crimes we must punish. (Father President Fermín Francisco de Lasuén, 1801, as cited in Archibald, 1978)

The Spanish missions mark the beginning of western education and cultural genocide for California Indians. Spain established 21 missions in tribal territories of California between 1768 and 1853. Each mission was about 15 square miles of land, and they regarded themselves as self-supporting agricultural and industrial schools. Missionaries sought to mold California Indians into a colonial labor force, through means of enslavement and indoctrination into Christianity. These means were arguably forms of education, in their effort to "civilize" indigenous people. Missionaries and their soldiers separated families and forced men, women, and children to work long hours to maintain the mission and military outposts. California Indians suffered many forms of torture, including laboring in chains, starvation, dog attacks, flogging, and rape (Dunbar-Ortiz, 2014). Resistance was prominent in the missions; every mission experienced an uprising or guer-rilla attacks from the outside (Dunbar-Ortiz, 2014).

Today, many textbooks say that the purpose of Spanish missionaries was to "improve" the lives of California Indian people. This motivation stands on the basis that California Indian people were inferior to European peo-ple, and that Indian religions, cultural values, economies, and governing structures needed to be civilized. In fact, the primary motive of missionaries was not to improve Indians' lives, but control the natural resources and hu-man capital to secure the Spanish empire in America. California Indians' forced labor at missions limited the costs of stationing soldiers in Califor-nia. Not only do social science and history curricula continue to idealize the California missions, but they also omit any Indian experience after the mission era, thereby keeping Indian people "stuck in time," validating old stereotypes of inferiority and extinction.

MANIFEST DESTINY

United States history books often begin with the glorified concept of Mani-fest Destiny, paired with an image of the painting *American Progress* by John Gast, where the *spirit of America*, depicted by a glowing white woman, leads settlers west. The U.S. government had to create stereotypes about Ameri-can Indians to justify the Manifest Destiny concept that led to forced and coerced relocation through treaties, among other destructive policies. To-day, these concepts, which are founded on the belief in American cultural and racial superiority, continue to be celebrated by history and social sci-ence textbooks.

One major piece of misinformation that supported the goals of Manifest Destiny and the "doctrine of discovery" was the view that few Indigenous people lived on the continent. Images of "virgin wilderness" and "roaming nomads" occupied the minds of Europeans and continue to occupy the pages of many textbooks. This inaccuracy serves to justify the "settling" of the land, rather than highlighting the violent conquest. This misrepresen-tation makes invisible the struggles and resilience of American Indian peo-ple. This puts American Indian students in the position to defend the truth and risk repercussions, or to keep silent and risk internalizing stereotypes.

THE GOLD RUSH

Today, the gold rush is often glorified in history textbooks, omitting the devastation that it caused California Indian people. The horrid reality of Manifest Destiny was particularly evident during the California gold rush of

1849. Some of the most degrading stereotypes were created during the California gold rush and "westward expansion," including the idea that Indians were violent and warlike. Other than attempts to protect their land, homes, and communities, there is no evidence that Indians made unprovoked war upon settlers (Henry, 1970). During the gold rush, the awful *digger* stereotype was applied to many central and northern California Indians (i.e., Maidu, Nisenan, Miwok, Washo, Tokut), portraying them as dirty impediments to progress (Lonnberg, 1981). These stereotypes justified genocidal policies such as legal enslavement of California Indians and federal troops and agents killing Indians to make land available to settlers. These policies created the public sentiment that it was honorable for pioneers to kill Indians (Aguirre & Turner, 2010). Many local municipalities offered bounties for Indian heads, Indian scalps, or Indian ears. The state of California authorized more than $1 million for the reimbursement of expenses for killing Indians. The Indian population in California in 1846 was estimated to be around 150,000, and by 1860 it was 30,000. The historical trauma of these events survives in the blood memory of California Indians today. By making invisible the trauma that occurred during the mission and gold rush periods, the education system rhetorically closes down opportunities for students to understand their communities' struggles, leading to increased silence around mental health issues caused by historical trauma.

BLATANT ASSIMILATION

Western education is built on the concepts of individualism, competition, and time, which are oppositional to traditional ways of life. Western teaching requires written word, daily classroom routine, and indoor study, which are far from the oral tradition and experiential learning that were the basis for traditional education (DeJong, 1993).

Government-funded, Protestant-influenced boarding schools mark the beginning of U.S. sanctioned educational assimilation of Indians into American society. In the 1860s, the federal government began establishing boarding schools and reservation day schools. These schools aimed to replace indigenous languages with English and traditional cultures with the White American way of life. In the words of Richard H. Pratt, founder of the first off-reservation Indian boarding school, Carlisle Indian Industrial School, boarding schools were intended to "kill the Indian and save the man." These schools forbade children to speak their indigenous languages and to practice their religions. The school administrators kept them away from other children from their tribe, and students were beaten if they spoke their languages. Prior to colonization, California was one of the most linguistically diverse places in the word, but California Indians were forced to learn to speak Spanish at the missions and then forced to only speak English at boarding schools and thereafter. A Bureau of Indian Affairs (BIA) employee stated that the boarding school system consisted of "penal institutions—where little children are sentenced to hard labor for a term of years for the crime of being born of their mothers" (Fraser, 1999, p. 99).

By the 1870s, the government operated schools at Hoopa Valley, Tule River, and Round Valley Reservations; as a result, resistance to schools quickly developed. In 1882, Indians at the Round Valley Reservation began a rebellion against the schools, burning the schools twice in 1883, again in 1912, and once more in 1914. Indians also destroyed a school in Potrero in 1888 and burned a school at Tule River in 1890.

Attendance at Indian schools was made mandatory in 1891. The BIA operated two boarding schools and twelve reservation day schools in California at this time. The Greenville Indian school was purchased by the government in 1897 and made into an agency with jurisdiction over American Indians in Butte, Plumas, Sierra, and Yuba Counties. Fort Bidwell Indian School was established in 1898, primarily serving the Pit River and Paiute Tribes as both a school and agency of the BIA until 1930. Perris Indian School opened in 1892 and was later transferred to the Sherman Institute in 1902 in Riverside, California.

California Indian people recognized the assimilative intentions of these schools. According to the United States Department of the Interior (1891), an agent from Tule River said that Indian parents were "indifferent if adverse to education" (p. 221), and an agent from Hoopa expressed that the parents "wish their children to grow up as Indians and they say 'school is no good to Indians'" (p. 224). Indian communities continue to deal with boarding schools' long-lasting and profoundly negative influences on their mental health and cultural connection.

Boarding schools continue to contribute to social dysfunction in American Indian communities in California today. Child abuse, including sexual abuse and corporeal punishment, scarred the victims of boarding schools. According to a study by Comant, Schultz, Robbins, Dorton, and Rivera-Colmant (2004), parenting became particularly difficult for survivors of abuse in boarding schools. One respondent said,

> My stepfather went to Riverside and he made us clean up. I learned later in life that he never learned how to nurture. All he knew was, basically, a military-type life he learned at boarding school. So I grew up, even at home, with someone who basically is a military person. So, I had to deal with that. (Comant et al., 2004, p. 28)

Another respondent reflected on the boarding school impact on erasure of culture:

My grandpa told us he wouldn't teach us anything because they used to wash out his mouth out with lye soap. . . . And my grandpa even said that they just cut his braids off. Made him wear those wool clothes, he said; made him wear those boots. And they couldn't talk. Even brothers and sisters couldn't talk. They wouldn't teach us. In fact, my grandparents would threaten us with Indian school if we acted up. (Comant et al., 2004, p. 27)

It was not until the 1970s that the assimilationist nature of these schools began to shift to incorporating culture and self-determination into its educational programming. Presently, Sherman High School hosts an average of 300 to 500 students who come from reservations throughout the U.S., and it continues to be funded entirely by the U.S. Department of the Interior, BIA, and the Bureau of Indian Education.

In 1887, to further the assimilationist agenda, Congress passed the General Allotment Act (Dawes Act) to dissolve Indian reservations. As a result, Indians throughout the U.S. lost 90 million acres of land. The Dawes Act contributed to the late 19th-century and early 20th-century efforts to integrate Indian students into public schools. In 1866, school districts were allowed, but not required, to admit *half-breed* children with White guardians into public schools. In 1874, as a result of Ward v. Flood, Indian children could attend White schools if no *colored* school was located in the district. These legal decisions did not require schools to be inclusive, though, and fewer than 100 Indian students were enrolled annually in non-Indian schools at this time (Wollenberg, 1978). Later, the BIA attempted to sponsor Indian students at non-Indian schools with little success. The few districts that accepted Indian students only cooperated because they were so small and needed the money. One agent reported that when Colusa County allowed one Indian student to enroll in elementary school with Whites in 1909, the White parents boycotted the school until the Indian child was withdrawn. The state legislature backlashed at the federal government's attempt to pin the education of Indian children on the state and created a law in 1921 that further limited Indian students' access by prohibiting Indian students who lived within three miles of an Indian school from attending non-Indian schools.

In 1924, Alice Piper was denied access to Big Pine School because she was an Indian, and her parents sued the school. Although the court ruled that her 14th Amendment rights were not violated based on her citizenship under the Dawes Act, Congress granted citizenship to all Indians the same day, allowing her and other Indian students to integrate into public schools. In 1931, more than 2,800 Indian students were enrolled in California public schools, while the seven Indian-only schools enrolled only 92 students (Wollenberg, 1978, p. 98). The Piper v. Big Pine case was later used as precedent in Brown v. Board of Education.

THE BEGINNINGS OF SELF-DETERMINATION

In the 1920s, the greater public began to acknowledge that the government's assimilationist agenda was not working for American Indians, in large part due to the Meriam Report, which had more influence on policy than other reports of its kind. In 1928, the Wright Institute published this report, bringing to national light the problem of forced assimilation that Indian communities were experiencing since the 1830s. The report criticized the Department of Interior's implementation of the Dawes Act and conditions on reservations and in Indian boarding schools: "It seems as if the government assumed that some magic in individual ownership of property would in itself prove an educational factor, but unfortunately the policy has . . . operated in the opposite direction" (DeJong, 1993, p. 134).

The report recommended many changes in federal policy toward Indians, including the replacement of the boarding school system with local day schools. The report called for culturally appropriate education in keeping with the philosophy of progressive education, which was becoming popular at the time. The Meriam Report reflected the accounts of the 1926 report by the Commonwealth Club that focused on Indians in California. The Commonwealth Club report had little positive to say about California's Indian schools, reporting that the Sherman Institute was "by far the best," yet it was still based on the "conception that the Indian is inferior to the Whiteman. . . . Every Indian girl is viewed as a potential house servant and every boy as a farm hand" (Kelsey, 1909, p. 422).

In 1934, the Johnson O'Malley Act (JOM) also represented movement away from the assimilationist agenda, which increased the BIA subsidies to pay for Indian students to attend public schools and allowed the BIA to consult with state educational agencies rather than dealing with individual districts as issues arose. The increased subsidies were intended to cover costs in lieu of local property taxes, and the BIA's statutory ability to work with state agencies was intended to more efficiently address Indian students' issues in public schools as community hostility and school administrators' indifference to Indian needs impacted public school teachers' treatment of Indian students (DeJong, 1993). California was the first state to sign a JOM contract, which phased out most of California federally run Indian schools.

Despite the lofty efforts of JOM to improve education for Indian students through easing the friction between Indian students and White school districts, effective implementation of the advocacy efforts proved bureaucratically difficult. Although many California Indians were satisfied with the program, the superintendent of Indian education in California, Mary Stewart, had severe difficulty in implementing the program, and when she retired in 1941, the state abolished her position (DeJong, 1993). The JOM funds were discontinued in the 1950s, and replaced by federal funds that attempted to relieve the burden of "impacted areas," including those with Indian reservations. Despite these programs' attempts at helping Indian students, the issue of schools' treatment of Indian students was not fixed, and there was never enough oversight to track whether schools actually spent the these funds on Indian students or if the funds went to their general expenses. Although Indian enrollment in public schools had greatly increased by the 1960s, dropout rates for Indians were as high as 50% in some counties, contributing to high unemployment and poverty rates in among our communities.

MOVING TOWARDS REAL SELF-DETERMINATION

With the 1960s and 1970s, the Indian self-determination movement spurred increased community involvement and action in Indian education. In the spirit of self-determination, the California Indian Education Association was founded in 1967 to elevate the voices of Indian communities in education. The association held the first all-Indian, Indian-controlled education conference in the U.S to discuss the problems of Indian youth in both Indian schools and public schools. The association successfully lobbied for restoration of the JOM funds.

In 1970, the American Indian Historical Society evaluated textbooks used in California schools and published a book in which 32 Indian scholars, historians, and students examined more than 300 social studies books. With this book, the American Indian Historical Society campaigned against the Indian stereotypes promoted in the public school curriculum.

Over the years, many universities and colleges have been incredible partners in improving Indian education. In the 1960s, Native American studies programs were established at several California colleges and universities, providing Indian students with much-needed services and support, in addition to allowing the Indian people to learn and tell their own stories. In 1966, Humboldt State University (HSU) established its commitment to Indian communities by establishing the Center for Indian Community Development to provide services and outreach to tribal communities. In 1969, the Office of Indian Education funded a program to increase the number of Indian teachers in public school classrooms, thereby making classrooms better for Indian students and influencing them to go to college. This program helped Native teachers acquire their bachelors and teaching credentials, with courses in Native American experience, Native American education history, and social historical implications. HSU later expanded the program to include other educational personnel because they felt that teachers were too isolated and did not have enough leadership influence. The Title VII funding for this particular program continued until the late

1980s. Today, HSU houses a support program for Indian students that provides outreach, academic advising, and advocacy for students. Additionally, HSU's Center for Indian Community Development continues to work to improve educational experiences for K–12 Indian students. HSU is not the only university to step forward in the name of Indian education, but it provides a prime example of how universities have been leaders in improving both education about Indian people and Indian self-education.

California's first tribal college was founded in 1971. Deganawidah-Quetzalcoatl University (DQU), near Davis, California was formally incorporated as a college for Indians and Chicanos to provide alternative ideas and methods of education. The purpose of DQU was to preserve and reinstitutionalize traditional Indian values, to perpetuate and exercise Indian religion and beliefs, to establish the Native American Research Institute, to develop field-based educational delivery systems to Indians who cannot attend the school itself, and to maintain social and personal support systems for DQU students and staff. DQU was the site of the first American Indian International Tribunal, which put the United States on trial. The government cut off DQU's financial aid and the institution ceased offering classes in 2005, but there is currently an effort to revitalize DQU.

Self-determination also became a goal at the national level. In 1969, the Kennedy Report criticized coercive assimilationist policies, pointing out the policies' harmful effects on the education of Indian children and strong negative influences on national attitudes towards Indians. This report urged increased Indian involvement in the education system but did not look beyond the scope of education. The report was of the thought that increased Indian involvement would be a cure-all for the poverty and health issues that the communities faced (DeJong, 1993, p. 196).

In 1972, the Indian Education Act was applied to the California education system. This act was the first legislation to provide direct financial support for the education of Indians students in public, tribal, and BIA schools. The Indian Education Act provided specialized programs in education for Indians through the establishment of the Office of Indian Education and the National Advisory Council on Indian Education and authorized a formula program and several competitive grant programs for Indian children and adults.

California enacted multiple pieces of legislation in the 1970s in an effort to improve Indian education. In 1972, California Assembly Bill 872 was enacted to establish the Bureau of Indian Education in the California State Department of Education, and California Senate Bill 1258 was enacted to authorize the Native American Indian Early Childhood Education Program for 10 rural school districts to raise the academic achievement of Indian students in kindergarten through fourth grade. In 1974, SB 2264 was enacted, establishing the California Indian Education Centers Program to improve academic achievement in basic skills such as reading and mathematics and to help Indians better develop self-concept. Additionally, the American Indian Higher Education Consortium was established to provide technical assistance to developing Indian colleges.

The federal government officially sanctioned the movement towards Indian self-determination in 1975, when the Indian Self-Determination and Education Assistance Act became law. The purpose of this act was to help tribes self-govern and control their own resources through contracts with the federal government for the operations of BIA and Indian health service programs. With respect to education, the Indian Self-Determination and Education Assistance did two things. First, it gave tribes control over the BIA-operated schools, which had little impact in California because there were few schools left that were operated by the BIA. Second, it made amendments to JOM, including a key amendment to create advisory boards made up of parents of Indian children for schools that receive federal funds through the program.

In 1978, the Education Amendments Act became law, declaring, "It shall be the policy of the BIA in carrying out the functions of the Bureau, to facilitate Indian control of Indian affairs in all matters relating to education" (Chapter 22). The act anticipated major changes, such as control of schools by Indian school boards and direct-line authority of the BIA education director over programs and personnel. This legislation was enacted due to the hard work of tribes and Indian organizations such as the Coalition of Indian Controlled School Boards, the National Indian Education Association, National Congress of American Indians, and the Native American Rights Fund. In California, The American Indian Education Council was reinstated to advise the California Superintendent of Public Instruction on Indian education concerns.

Although in many ways, tribal self-determination legislation did not translate directly into tribal control over education in California, Indian community members and leaders became more involved in education and successfully influenced the education of Indian students.

INTO THE NEW MILLENNIUM

Through the 1990s, efforts to improve tribal self-determination continued, but simultaneously policymakers were making efforts to downsize the federal government, leading to budget cuts. Despite the federal government's ongoing official trust obligation and government-to-government relationship with tribes, the Indian population continues to have problems with poverty, low socioeconomic indicators, and low educational achievement (Aguirre & Turner, 2010). Additionally, consultation has not been initiated on all matters that impact the wellbeing of Indian people. At times when tribes have been consulted with, they often do not have the resources to leverage their political power because there are no uniform mandates governing how consultation can be satisfied.

Title VII of the Elementary and Secondary Education Act of 2001 (now the No Child Left Behind Act, or NCLB) reinforced the intentions of the 1972 Indian Education Act. The funding provided by NCLB intends to support tribes, school districts, educational organizations, and postsecondary institutions to meet Indian students' unique academic and cultural needs. Similar to JOM funds, NCLB provides financial assistance to school districts that are affected by federal activities that reduce the tax funds available for schools, including those that educate children who live on Indian reservations. Critics of NCLB have argued that its inflexible requirements make it difficult to promote tribal consultation and that its standardized testing requirements prevent the promotion of multicultural education (Freng, Freng, & Moore, 2007).

In terms of Indian education, NCLB funding is primarily dedicated to American Indian education centers, which are organizations that serve school districts with American Indian students. They provide tutoring for Indian students, cultural programs, academic advising, student advocacy, and outreach to teachers to provide resources to make classrooms more inclusive. Unfortunately, there are fewer than 30 of these centers throughout the state, which does not accurately reflect the distribution of Indian students. In 2006, California Senate Bill 1710 required the California Department of Education to create the American Indian Education Oversight Committee (AIEOC) to provide technical support and administrative oversight to American Indian education programs in order to ensure that American Indian students in California public schools meet the academic standards set forth by the federal No Child Left Behind Act of 2001.

From 2007–2012, funding for language instruction in public schools was made available through the Esther Martinez Native American Languages Preservation Act, to counteract the assimilation committed by the U.S. government. According to the National Council of American Indians, language instruction can been shown to promote higher academic success for students who participate in Native language immersion programs compared to their peers. Language revitalization efforts have been growing throughout California, despite lack of federal funds to support the activities. Many tribes and tribal organizations are working hard to learn more about their languages through linguists and spreading the knowledge to their community members.

President Obama signed the Every Student Succeeds Act (ESSA) of 2015 on December 10, 2015, which reauthorizes the Elementary and Secondary Education Act of 1965 and replaces the 2001 No Child Left Behind

Act. ESSA requires states and local educational agencies (LEAs) to engage in meaningful consultation with tribes or tribal organizations in the development of state plans for Title I grants. Further, LEAs must consult with tribes before making any decision that affects opportunities for American Indian/Alaska Native students in programs, services, or activities funded by ESSA. Title of VI, or the Indian Education title, of ESSA can potentially fund Native language immersion programs in public schools. ESSA also allows tribes to enter into cooperative agreements with states and LEAs to run and operate Title VI programs on tribal lands. ESSA also requires that data from standardized achievement tests must be disaggregated, which will create an opportunity to hold the state accountable to American Indian scores.

Although policy-makers have made many efforts to address the impact of anti-Indian bias in education, much of the curriculum in K–12 public schools continues to affirm Euro-American narratives, and delegitimize cultural practices and knowledge of Indian people. Studies of Indian representation in textbooks have found that although blatant racist language has been removed, depictions of American Indians still promote stereotypes through omission, misrepresentation, and simplification of information regarding American Indians (Marquez, 2011). Studies of textbooks have found that representation often perpetuates the ideas of inferiority, the *noble savage*, and more recently the privileged *casino Indian* (Hawkins, 2005). When inaccurate historical information about American Indians is perpetuated in California classrooms, Indian students begin to accept this negative image of themselves. Additionally, the historical misrepresentation of California's history erases the historical trauma that California Indians suffer as communities and individuals and deepens the stigma around the mental health issues that we face and that impact our educational attainment.

Currently, California does not have any specific state laws that ensure that Indian history, culture, and governance are accurately represented in K–12 curriculum. This does not mean that all school districts or teachers uniformly teach without consulting the local tribal entity, an academic institution with supplemental resources. In fact, some teachers go out of their way to locate resources from these organizations in order to balance their history lessons.

Fortunately, our American Indian people remain resilient in their efforts to educate our American Indian youth about their true histories and culture. Over time and through hard work, the efforts of California Indian people and their allies will improve Indian education both for and about Indian people.

REFERENCES

Aguirre, A., & Turner, J. (2010). *American ethnicity: The dynamics and consequences of discrimination* (2nd ed.). Boston, MA: McGraw-Hill.

Archibald, R. (1978). Indian labor at the California missions slavery or salvation? *The Journal of San Diego History, 24*(2), 172–182. Retrieved from https://www. sandiegohistory.org/journal/1978/april/labor/

Blackburn, T. C. (1975). *December's child: A book of Chumash oral narratives.* Berkeley, CA: University of California Press.

Comant, S., Schultz, L., Robbins, R., Dorton, J., & Rivera-Colmant, Y. (2004). Constructing meaning to the Indian boarding school experience. *Journal of American Indian Education, 43*(3), 22–40.

Committee on Labor and Public Welfare. (1969). Indian education: A national tragedy—A national challenge (Kennedy Report). Retrieved from http://www. narf.org/nill/resources/education/reports/kennedy/toc.html

DeJong, D. H. (1993). *Promises of the past: A history of Indian education in the United States.* Golden, CO: North American Press.

de Lasuén, F. F. (1965). *The writings of Fermín Francisco de Lasuén* (Vol. 2, F. Kinneally, Ed.). Berkeley, CA: Academy of American Franciscan Library. (Original work published 1801)

Dunbar-Ortiz, R. (2014). *An Indigenous peoples' history of the United States.* Boston, MA: Beacon Press.

Education Amendments Act, 25 U.S.C, § 2011 (1978).

Fraser, J. W. (1999). *Between church and state: Religion and public education in a multicultural America.* New York, NY: St. Martin's Press.

Freng, S., Freng, A., & Moore, H. (2007). Examining American Indians recall of cultural inclusion in school. *Journal of American Indian Education, 46*(2), 42–57.

Hawkins, J. (2005). Smoke signals, Sitting Bulls, and slot machines: A new stereotype of Native Americans? *Multicultural Perspectives, 7*(3), 51–54.

Henry, J. (1970). *Textbooks and the American Indian.* San Francisco, CA: Indian Historian Press.

Kelsey, C. E. (1909). The rights and wrongs of the California Indians. *Transactions of the Commonwealth Club of California 1909, 4*(7), 422–423.

Locke, S., & Lindley, L. (2007). Rethinking social studies for a critical democracy in American/Alaska native education. *Journal of American Indian Education, 46*(2), 1–19.

Lonnberg, A. (1981). The Digger Indian stereotype in California. *Journal of California and Great Basin Anthropology, 3*(2), 215–223.

Marquez, B. (2011). *Who's left out? Representations of American Indians in social studies textbooks, 1959–2010* (Unpublished master's dissertation). Stanford University, Stanford, CA.

Meriam, L. (1928). Meriam report: The problem of Indian administration. *Institute for Government Research.* Retrieved from http://www.narf.org/nill/resources/ meriam.html

No Child Left Behind (NCLB) Act, 20 U.S.C.A. § 6301 et seq (2001).

United States Code, Title 25, Chapter 22, § 2011 (a).

United States Department of the Interior. (1891). *Annual Report of the Commissioner of Indian Affairs to the Secretary of the Interior.* Washington, DC: Author.

Wollenberg, C. (1978). *All deliberate speed: Segregation and exclusion in California schools, 1855–1975.* Berkeley, CA: University of California Press.

CHAPTER 3

NAVIGATING THE SYSTEM

Key Elements and Processes

Gerald A. Lieberman
State Education and Environment Roundtable, Poway, CA

GETTING THROUGH THE DOOR

A wide variety of interest groups is always pursuing access to schools. Whether they represent health, safety, the environment, or a local community interest, these well-intentioned people and organizations want to have an opportunity to present their information and, often, their prepared lessons to students of all ages.

Over the past two decades, with the growing focus on "standards-based" teaching and standardized testing, the requests for time by outside interest groups have come into direct conflict with teachers' need to keep their students focused on the target. This laser-like focus on standards is driven by several factors that are directly tied to student achievement, including evaluations of teachers and administrators and the funding of schools, districts, and state departments of education.

Keeping these issues in mind, it has become ever more important to take into account not just *our* interests and concerns, but to look at how we can

On Indian Ground: California, pages 33–47
Copyright © 2017 by Information Age Publishing
All rights of reproduction in any form reserved.

make it easier and more effective for teachers to incorporate our content into the school day. Simply put, this means that whether we work inside or outside of the formal education system, no matter how important the content and experiences we want students to have, our focus must be on instructional strategies and materials that connect to adopted standards and teach using the strategies identified in curriculum frameworks.

Using California as an example, this chapter will introduce the key elements that drive the work of teachers, schools, districts, and state departments of education: content standards, curriculum frameworks, adopted instructional materials, and student assessments. Each of these elements is explored using a California-based example that is focused on environmental content and issues. Table 3.1 summarizes the roles of the many entities charged with the responsibility of developing, adopting, and implementing these key elements.

Finally, this chapter provides guidance regarding how to become actively involved in decision making related to California's K–12 education system, a structure that exemplifies the general practices of educational management across the United States.

ACADEMIC STANDARDS—WHY ARE THEY HERE AND WHERE DO THEY COME FROM?

The 1983 release of the National Commission on Excellence in Education report, *A Nation at Risk: The Imperative for Educational Reform,* marks the starting point of the education reform movement that today, tomorrow, and for the foreseeable future will drive the functioning of every public school classroom in America—instruction targeted toward student proficiency with specific academic content standards. This report laid the groundwork for the transition to standards determined by states rather than instructional goals being set by school districts, schools, principals, and teachers. It also propelled the shift from locally determined student assessment into the wide array of state-established standardized tests—which, in many places, has resulted in monthly, biweekly, and sometimes weekly student testing.

By the late 1990s, most states and school districts had adopted academic standards for English/language arts, mathematics, science, and history/social studies. Now, practically all public schools and districts make their instructional decisions based on adopted standards and student assessment, including charter schools. They do this for two major reasons: the first related to federal and state education funding for schools and the second related to hiring and firing decisions for district superintendents, principals, and teachers—both of which are connected to students' achievement on state and local standardized tests.

TABLE 3.1 Summary of Roles and Responsibilities in the Development and Implementation of Academic Content Standards, Curriculum Frameworks, and Instructional Materials

Legislature and Governor

- pass laws that influence academic content standards
- pass laws that require particular educational program strategies

State Board of Education (SBE)

- sets policies and regulations that direct CDE in implementing laws
- adopts new standards or modifies existing standards
- sets criteria for implementing standards, curriculum frameworks, instructional materials, and student assessments
- guides, reviews, and approves curriculum frameworks
- guides, reviews, and approves adoption of instructional materials

Instructional Quality Commission (IQC)

- oversees and reviews development of curriculum frameworks, and recommends them for adoption by SBE (process includes a volunteer Curriculum Framework and Evaluation Criteria Committee [CFCC])
- reviews and recommends instructional materials for adoption by SBE (process includes a volunteer Instructional Review Panel [IRP])

California Department of Education (CDE)

- implements policies and regulations set by State Board of Education
- designs and directs programs and provides professional development that supports implementation of standards and student assessments by county offices of education and school districts as they implement standards
- manages the development of academic standards, curriculum frameworks, and adoption of instructional materials (among others, this process includes staff from the Curriculum Frameworks and Instructional Resources Division [CFIRD])

County Offices of Education

- oversee and support the development of local control and accountability plans (LCAP) by school districts
- provide professional development and other support to districts as they implement standards and student assessments

School Districts and School Administrators

- choose among instructional materials adopted by the SBE or other available instructional materials

General Public

- provides state-level input during the development and adoption of standards, curriculum frameworks, instructional materials, and LCAPs
- provides local input during the selection of instructional materials and development of LCAPs

The process of adopting new standards or modifying existing standards, in California, is under the purview of the State Board of Education (SBE). An 11-member body appointed by the governor, with the individual members serving staggered four-year terms, and a single student member. The SBE makes policy for the K–12 system in California and is responsible for academic standards, curriculum, instructional materials, assessments, and accountability.

The SBE is also responsible for adopting regulations that direct implementation of programs created by the legislature and signed into law by the governor. These regulations provide the policies under which the California Department of Education (CDE), county offices of education, and school districts are required to implement these programs.

In California, there is not a specific, legislatively required timeline for revising academic standards. Therefore, like most other states, until recently California's core academic standards have remained practically unchanged since the state's 1998 adoptions for English/language arts, mathematics, science, and history/social sciences.

The year 2009 saw the beginning of a major new endeavor led by governors and state superintendents across the nation, as a joint endeavor of the National Governors Association Center for Best Practices and the Council of Chief State School Officers. This effort led to the development of the Common Core State Standards (CCSS) for English/language arts and literacy, and mathematics, which were released in 2010 and subsequently adopted by over 40 states.

Then, in 2013 Achieve, Inc. and its partners released the Next Generation Science Standards (NGSS), the result of a development process that involved 26 state departments of education, the National Research Council (NRC), and many others. These new science standards were based on NRC's 2012 *A Framework for K–12 Science Education: Practices, Crosscutting Concepts, and Core Ideas.* They represent a new way of thinking about science education, using a strategy based on a three-dimensional structure composed of disciplinary core ideas, crosscutting concepts, and science and engineering practices. The NGSS also identify performance expectations that are designed to assess students' progress based on an extensive series of real-world tasks.

In the case of California, the English/language arts and mathematics standards adopted in 1998 were in place until the SBE adopted the Common Core State Standards (CCSS) in 2010. The mathematics standards were then modified in 2013, the same year that the SBE adopted its new science standards based on the NGSS.

Standards for history/social studies, both in California and nationally, have a very different status. In California, the history/social sciences standards were last updated in 1998. At a national level, no organizations have developed or promoted a comprehensive set of standards to parallel the other three core subjects. Development has been on more of a piecemeal basis that has been undertaken by various interest groups including the National Council for History Education, National Council for Social Studies, and the National Geographic Society. As a result, state boards of education and state departments of education across the country have developed and adopted a wide variety of different standards.

Content in California's 1998 history/social sciences standards related to American Indians appears at several grades, including 1st, 3rd, 4th, 5th, 8th, and 11th grades. A few examples include:

1st grade: 1.5.2 "Understand the ways in which American Indians and immigrants have helped define Californian and American culture."

4th grade: 4.21 "Discuss the major nations of California Indians, including their geographic distribution, economic activities, legends, and religious beliefs; and describe how they depended on, adapted to, and modified the physical environment by cultivation of land and use of sea resources."

8th grade: 8.5.3 "Outline the major treaties with American Indian nations during the administrations of the first four presidents and the varying outcomes of those treaties" (California State Board of Education, 1998).

Note: To fully understand the scope of California standards related to American Indians it is necessary to review the complete text of California's History/Social Sciences standards, available at http://www.cde.ca.gov/be/st/ss/documents/histsocscistnd.pdf.

The limited depth and coverage of standards-based content related to American Indians in California's academic standards means that it may be necessary to develop and adopt new strategies to achieve the goal of moving past historical approaches to American Indian education. A law passed in 2003 and signed by then Governor Davis provides an example of one alternative strategy that has proven effective. This law, which has come to be called the "Education and the Environment Initiative" (EEI, Assembly Bill 1548, 2003), came into being as the result of the interest and dedication of a California environmental group named Heal the Bay and its legislative director Leslie Mintz (Tamminen). This group sought to change California's academic content standards so that they incorporated more content about the environment, but ultimately discovered the complexity of the process and recognized the low probability that they would succeed through this approach.

They brought their concern to then Assemblymember Fran Pavley—a former classroom teacher and longtime supporter of environmental protection. Their discussions eventually resulted in a draft bill that called on the State Board of Education and the Department of Education to formally include environment-related content in California's standards. The state's education officials reacted negatively to the proposed approach, since they had only relatively recently completed the process of adopting California's academic standards and conforming instructional materials. Pavley and Mintz met time and time again with representatives of California's education and environmental agencies. Discussions that ultimately led Assemblymember Pavley to author Assembly Bill 1548, a compromise among all of the stakeholders.

Passed by California's Assembly and Senate in the fall of 2003, it was signed into law in October by Governor Gray Davis, this legislation did not create additional academic standards; rather it called for the development of "education principles for the environment." These principles were to be taught by integrating them with the state's existing science and history-social science standards and creating model instructional materials that could be used by California's teachers to help their students achieve proficiency.

Not surprisingly, the discussions, and in some cases arguments, did not stop with the signing of the bill. In spite of many conversations and compromises, the six agencies identified in the legislation as participants in this endeavor (SBE, CDE, Governor's Secretary for Education, California's Environmental Protection Agency, Integrated Waste Management Board, and Natural Resources Agency) had significantly different views about the details of what implementation should look like. The education agencies were primarily focused on their legal responsibilities, implementation of California's standards, using state-adopted instructional materials. Similarly, the representatives of the environment and natural resources agencies maintained their focus on the environmental content that they wanted students to receive under the EEI.

In spite of all these early difficulties and concerns, the agencies ultimately came together by recognizing the importance of each other's priorities—standards-based instruction, and environmental content and issues. Over the course of the next six years, these joint efforts resulted in the EEI curriculum, an 85-unit series of standards driven instructional materials that was approved by the SBE for use in California's classrooms (www.californiaeei.org).

At least in the short term, a strategy like the one used to establish California's Environmental Principles and Concepts, and the EEI curriculum may be the most effective way to broaden students' education about American Indians. Such a strategy could bring into California's classrooms the content and instructional materials that would help students learn about the diversity of tribes, tribal practices, and philosophies found among the 566 American Indian tribes who live across throughout the United States.

CURRICULUM FRAMEWORKS—WHAT THEY ARE, HOW THEY ARE DEVELOPED, AND WHAT THEY INFLUENCE

Curriculum frameworks provide the blueprints that teachers, administrators, school districts, and developers and publishers of curriculum programs and materials use as guides toward implementing California's State Board of Education adopted academic standards. These frameworks are developed under the auspices of the Instructional Quality Commission (IQC), a body that advises the SBE on matters related to curriculum, instructional materials, and content standards.

New curriculum frameworks are developed whenever the SBE adopts new academic standards. In certain cases, however, frameworks are updated or replaced even if standards have not been modified. For example, a science curriculum framework was adopted in 2002 in response to the 1998 standards, and then updated in 2004 based on the same standards but incorporating new criteria for instructional materials adoption. In this case, although there were no changes to the standards, there were substantial changes to the criteria directing how those standards were to be taught through adopted instructional materials.

The role of curriculum frameworks as the guides for teachers, administrators, and school districts is crucial in identifying and describing the instructional strategies that are to be used in classrooms. They build from the adopted academic standards that identify what students are expected to know and be able to do and provide educators with guidance about how they are supposed to help students achieve those learning goals. The frameworks also provide teachers and administrators with strategies for assessing student progress, assuring all students of equity and access to instruction, as well as vignettes and snapshots that are intended to give teachers insights into what classroom instruction should look like.

The second, but equally important, role of curriculum frameworks is associated with the work undertaken by the developers and publishers of curriculum programs and instructional materials. In addition to the overarching guidance on the standards, instructional strategies, and student assessment, the frameworks provide publishers with highly detailed and specific criteria that will be used to evaluate their submitted instructional materials for kindergarten through eighth grade. These criteria fit into five major categories related to alignment with standards, program organization, student assessment, access and equity, and instructional planning and teacher support. While all of these criteria are considered important, developers and publishers must meet all criteria of "Category 1 in full and [if they] do not show strengths in each one of the other four categories [their materials] will not be adopted" (California State Board of Education, 2017).

In the first instance, the Category 1 criteria require that the programs submitted to the state by developers and publishers focus on the SBE-adopted content standards. The other elements of this category of criteria vary substantially among the different subject matter disciplines; nonetheless, they cover equally important topics such as the requirement for using effective, research-based instructional methods, the need for grade-level appropriate materials, and, often, legislatively required content such as California's Environmental Principles and Concepts in the frameworks for science and history/social sciences.

California's curriculum frameworks are important in this state as well as many others across the nation because few of the other states go through such thoughtful and lengthy development process. The development of California's frameworks requires an extended period of time, sometimes up to two years, as a result of the complex development process, including an extensive series of meetings involving educational experts and several opportunities for public participation and input.

The frameworks are written by large groups of content and instructional experts; for example, the science framework writing team is led by the California Science Project. Throughout the development process, draft components of the frameworks are reviewed by an SBE-appointed Curriculum Framework and Evaluation Criteria Committee (CFCC). These committees include teachers, school administrators, and technical experts in the subject matter. After their work is completed, the documents reviewed and recommended by these committees are then submitted to the discipline-specific subject matter committee (for example, the Science Subject Matter Committee) within the Instructional Quality Commission. After their review, draft frameworks are distributed for a "field review," a follow-up revision by the subject matter committee, an additional public review, a final revision, and submission to the State Board of Education for their review and approval.

All aspects of the framework development process are open to public involvement and comment. This is especially important because of the crucial role that the frameworks play in focusing educators and instructional materials developers on classroom instruction in the SBE-adopted standards.

The work that is currently underway in the development of California's new Science Framework provides a useful example of how individuals and groups can become involved in the process. Since frameworks play such an important role in California's education system, there are always large numbers of applicants for the CFCCs—sometimes 100 to 200 applicants for the 20 positions on the committee.

The staff of the California Department of Education, specifically those within the Curriculum Frameworks and Instructional Resources Division (CFIRD), encourage and facilitate public participation from diverse stakeholders. Many different organizations, interest groups, representatives of other state agencies, and publishers are given access to all of the materials that the CFCC will be reviewing at their meetings. These stakeholders are welcome to make oral contributions during the meetings and can also submit written comments, as well as suggestions for edits and revisions.

The efforts of the team that has been working on California's Education and the Environment Initiative provide an informative example of opportunities for involvement in the development of the state's curriculum frameworks. In this case, several individuals participated in the process of developing California's new science framework. The CFCC leadership and members, as well as members of the writing team and CDE staff, were very welcoming. EEI team members observed all of the public meetings, reviewed and commented on draft documents throughout the process, and submitted a wide array of proposed additions for consideration by the CFCC. Several of the proposed edits and additions have been incorporated into the draft documents that will ultimately be reviewed by the State Board of Education.

It is particularly important for interested stakeholders to get actively involved in the framework development process because this opportunity typically occurs only once every 5 to 8 years for each of the major disciplines. In case this sounds like an overly bureaucratic process, it is nonetheless important as exemplified by the changes that occurred between the 2002 and 2004 versions of the science framework. This example demonstrates how substantial a shift can occur when interested people get involved. Based on input from science educators, the State Board of Education shifted the adoption criteria in 2002 from stating that hands on science activities "may represent up to a maximum of 20 to 25 percent of the science instructional time in grades K–8" (California State Board of Education, 2002) to the final criteria which state that "hands-on activities compose at least 20 to 25 percent of the science instructional time" (California State Board of Education, 2004). Indeed, a dramatic shift.

In many ways, the curriculum frameworks serve the function of gatekeepers, not just blueprints for best practices. In regard to American Indian education, whether it is the history/social sciences framework or one of the others, this is an opportunity for stakeholders to help define the highest quality instruction and content and the best instructional practices educators and publishers should use to bring this content into schools across California.

INSTRUCTIONAL MATERIALS: THEY ARE NOT JUST TEXTBOOKS ANYMORE—HOW THEY ARE DEVELOPED, REVIEWED, AND ADOPTED

For many, many years, the majority of content that students received came from textbooks selected by school districts and found in every classroom. Oftentimes, these books were old and out of date or damaged.

Over the past 20 years, there has been a shift from the classic textbook to a more diverse variety of materials, including textbooks, readers, maps, audio and visual aids, and, most recently, Internet-based information. All of these materials are now considered "instructional materials."

California's State Board of Education reviews and approves instructional materials for adoption and use by kindergarten through the eighth grade in the state's public schools. This process involves an intensive review by the SBE-appointed Instructional Quality Commission (IQC). In addition to the

IQC members, the review process typically involves well over 100 volunteers from across the state with both classroom teaching experience and expertise in the specific subject area. Their review and recommendations for the adoption or rejection of instructional materials, submitted by the publishers, are based on the SBE's adopted academic standards and curriculum frameworks. There is no state-led adoption process for instructional materials at high school grades; these decisions are made by the individual school districts. At all grade levels, California's education code, however, requires that the local school districts promote the involvement of teachers, parents, and other community members in the selection of instructional materials.

The authors and developers of instructional materials for K–8 schools typically start the process of developing new instructional materials by establishing "learning objectives" connected to one or more of the adopted academic standards. The best learning objectives are written in a style that specifies what students should be able to do as the result of one or more lessons. Two examples, from a 3rd-grade unit developed for California's Education and the Environment Initiative curriculum, demonstrate the form of these types of learning objectives: (a) "Describe how physical geography, including climate, affected the natural resources (goods and ecosystem services) upon which American Indian nations depended"; and (b) "Explain how the American Indian nations affected the natural systems where they lived" (Office of Education and the Environment, 2010). These two learning objectives are directly linked to California's history/social science standard 3.2.2, "Discuss the ways in which physical geography, including climate, influenced how the local Indian nations adapted to their natural environment (e.g., how they obtained food, clothing, tools)."

The process for developing and reviewing is constrained by the implementation timelines established by California's legislature and the State Board of Education. Publishers typically have 24–30 months after the discipline-specific curriculum frameworks are approved to submit their materials to the Curriculum Frameworks and Instructional Resources Division (CFIRD) of California's Department of Education for consideration by the SBE.

Members of the IQC, working with the CFIRD, train the volunteer members of the review panels in the review process, with an emphasis on teaching them how to evaluate the submitted materials based on the SBE-approved Criteria for Evaluating Instructional Materials. This training goes deeply into all of the criteria and processes, requiring about one week of the volunteers' time, after which they have several months to review their assigned documents. Several months later, they meet together for in-depth discussions of each set of instructional materials, focusing most of their discussion on deciding whether the lessons, activities, and supporting materials submitted by the publishers are designed to ensure that all students master the particular standard on which they are focused.

Although the IQC members and volunteer reviewers are required to consider a wide array of criteria, the most important, no matter what the discipline, are that (a) instructional materials are designed to ensure that all students master each of the (standards), as adopted by the State Board of Education; and (b) instructional materials reflect and incorporate the content of the (discipline specific) framework for California Public Schools, as adopted by the State Board of Education.

Reports from the review panels are submitted to the IQC for their formal consideration. During this process, IQC members review and, as needed, amend the reports to reflect their best judgment. The IQC then submits a formal report to the SBE recommending the adoption or rejection of each of the sets of instructional materials submitted by the publisher. These reports include recommendations for changes that, in their judgment, must be made by the publishers to meet California's adoption criteria.

Using the IQC report as its starting point, members of the SBE undertake their own reviews. Finally, the SBE as a whole conducts an open, public meeting during which they accept further input and make final decisions about which of the publishers' submissions should be adopted for use in California's public schools. Decisions for approval are typically made on a "subject to" basis, with specific required changes identified for the publishers. Prior to publication, CDE staff monitors the changes made by the publishers to assure that the requirements of the SBE are met.

During its 2013–2014 sessions, California's legislature made dramatic changes to the budget processes controlling funding for school districts. These decisions transferred many of the budgetary decisions that had been made by SBE and CDE to local school districts in collaboration with their county offices of education. This shift requires the state to provide funding for school districts through a local control funding formula (LCFF), eliminating the long-time use of instructional materials block grants and giving them much greater control over decisions about instructional materials. Although there is limited experience with the new LCFF process, most observers think that local school districts will continue to make choices about which instructional materials their teachers are to use, based on the adoption decisions made by the State Board of Education.

The LCFFs are accompanied by another new process, designated local control and accountability plans (LCAP). These plans lay out the strategies for how districts and individual schools will achieve progress in each of eight state priority areas, ranging from access to fully credentialed teachers to measuring student outcomes. The first two state priority areas identified by the legislature, much like the SBE's adoption criteria, require that "every pupil in (each) school district has sufficient access to the standards-aligned instructional materials," and "implementation of the academic content and performance standards adopted by the state board" (California Education Code, Article 4.5, para. 1).

Since these accountability plans tie directly to state funding decisions based on the LCFF, they will have major implications for every educational program that seeks to expand and strengthen American Indian education in California. Like all other subject-specific educational content, recently approved requirements will place new demands on the individuals and institutions working to further integrate American Indian education into California's classrooms. This includes nonformal educational programs developed and provided by one of California's many tribes or Indian museums.

As is the case with academic standards and curriculum frameworks, decisions about instructional materials are open to public involvement. Teachers and individuals with technical expertise about American Indians can apply for membership on the State Board of Education, Instructional Quality Commission, and instructional materials review panels. It is this level of participation that can help to bring about the institutional and policy changes that will give American Indian education a greater role in California's educational system.

STUDENT ASSESSMENTS—WHY, WHAT, AND HOW ARE THEY USED?

Measuring a student's classroom success was once in the hands of their teachers. Whether through writing assignments, oral responses, quizzes, or chapter tests, until about 20 years ago teachers used these tools to assign students grades on their report cards or to formulate their comments during teacher–parent conferences.

Most school districts also, at one time or another during the year, gave students standardized tests. Teachers and school administrators use the results of these tests to guide their work with individual students and their class as a whole.

All of this began changing after the release of *A Nation at Risk: The Imperative for Educational Reform* (National Commission on Excellence in Education, 1983). The movement toward state standards in the 1990s led to a major shift in student assessment from district decisions to statewide student assessments. This transition was further reinforced during the 2002 congressional reauthorization of the Elementary and Secondary Education Act, which also gave the act a new name, No Child Left Behind (NCLB).

The NCLB law included both "carrots" and "sticks." States could receive additional funding from the U.S. Department of Education to help them increase student achievement as measured by the statewide student assessments. At the same time, however, departments of education whose students did not meet the agreed-upon goals for annual yearly progress (AYP) were in jeopardy of losing some of their federal funding. Not surprisingly, loss of this state-level funding also put the budgets of individual school districts in jeopardy. In many districts, this progression trickled down to school principals who were being judged based on the AYP at their schools.

In planning how to work effectively with teachers and educational administrators at all levels, it is crucial to take into account this direct connection between their students' success on statewide standardized tests and the funding at the levels of states, districts, and even schools. These are the current circumstances in California, even in this new era of local control funding formula and local control and accountability plans—both of which tie directly to state decisions about school district funding.

This situation reinforces the need to develop strategies for integrating the goals of American Indian education into state-driven student assessment systems, not just standards, frameworks, and instructional materials. Whether in California or any other state, whether or not we value or support the use of statewide standardized tests, overlooking the student assessment system ignores a concern that drives decision making by teachers, school administrators, and school districts.

WHEN TO ACT—THE TIME IS NOW

The formal education system is a constantly moving target. In 2009, for example, California's State Board of Education and the State Department of Education began to work on updating the history/social science curriculum framework, which would then have led to the development and adoption of new instructional materials. However, due to the state's budget shortfall, this process was put on hold, stopping the development of the revised framework mid-process and putting the adoption of new history/ social science instructional materials on an indefinite hold. The revision process was restarted in 2014 based on the framework materials that had been drafted in 2009. Then, in 2015, the history/social science process was again put on hold, but after much work, a revised framework was adopted by the State Board of Education in 2016. In the short term, this means that California's kindergarten to 8th-grade students will continue using instructional materials that were originally adopted by the State Board of Education in 2005.

Legislation was recently introduced in California that would establish a more formal schedule and specific processes of updating and revising standards, developing revised frameworks, and, as a result, undertaking new adoptions for instructional materials. In the meantime, the curriculum frameworks for English/language arts and mathematics, based on the Common Core State Standards, are guiding the adoption of new instructional materials. And, as described above, the process of finalizing the new science curriculum framework is currently under way and will lead to the adoption of new science instructional materials in 2018.

All of California's academic content standards related to educational topics about American Indians currently appear in California's history/social sciences standards. The logical first step in expanding the coverage of these topics in California's schools therefore starts with those standards. This raises several questions, among the most important of which is: Do the existing standards include appropriate and sufficient content related to American Indians in California and elsewhere? If the answer to this question is no, then efforts should be made to work with either the legislature or the State Board of Education to ensure that additional content is incorporated into the standards when they are updated.

Given the current status of California's history/social science framework—under revision yet currently on hold—it is important regardless of the current standards to become actively involved in the revision process once it is again underway. Representatives of California's Indian community can get involved in many ways, including seeking membership on the State Board of Education, Instructional Quality Commission, or, if it is reinstated, the SBE-appointed History/Social Science Curriculum Framework and Evaluation Criteria Committee. (Note that Professor Patricia Dixon [Luiseño], the recently retired chair of American Indian Studies at Palomar College, served as a member of the Instructional Quality Commission.) Even if it is not possible to become a member of one of these groups, one or more representatives of the Indian community can participate as a member of the public, attending the meetings, observing the activities, or even becoming more active as I have done by making direct contributions to the content of the draft science curriculum framework.

WORDS OF ENCOURAGEMENT

As complex and formidable as this process appears to be, it is possible to influence the K–12 education system. The 2003 legislation that established the Education and the Environment Initiative and the 2012 legislation that required the inclusion of organ and tissue donation in the science and health curriculum frameworks are just two examples of success in influencing the system.

Although it will certainly take a substantial effort, it is equally possible to strengthen American Indian education in California—a worthy goal that could, for all California students, deepen their understanding of the cultures, traditions, achievements, beliefs, and histories of American Indians in California and across the continent.

REFERENCES

Assembly Bill 1548, Pavley, Chapter 665, Statutes of 2003.

California Education Code, Article 4.5. Local Control and Accountability Plans, 52060.

California State Board of Education. (1998). *History–Social science content standards for California public schools, kindergarten through gradet twelve.* California Department of Education. Sacramento, CA.

California State Board of Education. (2002). *Science framework for California public schools, kindergarten through grade twelve.* California Department of Education. Sacramento, CA.

California State Board of Education. (2004). *Science framework for California public schools kindergarten through grade twelve.* California Department of Education. Sacramento, CA.

California State Board of Education. (2017). *Science framework for California public schools, kindergarten through grade twelve.* California Department of Education. Sacramento, CA.

National Commission on Excellence in Education. (1983). *A nation at risk: The imperative for educational reform: A report to the Nation and the Secretary of Education, United States Department of Education.* Washington, DC: National Commission on Excellence in Education.

National Research Council. (2012). *A framework for K–12 science education: Practices, crosscutting concepts, and core ideas.* Washington, DC: National Research Council.

Office of Education and the Environment. (2010). *California Indian people: Exploring tribal regions.* State of California, Sacramento, CA.

CHAPTER 4

TOKOY

A Circle of Promise for the Santa Ynez Band of Chumash Indians

Nicolasa I. Sandoval
Santa Ynez Band of Chumash Indians

kɨPɨ': NOW

The days of imposed governance in education for Native peoples are fading. Slowly. Our memories burn still when we confront assumptions, attitudes, and biases rooted in educational systems not of our own design. Native peoples are engineering promising futures through education in ways that are culturally relevant and consistent with unique community realities. Among Native California's 109 federally recognized tribes, several have established education departments. These departments occupy different but important places in their respective communities, along a rich spectrum that encompasses activities from academic support, career development, cultural learning, and language revitalization, to substance abuse prevention and wellness.

The Santa Ynez Band of Chumash Indians (SYBCI) is one tribal government exercising sovereignty by choosing to invest in systems that ensure each community member has clear access to educational pathways from birth through career.

On Indian Ground: California, pages 49–60
Copyright © 2017 by Information Age Publishing

By educating tribal community members and providing them with employment and leadership opportunities, the SYBCI is positioning itself for a strong future of economic independence and self-governance. Through tribal entities led by educated and invested citizens, the SYBCI is stimulating enhanced performance that is intrinsic to self-determination. "Today it is about politics. Then it was poverty. Today we support our education programs tenfold. We've got probably over 1,000 kids—and adults—who are eligible for education assistance. [These are the descendants of tribal members.] We pay 100% of their college tuition. In the last eight years, the number of our college graduates has tripled because of the scholarship," said Kenneth Kahn, tribal chairman (Brugger, 2016).

The Santa Ynez Reservation is located in northeast Santa Barbara County and was established on December 27, 1901 under authority of the act of January 12, 1891. The residents of the Santa Ynez Reservation are members and verified lineal descendants of the Santa Ynez Band of Chumash Indians. Today there are 249 residents on the Santa Ynez Reservation (126 acres) and 97 homes, with a surrounding community population of approximately 20,000 people. The Santa Ynez Band of Chumash Indians is the only federally recognized Chumash tribe in the nation, comprised of 1,771 citizens.

The SYBCI education committee leads educational initiatives and policy. This governing body is made up of eight tribal members. One member is a representative of the business committee. Seven members are elected by the general council to two-year terms that are renewable for up to four terms (8 years) before requiring a one-year absence.

The SYBCI education committee has established written concepts, principles, policies, and practices that guide educational initiatives. Members engage in continuous improvement through an annual strategic planning process, needs assessment, and ongoing program evaluation. Education Department staff members conduct a summary evaluation of each event and program, ensuring the inclusion of formative questions for participants in an effort to support future program development. SYBCI also engages external partners in evaluation. Graduate students from UCLA's Luskin School of Public Affairs conducted an applied policy project that evaluated the effectiveness of SYBCI's educational initiatives in spring 2014. Various forms of community-based research results inform decision makers as they work to solve problems through sound policy.

FOCUS ON SYSTEM CHANGE VS. PROGRAM

System Change

The Santa Ynez Band of Chumash Indians is investing in long-term, sustainable change on a policy level. This departure veers from a program model that depends upon a staff member or champion to carry and protect the effort and moves towards a lasting and strategic action that is collectively decided upon by voting members. Effecting change on a policy level ensures tribal community awareness, engagement in the decision-making process, and the benefit of many good minds thinking about implications for future generations.

Long-term and sustained investment in education has resulted in measurable outcomes visible in leadership positions held by graduates. By providing leadership opportunities through employment, the SYBCI is building a nation led by community members who introduce new knowledge and diverse experiences, challenge assumptions, and propose positive change. Chumash leadership throughout tribal enterprises ensures that governance is culturally grounded and relevant to contemporary contexts.

Several SYBCI graduates have returned to help build the nation. Tribal descendants leading departments report on a weekly basis to elected government officials but are responsible for managing day-to-day operations. This governance structure ensures fiscal and programmatic accountability through a system of checks and balances while enabling elected decision makers to focus on strategic policy issues. Following is a partial list of college graduates working in leadership capacities:

- The SYBCI Foundation administrator earned a vocational certification and has worked in tribal entities for more than 17 years.
- The tribal administrator earned a bachelor's degree and has served the Nation for more than 14 years.
- The education director (and author of this chapter) earned a doctorate and has led the Education Department for more than 8 years.
- The Tribal Health Clinic's behavioral health director earned a doctorate and is working to build this growing department.
- The manager of one of SYBCI's fine-dining restaurants earned a bachelor's degree.
- The environmental technician/field lead earned a vocational certification and is leading an emerging division in the Environmental Office.

Leadership development for tribal youth is also a focus throughout tribal government. Twelve high school students have served as youth ambassadors for the California Indian Conference on Education. Twenty youth have successfully completed a rigorous youth internship in one or more tribal enterprises, resulting in employment opportunities after graduation.

Academic Incentives and Services

As the majority of tribal community members live off of the Santa Ynez Indian Reservation, the SYBCI educational system is comprised of academic incentives and services that reach community members wherever they are geographically. The focus is on supporting individuals from birth through adulthood by investing in kindergarten readiness, educational attainment, and advising on career transitions. Of individuals affiliated with the SYBCI, 1,771 are eligible for these academic incentives and services:

- **Graduate Awards:** Graduates are eligible for monetary rewards, from $100 for 8th grade completion through $3,000 for doctorates. As a result, the number of graduates has grown steadily. At the conclusion of the 2015–2016 academic year, 97% of Chumash high school students graduated in four years with their freshman cohort, and 28% of Chumash adults have earned college degrees or vocational certifications since 1996.
- **College Planning:** Precollege consultations between college-bound adults and the education director result in an individualized academic plan that outlines academic and professional goals, grade expectations, financial aid application requirements, and the degree completion timeline. Staff members organize college visits, disseminate current scholarship information resources, and draft letters of recommendation for college admission and scholarship applications. One member of the tutorial team is also an experienced high school guidance counselor. He assists middle and high school students and their families with college planning advice. The result is increased college participation and graduation rates. Tribal students have participated in college visits to UC–Berkeley, UC–Los Angeles, UC–Riverside, UC–Santa Barbara, Humboldt State University, California State University–Long Beach, Cal Poly–San Luis Obispo, Pepperdine University, and Western University of Health Sciences.
- **Advocacy:** The education director supports students and families by participating in IEP/504/Student Success Team meetings and drafts letters to school officials to ensure that Chumash students are accessing all resources they are eligible for under the Individuals with Disabilities Education Act. A key goal is to help students and families navigate a complex legal system so they may self-advocate confidently in the future. A growing number of Chumash adults are engaging with local school systems through school board service. One parent serves on the board of the local elementary school district and two others are board members for local independent

schools. Tribal parents and family members also volunteer time in
local classrooms, on school field trips, and as athletic coaches.

- **Tutorial Services:** The Education Department received a multiyear
Federal Demonstration Grant for Indian Children in 2013. The grant
is funding the assessment of 3–4-year-old Chumash students in Santa
Barbara County, individualized tutorial and speech/language services
focused on school readiness. The grant also supports individualized
tutorial services, college preparation, and frequent academic coach-
ing for high school students. Each tribal community member, from
preschool through college and career, is eligible for individualized
tutorial services from credentialed teachers. SYBCI maintains a policy
that all tutors must possess a valid California teaching credential, pass
a criminal background investigation, and complete a drug test prior
to working with students. The tutors are paid as independent contractors who work with students based upon required subject matter
expertise, geographic proximity, and availability. Tutorial services are
student-centered and continuously evaluated. Formative, interim, and
summative assessments include notes on the content of each tutoring
session, three tutoring progress reports per year for distribution to
student families, an analysis of standardized test scores, school progress reports and report cards, and a Brigance Comprehensive Inven-
tory of Basic Skills for students ages 5 through 12. The results inform
appropriate academic intervention and tutor matching.

The SYBCI offers direct financial aid that supports tuition for preschool,
private school, vocational school, college, and professional development. Financial aid recipients for college and vocational school tuition are required
to complete a prescholarship appointment with the education director that
results in an individualized academic plan with specific goals and timelines.
Financial aid recipients must earn a grade of C or better to remain eligible
for future assistance. Students pursuing undergraduate degrees have up to 5
years for completion. Students seeking graduate degrees have a maximum of
four years. All coursework must be in fulfillment of a degree or certification.
Tribal leaders designed the financial aid policies to support the attainment of
one degree or a series of successive degrees. The goal is to be prepared for a
career that is rewarding and sustains self-sufficiency.

EDUCATION PROGRAMS

The Santa Ynez Band of Chumash Indians opened a 5,000 square foot
learning center on the reservation in November 2012. Start-up and annual
operational costs for the facility are paid by the tribe. The learning center

has a computer lab, library, curricular resources for tutors, and seven study spaces to accommodate individual and small group tutorial sessions. The classroom accommodates 35 people for meetings, workshops, and larger group tutorial sessions. Copy machines, computers, printers, scanners, wireless connectivity, telephone service, and utilities are paid by the tribe. An edible garden and greenhouse is on-site, which creates outdoor learning opportunities. The garden and greenhouse project was funded in part by a Community Development Block Grant, administered by the Northern California Indian Development Council. The Education Department offers transportation from the local high school to the reservation's learning center Monday through Thursday to facilitate access to drop-in tutorial services. As the majority of tribal students do not live on the reservation, the tribe works in partnership with local public and private schools by funding on-site academic intervention for students in need.

SYBCI's academic programs and services engage tribal entities such as the Culture Department, Environmental Office, and Tribal Health Clinic in several programmatic areas. This ensures that Chumash community members build a strong cultural foundation that supports them on their journey from birth through career. The Culture Department offers language classes twice weekly to participants in the after-school program, the Environmental Office brings culturally relevant environmental education to programs throughout the year, and the Tribal Health Clinic facilitates talking circles and counseling on a weekly basis.

Education Department staff members organize monthly family Fridays, quarterly college visits, skill building workshops for youth and adults, and intergenerational excursions. Chumash cultural practices and community building are embedded in each program. To stimulate lifelong learning, the Education Department offers adult workshops addressing a wide range of topics from parenting strategies, financial literacy, and small business planning to gardening and photography. For adults who intend to complete their GED or high school diploma, the Education Department directs them to local resources offered through adult education and community colleges and/or pairs the student with a credentialed teacher to guide test preparation.

During the academic year, Homework Club is available to Chumash students on a drop-in basis Monday through Thursday at the learning center on the Santa Ynez Indian Reservation. Students work in small groups with a credentialed teacher to complete homework and build academic skills. The Education Department is joined by community-based partners to offer experiential learning opportunities during Homework Club hours. Five certified therapy dogs affiliated with Love on a Leash visit the learning center for a monthly reading hour that helps students build literacy skills.

The Education Department offers academic intervention and resources to tribal students throughout the year. Services occur at schools, in homes, in libraries, and at the Learning Center located on the Santa Ynez Indian Reservation. Staff members have organized annual intensive workshops to support literacy development, and the building of math and science skills for students in grades 1 through 12. Partnering with local non-profit organizations and businesses, the Education Department has hosted hands-on rock music, robotics, and financial management workshops.

The Education Department has worked to stimulate social enterprise, understanding that youth today are tomorrow's leaders. In 2010, a student-curated exhibition of original photography resulted in sales proceeds of more than $2,000. The young photographers contributed 100% of the proceeds to local agencies serving homeless people, animal shelters, and indigenous plant restoration. In 2011, youth hosted a lunch and silent auction that yielded $2,439 for a local social service agency. Tribal leadership is committed to continuing the spirit of *amuyich*, meaning generosity.

Supporting the Work

The Education Department is comprised of five full-time staff members and 47 independent contractors who are credentialed teachers. The Education Department provides professional learning opportunities for staff members and contractors who support academic programs and services. Professional learning activities have included:

- Tribal orientation for tutors and teachers regarding Chumash experiences of education (historic and contemporary)
- Curriculum development workshop for tutors, teachers, and parents
- Child abuse prevention workshops
- Substance abuse recognition workshop
- Behavioral challenges workshops
- Organizational skills for students' workshop
- Check and Connect drop-out prevention implementation training
- CPR certification

Individual development plans are included in each year's performance review for permanent, full-time staff members. Staff members work with their supervisor to identify professional learning goals for the next year. The tribe pays time and registration fees for seminars and courses related to improving capacities to meet student needs.

Education Department staff members and education committee members participate in the annual California Conference on American Indian Education. Staff members have presented workshops regarding advocacy, best practices, and youth activities. Staff and education committee members also participate in the National Indian Education Association Convention. Both venues offer a platform for disseminating information about lessons learned and best practices on a statewide and national level. Participation ensures that appropriate resources are brought back to the tribal community. The education director also participates in meetings with other tribal education directors and facilitated a data collection report on behalf of 20 state-funded American Indian Education Centers in 2011 and 2012 for submission to the American Indian Oversight Committee and State Superintendent of Public Instruction.

EVALUATION

Family engagement is integral to all aspects of SYBCI educational initiatives. Educational leaders in the tribal community define family involvement in education as the actions initiated by family members (parents, guardians, siblings, grandparents, aunts, uncles, cousins) to support student learning. This learning occurs at home, in school, in nature, and in community. The Education Department conducts an annual parent/guardian meeting to describe academic progress and jointly identify areas of need. Parents have shared their concerns about student achievement. Their contributions have informed program development and resulted in enhanced educational support. Following is a summary of parent/guardian recommendations from 2011 through 2016:

Strategies for supporting students in math and reading:

- Workshops in literacy, math, organizational skills, and overcoming test anxiety
- Incentives (gift cards, prizes) to encourage reading and homework completion

Strategies for supporting students and families:

- Academic counseling for incoming high school freshmen
- Advocacy (at school and teaching self-advocacy)
- Classes regarding Chumash history and culture
- Include parents in teacher workshops to build understanding of Native realities

Strategies for helping teachers:

- Consistent and frequent communication, particularly in high school
- Reservation-based professional learning opportunities that include parents

The SYBCI education committee initiated a strategic planning process in 2005 and conducted an educational needs assessment in 2007, focusing on the educational and cultural service needs of its educational leaders, parents, and students. Education committee members continued strategic planning self-study assessments in 2009, 2011, 2013, and 2015 to further identify gaps and weaknesses in educational outcomes and propose ways to increase student preparedness and improve student achievement in post-secondary schools.

Participants ranked the following educational needs in order of priority:

1. Need for early intervention (preK)
2. Need to improve academic achievement and postsecondary preparation
3. Improve student attendance/drop-out prevention
4. Enhance special education services
5. Provide professional development for teachers
6. Strengthen substance abuse prevention programs and services
7. Provide student and parent rights training
8. Provide parent and/or student advocacy/training
9. Integrate American Indian materials into curriculum

Each educational priority has guided strategic directions of academic initiatives during the past 8-year period. While significant progress has occurred in all areas, the integration of American Indian materials is in need of focused attention, particularly as it relates to local Chumash culture, history, and contemporary life.

Return on the Investment

The SYBCI's academic initiatives support community members from birth through adulthood by investing in kindergarten readiness, educational attainment, and support of career transitions. The Santa Ynez Band of Chumash Indians (SYBCI) has directed financial and human resources to support education with the following results:

- 23% of Chumash adults (250) have earned a college degree or vocational certification (6 doctorates, 18 master's, 80 bachelor's, 63 associate's, 80 vocational) since 1996.
- 6% of Chumash adults (63) who have not previously earned a degree or certification are currently pursuing postsecondary education (63 at a college or university, 2 at vocational school).
- 97% of Chumash students graduate high school in four years with their freshman cohort.

- 86% of 30 students (Grade 1–6) improved by at least one level in one or more subject areas in 2016.
- 70% of 30 high school students improved their grades in Language Arts, Math, or Science in 2015–2016 (an increase from 44.44% in 2014–15, and an increase from 37.5% in 2013–2014).
- 100% of 11 high school graduates who received academic services successfully completed and met college entrance requirements in 2016. Six graduates are enrolled at 4-year colleges: UC Los Angeles, UC Santa Cruz, CSU Sonoma, Cal Lutheran, CSU San Bernardino. One transfer student was admitted to Humboldt State University. Five graduates are attending community college.

A returning student pursuing a master's degree while working as a full-time, professional musician wrote, "I am very grateful for the financial support I receive from the Education Department of the Santa Ynez Band of Chumash Indians. Their help makes my graduate education possible, and I greatly appreciate the support they are providing. I hope it will make my relatives and ancestors proud when we have another MA or PhD in the family" (personal communication, 2015).

These educational attainments continue to rise in spite of historical and contemporary realities. Two of ten local Chumash students (20%) is eligible for special education services or has been diagnosed with a learning disability, compared to 11% of California's general student population. This fact demands culturally sensitive, individualized, and extensive support services that span academic, health, and social spheres. Through student-centered academic and social/behavioral intervention with community-based partners, Chumash students presenting learning differences are supported in meeting goals, attaining diplomas, and earning college degrees. "Just two and a half years ago my daughter was being assessed for a learning disability . . . and now she made honor roll! What a blessing to have the opportunity you are giving my daughter—it is making a difference in the lives of our little ones," wrote a parent to members of the education committee.

KA ŠTAPIN: YESTERDAY

The Santa Ynez Reservation was established on December 27, 1901 under authority of the act of January 12, 1891. The Articles of Organization were approved in 1964. While the archeological evidence confirms a continuous human presence in this region for more than 13,000 years, oral histories describe Chumash persistence in this region since time began.

Historically, American Indian students in the United States have experienced profound educational challenges. While the majority of school-age reservation residents since 1901 have been enrolled in local public schools, several children were sent to board at the Sherman Institute in Riverside, California in the 1940s. Survivors of this experience are still alive today and many are great grandparents of Chumash students. They are esteemed elders who endured the legacy of Estelle Reel's Uniform Course of Study, which emphasized the indoctrination of domestic life and habits while grooming generations of Native students for manual labor (Lomawaima, 1996). Elders have spoken about spending most of the day engaged in vocational curriculum and focusing on domestic work to support lifestyles of the upper class. The jobs that boarding school prepared them for included laundress, waitress, and housekeeper (Sandoval, 2007).

Disparities have prevailed in recent times. "Just a generation earlier, only a handful of tribal students were able to pursue higher education due to a number of factors, including economic obstacles," said Richard Gomez, former tribal vice-chairman (2010).

WA SʰɨKɨN: TOMORROW

The SYBCI has worked to ensure fiscal and systematic sustainability for future generations and has secured approximately 10% of the education budget from external sources. The business and education committees have exercised prudent fiscal responsibility by establishing an education fund that serves as an endowment and working closely with the education director to monitor budgets on a quarterly basis. Due to conservative and thoughtful growth, less than 12% of the Education Department budget goes to administrative costs; more than 88% goes to direct services. Frequent and tailored support prepares community members for rewarding academic and professional lives. Sustained academic initiatives minimize remediation costs for schools, universities, and the SYBCI in the future.

A wide achievement gap continues for Native students throughout California. Less than 25% of California Indian high school graduates meet entrance requirements for the University of California or California State University system, compared to more than 38% of the general population. Nearly 19% of California Indians leave high school, compared to 13% of the general population (Proudfit & Gregor, 2014). As long as these educational disparities persist, they guarantee a cycle of poverty, disease, and high unemployment.

For California's Native cultural, educational, and governmental leaders, this fate is not acceptable. Change is unfolding in policy that is informed by community-based research, systemic focus, and strategic investment of human and financial capital in education. Native peoples in California are poised for a new era of self-determination, fueled by the fire of our intelligence and spirit.

REFERENCES

Brugger, K. (2016, July 28). New Chumash Chair Kenny Kahn. Santa Barbara Independent. http://www.independent.com/news/2016/jul/28/new-chumash-chair-kenny-kahn/

Gomez, R. (2010, June 10). Academic efforts rewarded each year. *Santa Ynez Valley News*. Retrieved from http://www.santaynezchumash.org/news2.html

Lomawaima, K. T. (1996). Estelle Reel, Superintendent of Indian Schools, 1898–1910: Politics, curriculum, and land. *Journal of American Indian Education, 35*, 1–20.

Proudfit, J., & Gregor, T. (2014). *State of American Indian/Alaska Native education in California*. San Marcos, CA: California State University.

Sandoval, N. I. (2007). *Bridging generations: American Indian family perceptions of home/school partnerships* (Doctoral dissertation). University of California, Santa Barbara, 2007. Retrieved from Pro Quest. http://media.proquest.com/media/pq/classic/doc/1390281281/fmt/ai/rep/NPDF?_s=ITxHicCwSAJ%2Be2IrZQkdlfr7YrI%3D

CHAPTER 5

EARLY LEARNING AND BEST PRACTICE IN A NATIVE AMERICAN HEAD START PROGRAM

Tamara Alexander
Karuk Indian Tribe

Kristy Harmon
Tribal Head Start

Mikela Jones
Little River Band of Pomo Indians

Tribal Head Start programs have been the foundation for early education for Native children and families living within tribal service areas for many years. This most definitely has been the case for the Karuk tribe, and our tribal Head Start program has been providing services to the Native community within Karuk ancestral territory since 1978. In 2016, the Karuk Tribal Head Start now has two centers and serves approximately 60 children

On Indian Ground: California, pages 61–70
Copyright © 2017 by Information Age Publishing
All rights of reproduction in any form reserved.

and their families every year. Since the Karuk tribe is largely situated in rural areas, the services that the Head Start program provides are particularly vital to our communities we serve.

We value our role as educators of our communities' youngest students. As well as adhering to federal guidelines, the Karuk Tribal Head Start implements a curriculum based on what we consider best practices. Within our program we have defined "best practice" in a constructivist manner, regarding the developmental stages and characteristics of children's cognitive processes as invaluable and emphasizing the importance of interaction between children and the environment, as children construct what they know for themselves. Emphasis is also given to the significance of play as an important medium for learning (DeVries & Kohlberg, 1987; Frost, Wortham, & Reifel, 2008).

Teachers of the Karuk Tribal Head Start put these theories into practice by recognizing that the parents, or family unit, are a child's first and best teachers. Our best practices work when the child and family's interactions within the program begin to promote the child and family's social-emotional, cognitive, physical, language, and literacy growth. In order to implement this idea, we have learned that, as teachers, it is most effective to first make sure that a family has the knowledge and supplies that it needs to be motivated to bring their child to school. That is why Head Start works! In addition to being a nutrition-based program, our tribal Head Start centers provide quality care and learning environments for not only the school-aged child, but also the family as a whole. Our teachers begin each year with a home visit that immediately helps to make a connection between the family and the Head Start staff. At our home visits, we make certain that our families are given respect and feel comfortable sharing in an environment that is both culturally sensitive and thoughtful to various economic statuses. Ensuring a safe environment helps to build a relationship that will allow us to help in ways suitable to each family's unique needs. One of our personal favorite scenarios is when we can help families apply for WIC. Often in rural areas, it is unknown to families that these services are available and only a phone call away.

One of the best things about being a part of a tribally run Head Start program is that we are able to truly realize another best practice, which is cultural sensitivity. Working for a tribe allows us to be able to use our Karuk language and culture in the classroom, and it is represented throughout classroom decor, curriculum materials, and lesson plans. Each family should feel welcome and honored to express and share their own unique cultural traditions, whether it is Native American or any other culture. It is very important that each family feel the respect that they are entitled to, and a teacher's biggest role is to be an advocate for the child and family while teaching the family to self-advocate. Working in a tribal community, it is imperative that teachers are mindful of the history that Native people have experienced, especially in regards to education. Only a couple of generations ago, Native American children were routinely stolen from their family homes and placed in a government-funded boarding schools whose main goals were to eradicate Native culture, religion, language, and identity. It has taken many years for Indigenous peoples to gain back some of what was lost and to gain the ability to display their roots without being discriminated against. As such, many tribal elders continue to be apprehensive of being involved in schools, and unfortunately for many, schools still carry a stigma. In order to address this issue, we at the Karuk Tribal Head Start have taken it upon ourselves to invite elders from our program's extended families, as well as tribal elders from our community at large, to volunteer and be a part of our classrooms. It is also an important part of teaching our children to have love and respect for our elders, while providing a forum for intergenerational teachings to be passed on to our students.

The Karuk Head Start Program honors each family's own educational journey, and we always make ourselves available to support each family, as they grow in any and all ways. Each day, we remain organized and child-centered. Each day we provide stability and promote growth. Our center is a fun-loving, family-nurturing, and culturally sensitive part of the community that we can be proud to be a part of as we continue to take our children's education back into our own hands.

Alexander's experience with a tribal head start program highlights the personal perspective of hands-on education for tribal youth as they begin an education journey. Jones, in the following section, describes his experiences from the perspective of an administrator of older youth as he shares perspectives that he envisions educators actualize every day, regardless of the age of the student.

PERSPECTIVES AND PHILOSOPHY
Mikela Jones

In order to address the many challenges of education, let alone Indian education, there are some things that you just need to accept as truth. If you cannot, or if you have a hard time accepting these, you will be someone who is continuously attempting to fit a square peg into a round hole, and trust me, it will just make you frustrated; I've tried it on a dare. First, not all students are ready to learn. Repeat after me: "Not all students are ready to learn." Good job! Now, students may show up to your class every day; however, that does not mean that they are ready to receive information. Second, there is not a one-fix-all recipe for reaching all students. Please keep reading! I know, I wish there was a quick fix! If there was one, I'd bottle it and send it all around the world! You still with me? Good, we can move on. We have to utilize many tools to address each child. However, the effectiveness of the tools we utilize stems from one foundational concept...which we will address shortly. Once we accept these two items as truth, we can move forward and stop banging our heads against the wall. Furthermore, if we do not accept these as truth, we risk the possibility of resenting our students and creating negative perceptions about our students or even a group of people, in addition to continuing to fail horribly when it comes to serving Native children.

Now that we have gotten that out of the way, let us begin. I was once told that in order to know where we are going, we must know where we are, and in order to know where we are, we must know where we have been. This is essential for addressing the educational needs for Native children. In order to know where we are going and where we stand within Indian education, we have to look at history. Unfortunately, history is an unpleasant experience for Native children when it comes to the concept of institutionalized education. However, when we look at the history of education of Native children precontact, the history is one that is of extreme importance, value, and essential for life, and the proof is in the long-lasting success in the livelihood of tribal people. There we will find the true essence of an indigenous pedagogy; there we will find elements that will support us in effectively reaching our native populations.

Institutionalized Education

The history for Native people when it comes to institutionalized education systems is not a pleasant experience. Institutionalized education was not to inspire or promote inquiry or creativity among Native children; institutionalized education was used to further colonize tribal people. Many tribal people were forced from their communities to go to boarding schools. These boarding schools were used to strip the tribal children of their indigeneity. These "schools" were tools to colonize Native children. The old saying was, "Kill the Indian, save the man" (Pratt, 1892). Native children were forced to go to these schools; they were not allowed to speak their language or practice their culture; and they were abused physically, mentally, emotionally, spiritually, and sexually. Furthermore, children who attended these schools were not allowed to choose what field of work they would enter; they were not learning how to be lawyers, teachers, or doctors, but rather, they were learning positions of servitude. Girls were learning how to be housekeepers and boys would learn blacksmithing and shoemaking. Children were also forced to learn Christianity. This was the first experience Native children had in a classroom. This trauma has created a wound that surpasses time and generations and will continue until it has been healed. As a young man I was angry—I always wondered why I didn't know my language, or songs, and traditions. Then I learned about the history of our people and what happened to my ancestors that led us to where we are today. I recall my mom telling me about asking her grandma why she didn't teach my mom the language. Granny said, "I'm doing you a favor by not teaching you the language, knowing the language will only bring you harm." When I learned the history, yes, it hurt, but in the end it gave me understanding. With understanding comes acceptance, with acceptance comes healing, and with healing comes the ability to move on. Many of our Native families are angry because they don't know their culture as an indigenous person and more importantly they do not understand and cannot move on. Regardless of how much you can encourage institutionalized education, until there is healing, it will forever be a place that once took our children, raped them, took so much from their identity and their birthright, and changed our communities forever. This is why so many of our Native children and families struggle with institutionalized education. It was not built for us, and the history of educating Native children is dark and ugly and has left us with the feeling of not belonging in educational institutions. Until we acknowledge this history, embrace this history, both Native and non-Native alike, we will continue to suffer from and perpetuate the challenges that many of our people have faced while sitting inside of a classroom.

Education Precolonization

Again, regardless of how unpleasant and how impactful boarding schools were, it is a small part of the educational experience of tribal people. The impact is great; however, it does not need to define Native people. For many of the challenges we face, there is support when we look at traditional education practices prior to contact. Traditional education among tribal people was beautiful! Imagine being taught by someone that you loved, someone that you cared about and trusted. You were taught by your auntie, uncle, father, and grandmother. Someone that you also knew loved you. Furthermore, the lessons were essential to the continued survival of the community. America is all about independence, whereas tribal people are all about *inter*-dependence. Here you were given your role and value to the community. Without you the community will not be as strong; the community will hurt or not be able to function. Therefore, the lessons you were learning were essential to life. Traditionally, we were taken by a loved one and experienced the lessons and the passing on of a responsibility. This created a value in the instructor, a value in the content, and a feeling of being valued to carry out this role or responsibility. Tribal people like the Sioux not only survived harsh winters but they flourished. The Navajo people did the same while living in the harsh conditions of the desert. The point is that education was a part of daily life for our people and when accompanied by true relationship, content-related, or connected to a student's life, and the student was valued and given responsibility based on particular skillset; students flourished. Here we have identified the foundation for an effective pedagogy for Native children:

1. Establish true, sincere, and meaningful relationships
2. Connect materials through content related or connected to students' lives
3. Value the learner, create and appreciate the role
4. Include hands-on experiential learning

Effective Practices for Tribal Children

The following sections in this chapter will outline ways in which we can incorporate the traditional concepts to effectively reach and support Native students. These concepts are the importance of building sound *relationships* with students, creating a sense of *belonging* for Native children, healing from *trauma*, and establishing *anchors*. Please continue to consider our two truths we originally accepted; this is important in our efforts that we make toward supporting native students. I will also encourage you to keep trying. The old adage of "you can bring a horse to water, but you can't make him drink" may be true; however, I always say I'm going to offer that horse water every day that I can; eventually that horse will be thirsty. And that is what you have to be willing to do, continue to offer, every day, and eventually someone will accept.

Relationship

I have found in my experiences both as a Native student and as an educator that many of our students tend to do well up until middle school. In elementary, students do well, but they have a significant dip upon entering middle school. I believe a great deal of that challenge is due to the change from a homeroom teacher to many teachers. I wish I had some great advice for you reading this; however, the answer is easy. Just like if I asked you how to lose weight... how do you lose weight? I'm sure right now you're thinking: exercise, eating well, cutting off the junk food. We all know the answer; the answer is the easy part! The hard part is doing it! Same thing here— my golden nugget, secret recipe, is not much of a secret after all. It is *relationship*! Our children need to trust you, care for you, and the relationship needs to be reciprocal. You need to care for your children, show it to them, and prove it to them. And believe me: Students will definitely test your level of commitment with their actions. Students want to see if you'll give up on them—when things get tough, will you care enough to stick around? They need to feel that it is a solid, sincere, real, meaningful relationship. Create relationships with children, and they will follow you to the end of the earth. And in some ways, with the expectations we place on children, we might as well be asking them to follow us to the end of the earth. We are asking them to trust in us, to believe that what they are learning in school is of value. Especially when we focus on subjects and emphasize, for example, that algebra is important, even though they have to deal with issues at home. They have to weigh, determine, and trust that this school work is worth their time and energy. I'm not saying that every staff in the school or person in the community has to do this, though imagine how great that would be if they did. I understand people, and there is a natural process that takes place when building relationships. None of us is going to click with every person. But it is vital, for our students to be successful, that they have at least one person that they have created a meaningful relationship with. I think it is obvious to say, and I will say it anyway, that the more meaningful relationships a child has, the more likely they will be connected to school or willing to listen and follow through with that person. For a student who is on the fence when it comes to education—I know I did this—for teachers they dislike they will not perform for and for the teachers they do like they will make an effort to complete their work. Spend time getting to know your students and having conversations with them. Inquire about them, what they like, what they want to be. Listen to their music, shoot hoops with them, bring food and eat with them. Create opportunities to learn about each other.

Belonging

Belonging is an Indigenous value as much it is a human value. Belonging is one of the biggest drivers in behavior. We constantly seek out, find, and create the sense of belonging. Until we feel that we belong, until schools make efforts to create belonging, we will continue to struggle. Education systems do not acknowledge what has been done, they do not acknowledge tribal heritage, we are mascots, we are in the history books, and we are forgotten. As a teacher, we first start by creating a sense of belonging in the classroom. Again, let's look back at one item we accepted as truth, that not all students are ready to learn. We must prepare our students to be in a place to receive information. We do this by establishing expected behaviors in the classroom and reminding students of these when they enter in a variety of ways such as verbally in the classroom, having a list on the wall, or giving students a handout. Whenever I work with a group of students, I start each day with a physical activity, small and short energizers that provide movement, focus, and fun. I then follow it up with creating norms, expected behavior that we collaboratively create. I often say, what norms do we need to create that will allow us to have a good day? What do you need to feel safe, supported, and willing to work together? When we work together to create the expectations, when someone is not following I remind them that we created these together. This is the foundation to creating a sense of belonging in the classroom. Again, referring to our second truth, there is not a one-fix-all recipe for reaching all students. This is not going to work with all students, but this is where building relationship is key. When we get to know our students, we know what works, what does not work. We are more effective at motivating, encouraging, and supporting our students. The initial "get to know each other" process is slow. But relationship is key to creating and maintaining that sense of belonging. When students feel that they belong and they are in a safe environment that accepts and appreciates them, they will take healthy risks, be more willing to fail, and ask for help.

Trauma

Due to history, Native people have experienced a life-changing trauma. This trauma was so significant that it truly has impacted generations of tribal people—that regardless of time, if a person has not dealt with the trauma by healing, is continually passed down from one generation to the next. In the article, "Trauma May Be Woven in the DNA of Native Americans," Pember (2015) speaks of epigenetics, identifying evidence that traumatic events are passed down through your DNA. Our children deal with this trauma in addition to their day-to-day challenges. This trauma has created a loss of identity for our children—for some an embarrassment of their own tribal ancestry. I know you may be asking yourself, this isn't my job, how do I help, this is too deep... regardless, this is what our children are facing. This is what prevents them from creating relationship, from trying their hardest, from caring about their future or what happens to them. Introducing children to wellness models is essential to their overall success in life. Whether it is success in education, having a job, raising a family, or just being a contributing member of society. Introducing students to wellness models in addition to identity development will support their healing. Due to the limits of this chapter, I cannot go into the concept of wellness, which is a book in itself. However I encourage you to identify wellness models to utilize with Native children. There are great programs out there: GONA (Gathering of Native Americans), Native Wellness Institute, and programs like Sons of Tradition. You can find helpful webinars on the GONA on the Substance Abuse and Mental Health Services Administration (http://www.samhsa.gov/tribal-ttac/resources/webinars). Find more information about Native Wellness Institute at their website, www.nativewellnessinstitute.com, and finally, www.whitebison.org has great resources for wellness training. Children with trauma are not able to reach their full potential due to a lack of wellness, a sense of identity, and that understanding that leads to healing. We cannot expect our children to be their best when they are deal- ing with Trauma. It is absolutely necessary to include a wellness program in our menu of services for Native students to further support their healthy growth and development in all areas of life.

Anchors

Students—heck, all people—need anchors! Anchors are what hold us in place and keep us where we need to be. When I look back at my educational career, I can clearly identify all my anchors. These are important reasons for staying in school. To use myself as an example, my mother was an anchor, sports were an anchor, and OK, sad but true, but girls were an anchor! These are things that kept me in school. The more anchors the better—the more likely you will stay on track. Helping students identify and develop anchors is essential for them to do well. As I got older and more advanced in my edu- cational career my anchors changed over time; sports eventually fell off but then I added my tribe, passion, career, even money. Helping students identify anchors will keep them connected to school and increase the likelihood of completion. For some children, it is difficult to find anchors, so you will need to help them. Work with your students to create a list of anchors, reasons why it is important for them to do well in school. One anchor for me that I added later was the fact that there were so few Natives going to college. I wanted to change the numbers! Having students regularly check and update their anchors is valuable to keeping them on track. Sometimes that finish line is so far away, we lose sight of why we are doing what we are doing in the day-to-day. Visiting our list will inspire, motivate, and remind us why we are on this path.

All of these items are interrelated. They work together; for example, *an- chors* are important to keep students in place and if you take the time to get to know and understand your student anchors that also will support *relation- ship* building and *belonging*. Utilize these tools to set the foundation for stu- dent readiness and support. Not every program is going to be able to change the curriculum to meet the needs of all Native children; however, when we build trust and relationship with children, create a sense of belonging, pro- mote healing, and develop anchors, students will persevere regardless of the lack of cultural fit of the content. It is evident in the number of Native students who have graduated or achieved regardless of that cultural fit. I am speaking from experience as a student and experience as an educator.

REFERENCES

DeVries, R., & Kohlberg, L. (1987). *Constructivist early education: Overview and com- parison with other programs* (Vol. 1987). Washington, DC: National Association for the Education of Young Children.

Frost, J. L., Wortham, S. C., & Reifel, R. S. (2008). *Play and child development.* Upper Saddle River, NJ: Pearson/Merrill Prentice Hall.

Official Report of the Nineteenth Annual Conference of Charities and Correction (1892), 46–59. Reprinted in Richard H. Pratt, "The Advantages of Mingling Indians with Whites," Americanizing the American Indians: Writings by the "Friends of the Indian" 1880–1900. Cambridge, MA: Harvard University Press, 1973, 260–271.

Pember, M. A. (2015, May 28). Trauma may be woven into the DNA of Native Americans. Retrieved from http://indiancountrytodaymedianetwork.com/2015/05/28/trauma-may-be-woven-dna-native-americans-160508

Pratt, R. (1892). Kill the Indian, save the man. In *Official Report of the Nineteenth Annual Conference of Charities and Correction* (pp. 46–59).

CHAPTER 6

K–12 BEST PRACTICES

Creating Successful
American Indian Students

Melissa Leal
Wilton Rancheria, Elk Grove, CA
and Sierra College, Rocklin, CA

In January of 2001, I started working as a tutor for Capitol Area Indian Resources (CAIR), an Indian education program that serves American Indian and Alaskan Native students in the greater Sacramento region. This was my first job out of high school and I was excited and nervous at the same time. I grew up knowing that I was California Indian, a descendant of the California Judgment Roll, a "mission Indian" from Carmel and San Juan Bautista, Esselen and Ohlone, but I had only known one other California Indian family, two Miwok boys that I had gone to school with since 3rd grade. I also began attending California State University–Sacramento in January of 2001. Little did I know that these events in my life's history would lead me to be writing this chapter on K–12 best practices for American Indian students.

When I started tutoring, I began to notice how similar my family was to the rest of the families that I was serving: same foods, lots of kids in and out

On Indian Ground: California, pages 71–81
Copyright © 2017 by Information Age Publishing

of the house, so many cousins, often a lack of resources, but most importantly parents who genuinely wanted their children to succeed. Unfortunately, due to factors that were out of their control and some that were in their control, these parents (much like my own) didn't have the ability to help their children with their school work, especially the older children. Education was a priority for their household, but they didn't have the tools to assist in a way that was beneficial to their children. These similarities allowed me to understand my situation a little more clearly. I was the first person in my family to go to college, let alone graduate and earn a PhD. My mom, an amazing woman, did not graduate from high school. My father graduated from high school and then spent his life working as a contractor, which took a toll on his body, mind, and spirit. We were poor. I had a love for reading and learning. School was easy for me. Life was a little more difficult.

This was the case for many of the students I began working with. They were intelligent and had the ability to learn. What they often lacked was confidence and stability. For many of my students, I acted as more of a mentor than a tutor. I spent time talking to them about what they wanted to be when they grew up, how they planned to achieve that, what they were good at, and so on. Sometimes I even played basketball with them after our tutoring sessions. I wanted them to make a commitment to themselves and to me that they would always care about their education, that they would continue with school and graduate from high school. I even started promising them $100 when they graduated high school. I can proudly say that I have had to shell out a few hundred dollars over the years. Tutoring and Indian education became more of a way of life for me than an occupation. I owe whatever success that I may have in educating others and my own continuing education to Capitol Area Indian Resources. The director, Cindy La Marr; the families that I worked with; and the program structure have influenced me and molded me. They have allowed me to become an advocate for education, not in *their* traditional sense but in *our* traditional sense.

My understanding, academically and personally, of a successful Indian education program includes the goals and mission of CAIR. CAIR operates from these premises:

1. Development of programs with purpose that embrace and respect American Indian cultural traditions.
2. Build positive and individualized connections with American Indian youth and their families.
3. Development of mutually supportive relationships with schools to promote an understanding of Indian student needs.
4. Build strong, positive connections with participants' families to further cultural and academic growth and achievement.

5. To engage community members, groups, organizations and institutions in programming that positively affects the American Indian community.
6. Incorporation of a variety of engaging program activities that honor the cultures and traditions of Indian people. (CAIR, n.d.)

These six premises have become the foundation of what I strive to do in my current position as the director of education for Wilton Rancheria. They are goals that I have attempted to lay out in other positions as well, including at the Elk Grove Unified School District and the Greater Sacramento Urban League. As I was being trained and molded by CAIR, I was also acquiring my own education, first at CSU–Sacramento and then later at UC–Davis. I was learning about Native American history, issues, laws, and programs. I was also becoming more familiar with my own tribal heritage, including learning the Esselen language. All of these things were pivotal in my development as an educator and play a huge part in the framework and pathways that have been created for K–12th grade American Indian students.

The following paper will describe an outline of best practices in Indian education for kindergarten through 12th grade students and an example of a successful after-school program designed and implemented by California Indian students, NERDS (Native Education Raising Dedicated Students).

CREATING A FRAMEWORK AND PATHWAY FOR EDUCATIONAL SUCCESS

There are four key factors that make a successful California Indian student (Figure 6.1). They include culture, academics, community, and family. A program can't simply focus on academics and ignore culture. The reverse is true as well. We speak about a holistic approach a lot within wellness programs, but the reality is that an education program must be designed and implemented just like a wellness program. Every part of that student's life has to be addressed before the student can begin to excel academically.

The following is an outline of how the Department of Education at Wilton Rancheria serves its tribal members. (Note: Wilton Rancheria has approximately 710 enrolled members, half of whom are children under the age of 18. The director of education is responsible for assisting every tribal member who is enrolled in school or planning to attend school or receive training. This means, essentially, that the Department of Education serves every single tribal member including those who are incarcerated.) This framework can be used and modified for any tribe or Indian education program. It is simply an outline for the areas that need to be addressed in order to raise and educate successful students.

Figure 6.1   Four key factors that make a successful California Indian student.

I. Tribal Individualized Education Plan (TIEP)—Each tribal member student is tracked in a system/spreadsheet that allows the director of education and other employees to monitor their progress or lack thereof. This tracking begins with a survey that is sent to each household, whether the household has small children or not. Sometimes grandparents are taking care of their grandchildren and may have more information than the parents. The goal is to get as much information as possible about the students as we can so we know how to help them. The survey asks for name, age, grade level, school names, school district, current GPA, address, phone number, and email. In addition, the survey asks if the home has a computer and Internet access. The final question is, "How can the tribe assist your child?" We encourage parents to send their child's most recent report card or progress report. All of this information will be entered into a student profile. The information here helps us in many ways. For example, if several students are in homes without a computer or Internet access, we need to start looking for funding to help buy computers, and so on. We can create email lists and disseminate information easily to households with students.

The survey is a great tool and has been the foundation for the TIEP at Wilton Rancheria.

II. Scholarships: Higher Education, Adult/Vocational, and General Education—The tribe currently offers three different types of scholarships and funding for students who have completed high school or who are taking college/vocational classes. The higher education scholarship program's aim is to promote and emphasize the value of education. It provides financial assistance to tribal members attending graduate school programs, universities, colleges, and community colleges. The purpose is to promote access to higher education opportunities and assist tribal members to achieve their educational goals.

The adult and vocational assistance programs aim to assist youth and adult tribal members attempting to obtain their high school diploma, GED, or a certificate in a specific skilled trade (mechanics, nursing, cosmetology, etc.) The purpose of these two programs is to promote further education and/or increase access to employment opportunities.

The general education program is a small fund available to tribal members, specifically high school students to assist with the cost of things like SAT testing, summer school, or field trips. It is a fund set up to assist students whose parents are low income and can't afford extra expenses that may be necessary for their child's education.

III. Summer Program—Each year in the months of June, July, and August, we provide a 3- to 4-week summer program for tribal member students. The summer program consists of academic, cultural, artistic, athletic, and other extracurricular activities. For example, last year we did a week of language learning and math/reading review, a week of empowerment activities and talking circles, a camping trip, and a field trip to the state fair; the students wrote, produced, and directed a song and music video titled "Miwok Pride" in four days, and we went on a field trip to the Bowling Alley. We typically end the summer with a back-to-school BBQ and backpack giveaway. One of the requests from tribal members is assistance with school supplies, so we fill the backpacks with school supplies and give them away at the BBQ. The BBQ acknowledges all of the students who were promoted or graduated at the end of the school year, and we showcase any of our language learning or art at this event as well. (Language learning is woven into every activity.)

IV. Language and Cultural Classes—We hold weekly Miwok language classes utilizing language teachers and tech experts from other tribes. The language classes are open to tribal members, and we encourage the very young children to participate as it is often much easier for them to learn than the adults. In providing the classes, we are also training tribal members who are interested in becoming language teachers.

V. Socialization and Team Building Activities—These activities include field trips or special presentations that are interesting and informative, and they create a space for families to come together. Recently we hosted a reptile show in collaboration with the local school district's Indian education program. It was a well-attended event, and the families loved it. Having events like this allows for the families to get to know each other better, bond over the excitement that their children possess, and allow them to become familiar with the Department of Education staff. The parents' ability to trust the staff is a key factor in a tribal education program. We are often the neutral party and advocate for the tribal members when dealing with teachers and schools; therefore, a parent has to know that we are not just another "person working in the tribal office," but someone invested in their children.

VI. Tutoring—The tribe hires tutors and offers tutoring for students who are in need of it. It is important to work with the Title VII programs as well because they often have tutoring services and resources for tutoring within the students' respective school districts.

VII. Mentoring/Empowerment/Educational Planning—This occurs on an everyday basis and is most often implemented during the summer program. Workshops and individual meetings occur throughout the year to assist students with motivation and goal setting. It is necessary for the older students (middle school and high school) to gain trust in the person who is providing these services. The staff person in charge of this needs to be experienced and trained in wellness and education. They also need to be relatable to the students, which often means someone who is Native American and possibly closer to the student's age.

VIII. Partnerships—The most essential partnerships are with the schools and school districts that the tribal member students are attending. This can be a difficult task as we have tribal members spread out across the west coast. The TIEP allows us to see where a majority of our students are going to school, and we can ensure that we have formal partnerships with those schools/districts and possibly informal, but working partnerships with the other schools/districts. These partnerships can be developed through MOU's or basic email/letter outreach and introductions. This would depend on the type of program that is being run. Other partnerships would include Native American Health Centers, funding agencies or organizations, local businesses that can provide services or coordinate activities, Title VII programs, colleges, universities, private schools, and vocational training centers.

IX. Prison/Juvenile Hall Outreach—We often forget about serving the individuals who are incarcerated, but we must be able to provide them with as many services as the institution allows them to receive. This means that correspondence between inmates and the Director of Education must be allowed. Currently, Wilton Rancheria provides scholarships for tribal members who are incarcerated and have the ability to take correspondence courses. Educational and career planning can also be done through correspondence, especially necessary for those who are close to their release date. This outreach and educational assistance is essential but also comes with many barriers. This best practice is still in its beginning stages and will hopefully grow to be more effective and helpful for juveniles who are incarcerated.

X. Social Media—It is essential to have a presence on a social media platform like Facebook as it allows parents, families, students, and anyone interested to see what is going on in the community or within the tribe. Typical uses include posting announcements for workshops, scholarships, and community events, highlighting tribal members and students who are making positive strides in their educational goals, motivational quotes, and pictures of students participating in activities. Facebook has been extremely beneficial to Wilton's Department of Education and the parents and tribal council are extremely happy with its use.

XI. Department of Health Joint Ventures—As mentioned previously, wellness programs are absolutely necessary within an education program. Many of the activities that our Health Department plans, implements, and evaluates are youth centered, specifically Diabetes and Tobacco prevention. A great working relationship between the two departments and/or organizations is essential.

XII. NERDS—Native Education Raising Dedicated Students (NERDS) is a leadership program for 7th through 12th grade students (NERDS, n.d.). It fosters intellectual and academic development, paying attention to cultural values and tribal heritage. This is an after-school program that has been shown to have amazing positive effects on Native American youth who participate. NERDS will be discussed in more detail later. Each tribe and/or education organization can benefit from implementing a NERDS program or a program similar to NERDS.

XIII. Safe Spaces—Students should have a communal space that they can come to, to do homework, study, interact with their peers, and feel safe and wanted. Wilton Rancheria has an Education Department Center that includes the director's office, storage, a main area with laptops available for use, comfortable chairs for lounging and studying, a small library, and library "chill space." The office is decorated with fun and uplifting colors and is still in the process of being decorated, but the decorations will be designed by the students. In addition to this space, we are planning to create another space that we will call the "Usu:mati Hol:awu" (bear cave), which will be more of a social space where older students can gather to play games, listen to music, watch movies, and have talking circles. A student recently said to me, "I wouldn't smoke weed all of the time if I had more to do." Ideally this space would be open every day of the week; however, even 2 days a week can be beneficial to the students in an effort to prevent risky behavior.

XIV. Transportation—This can be the biggest challenge for any successful education program. Lack of transportation is a barrier for many families. A vehicle designated to the program and a person who is responsible for picking up and dropping off students is ideal. Unfortunately, it isn't always a reality. However, the Facebook page has begun to assist in this process as parents can figure out ways to carpool or share the transportation duties. Sometimes we are able to use the tribal van and van driver to help with transportation, but it is not always available. Often the director of education transports students in her personal vehicle. Acquiring funds to afford a vehicle and an employee to have that responsibility is possible through grant funding and other types of governmental resources, but it takes time.

All of these best practices require financial support and an experienced and relatable staff that can work with students to inspire, motivate, and educate them differently than their teachers and schools do. The most common ways to acquire funding are through partnerships where other departments and/or organizations are providing services to students and by writing and acquiring grants that support program development and implementation. However, even if there aren't a lot of resources available, a successful Indian student is one who is given time and a listening ear. The NERDS program is an excellent example of a student-developed and -run program that started with nothing but an idea and a commitment.

NERDS

NERDS began in the 2011–2012 school year when Wilton Rancheria tribal member Dahkota Franklin Kicking Bear Brown was in 8th grade. He witnessed family members and friends begin to withdraw from school activities and fall behind in the classroom. He learned about the current statistics regarding education and suicide for Native American students, and he wanted to do something to help his peers persevere and change those statistics. NERDS is now a nationally recognized nonprofit with numerous clubs operating all over the United States under the original executive board. The mission of NERDS is to "support the peer-to-peer mentoring clubs currently in place that focus on education, culture, and community service" (NERDS GoFundMe, n.d., para 2). NERDS hosts an annual conference in California and invites 7th through 12th grade Native students from all over the state to participate. NERDS has begun to encompass an even more holistic approach that is now focused on empowerment rather than solely education.

Dahlton Brown, Dahkota's older brother, recently completed his undergraduate honors theses in the Graduate School of Education at Stanford University. His theses was titled *Culturally Immersive Programming for Native American/Alaska Native Students: Benefits, Impacts, and Implications Based Upon a Survey of NERDS (Native Education Raising Dedicated Students)*. His study evaluated "the ways in which culturally immersive extracurricular programming affects attitudes towards education in NA/AN youth. More specifically, the study analyzes the ways in which a non-profit organization has been able to work with NA/AN students to provide a culturally responsive atmosphere that advocates for educational achievement" (Brown, 2015, p. 2).

His study proved that a culturally responsive program can positively impact student attitudes towards school and their education. He surveyed new and veteran NERDS participants in Amador, California. He based his study on five areas that were previously defined as the focus for the NERDS program: education, culture, community, service, and future. The findings that he reported are that students who participated regularly in the NERDS program had a greater sense of personal and cultural belonging, which resulted in a better and more engaged classroom experience. Students were able, through advocacy, tutoring, and being held accountable by their peers, to improve their grades/GPA and genuinely feel better about themselves as a student. Brown concluded,

> Participation in a culturally immersive extracurricular program is absolutely beneficial in engaging NA/AN youth in public school settings. As evidenced by the NERDS model, bringing together NA/AN youth in a culturally responsive setting allows them to effectively engage in the learning environment and feel accepted in a space that for so long has not welcomed their presence. The majority of students sampled indicated a greater sense of community, identity, and culture since joining the NERDS program. (2015, p. 55)

NERDS has proven to be a successful program for students in Amador County and other counties in the region. The annual NERDS conference is something that students look forward to each year. They have expressed that they feel a sense of belonging and importance at the conference and they leave feeling like they have made new friends and have goals to accomplish. In order for students and programs like NERDS to be established in a culturally responsive way, school districts and Native communities need to come together in partnership and collaboration to promote the advancement of Native American youth academically and socially.

CONCLUSION

I have learned through working with Native American youth for 15 years that no two students are going to respond the same to attempts at assisting them in their education. There is not one best practice, but a circle of activities, methods, pedagogies, and teachings that I hope to have illustrated here in this chapter. There are several excellent educational programs in California that are run through tribes, Indian Education programs, and schools. The key to the success of these programs is that the student is at the center and that the community, family, academics, and culture surround that student acting as a weapon and a shield to their success. Community, family, academics, and culture protect and empower Native American students. A framework without one of those pieces will not be successful. I mentioned previously that a student confided in me that she didn't want to smoke weed anymore and that if she had more to do, she wouldn't smoke weed. This confession occurred at the last NERDS conference. I sat and talked with this student (along with another student) for a couple of hours. I listened more than I spoke, and I offered suggestions about what she can do to occupy her time in a positive way. I am happy to say that this student has been able to abstain from marijuana since that day. She had all of the answers. I gave her nothing but a shoulder and an open heart, and NERDS gave her a safe space to have that discussion. Traditionally we were educated through watching our parents' and older siblings' actions and through stories and song. Those are our Native Ways of Knowing. Those epistemologies have not changed. In order to guarantee the success of our students in kindergarten through 12th grade, we must show them how to be successful. We must tell those stories and sing the songs that allow them to see their own greatness.

REFERENCES

Brown, D. (2015). *Culturally immersive programming for Native American/Alaska Native students: Benefits, impacts, and implications based upon a survey of NERDS (Native*

Education Raising Dedicated Students) (Undergraduate Honors Thesis). Graduate School of Education, Stanford University, Stanford, CA.

Capital Area Indian Resources, Inc. (n.d.). *About us.* Retrieved from http://cair.us/?page_id=81

Native Education Raising Dedicated Students. (n.d.). *History.* Retrieved from http://www.nativenerds.org/contact—history.html

CHAPTER 7

TEACHING TRUTH

Social Justice for California Native Students

Joely Proudfit
California Indian Culture & Sovereignty Center

Nicole Quinderro Myers-Lim
National Indian Justice Center
and California Indian Museum and Cultural Center

Native educators throughout California are faced with many challenges in advocating for change in curriculum, combatting stereotypes, correcting misconceptions, challenging romanticism, and keeping Native youth engaged in an educational system that typically marginalizes their histories, cultures, and contemporary issues. These educators and colleagues are motivated by a sense of social justice and an inherent desire to make the experience of Native youth better than the one they had endured. As these educators become parents a sense of urgency rises to the surface. There is pressure to make your child's world a better place.

My [Nicole Lim] daughter is currently a high school freshman. Since she was in preschool, I have worried about the impact that fairytales, cartoons,

On Indian Ground: California, pages 83–100
Copyright © 2017 by Information Age Publishing
All rights of reproduction in any form reserved.

children's storybooks, and elementary and upper school curricula would have on her psyche. It seemed overwhelming, as if there was too much to combat and counteract. She was surrounded not just by Hollywood images but by the misconceptions of her peers and teachers alike. She would continually have to speak up to, correct, and educate those around her. She would be labeled as overly sensitive or aggressive and would have to get used to her classmates reacting with sighs and eye rolls. How could I raise a confident Native leader in a world that continued to minimize, question, and negate her identity? Needless to say, I worried about the toll these repeated negative interactions would take on her. I was all too familiar with the circumstances and the anxieties they had caused me when I was in her same situation. I found that the wheels of justice turn slow, but she had her hands on the wheel. When she was in the 7th grade, she wrote the following editorial for her English teacher.

"Redskins": A Compliment? (California Native Youth 7th Grade Editorial)

The lake was painted red with the blood of her family. She looked up to see the sun peering through the rippling water. She could see the black boots that belonged to the U.S. Cavalry stomping through the water and breaking the silence. She shook underwater with the fear of discovery. What if they find her? Will they kill her? She held the tule tightly between her two chapped lips. This plant was the only chance at survival. She took deep breathes through the straw like plant. She tried to calm herself, but it was impossible. Calmness and slaughter don't quite go together. This was the 1850 Bloody Island Massacre she was experiencing. She was among the very few child survivors.

In the fall of 1847, Andrew Kelsey and Charles Stone bought Salvador Vallejo's cattle operation. Vallejo had trained the local Pomo natives as vaqueros (Indian cowboys), but Stone and Kelsey's treatment of the Native community in Big Valley was extremely brutal. Natives were outraged in the fall of 1849 when, in the grip of gold fever, Kelsey forced 50 to 100 Native men to accompany him to the gold fields. Only two returned alive. Stone and Kelsey became more careless and brutal as ever. Shootings and beatings took place regularly. Women and children were raped and enslaved. When Chief Augustine's wife became the subject of attention, he organized an attack. From within, his wife poured water onto the powder charges of Kelsey and Stone's firearms, and Natives burst into the house at dawn. Kelsey was killed, but Stone had leaped through a window as an act of desperation. Stone's body was later found, he had been brained by a rock.

In the spring of 1850, the U.S. Cavalry came to "punish" the Natives for their "misbehavior." Two hundred Pomo people were slaughtered. During the attack, one of my ancestors, Napo, had told her children to hide in the lake and breathe through the tule. They ran to the lake while Napo tried to find another way to escape. Napo's children were child survivors of the Bloody Island Massacre. Many of the children lived through adulthood. Elizabeth Posh, a grandchild of a child survivor of the massacre, gave birth to nine children. Only six of the nine children lived to adulthood, one of which was my great grandmother, Matilda Myers. She had a child at fifteen years old and named him Joe Myers.

Joe has spent his life fighting against the injustices, violence, and poverty he experienced living on the Pinoleville reservation near Ukiah, CA. He spends his time educating non-Natives who need to better understand the misconceptions and stereotypes that Natives face. Native people suffer from stereotypes in addition to the external traumas that shape their lives. The instinct for survival has guided our people through generations of painful experiences. Though the pages of our history are sad, the ability of our ancestors to overcome these challenges and save our culture gives us strength and purpose. From my ancestors I have inherited the ability to survive, adapt, dream, excel, and beat the odds at all costs. I am not a princess, animal, savage, drunk, stupid, or extinct.

Before fourth grade, most children think that Native American women are princesses and the men are buff killing-machines. Thanks to Disney's Pocahontas, even some children that are older than 10 years of age still believe the misconceptions. They also believe that we have mystical powers and that we can't count beyond one hundred. This shows how Native Americans are classified as "characters in a fairytale." These classifications over simplify who we are and take attention away from the more important issues. What's the truth about Native American women? "Native American women are also at a high risk of sexual and physical abuse, recorded at three and a half times higher than the national average. This estimate is very low because 70 percent of abuse cases go unreported, often due to mistrust Native American women feel towards government and police. Seventy percent of the violence experienced by Native American women is from non-Native American men." (*The New York Times*)

The Hollywood Indian is the most common stereotype. Headdresses, moccasins, buckskin and beads are "common accessories." They also enforce stereotypes because they are those most common representation of Native Americans offered to the public eye. These false images are engraved into young minds. These pictures appear on beer bottles, movies, books, and sports mascots. Our ceremonial dances are also turned into popular dance moves. For example, the "Party Rock Anthem" shuffle is really a smoke dance. After this song and shuffle became popular, LMFAO later tried to sue the Natives for "copyright infringement." The smoke dance was originally a war dance only performed by men. People don't understand the value of these dances to Native people. These ceremonial practices represent our cultures, connect today's tribal communities to the past. The "Hollywood Indian" stereotype is for the movie obsessed, but there is another common stereotype among the knowledge obsessed.

"Native Americans came across the land bridge called the Bering Strait." This is the typical hook or introduction for starting a lesson on Native Americans.

This theory has so many inconsistencies. Where is the evidence that supports this theory? There is no evidence. Though there is evidence that it did not happen. The Natives were supposed to have come across the Bering Strait about 15,000 years prior to Columbus' arrival in 1492. If we are using science as our "measuring stick," there are ruins that are over the age of 20,000 years old in America. The Bering Strait theory is also offensive because it goes against the religion of Native people. The religion states that we, Native Americans, have always been here. The late Standing Rock Sioux scholar Vine Deloria, Jr., has significantly challenged this theory and referred to it as, "scientific language for I don't know, but it sounds good and no one will check." He went on to say in his book, *Red Earth White Lies: American Indians and the Myth of Scientific Fact*:

> An examination of the Bering Strait doctrine suggests that such a journey would have been nearly impossible even if there had been hordes of Paleo-Indians trying to get across the hypothetical land bridge. It appears that not even animals or plants really crossed this mythical connection between Asia and North America. The Bering Strait exists and existed only in the minds of scientists.

Why is this theory presented as fact? Is it to promote the romantic notion that America is a country of immigrants? Why are other theories or cultural beliefs not presented? Are we ignoring a discussion of what happened to aboriginal peoples? I understand that it may protect children from the reality of what occurred and will prevent questioning, but does it really help them in the long run? Preparing our youth for the future is what childhood is supposed to do. Rebecca Stead says, "Everyone is born with a 'veil'." This "veil" is like a bride's veil and is somewhat see-through. It causes the world to look blurry, but we like it that way. Sometimes the wind lifts the "veil" so we can see the world for what it truly is. We can see glimpses of the good and the bad in the world. We need to lift the "veil" that our children wear so they can see the world for what it truly is.

There are many essential understandings that one must possess to teach accurately and sensitively about Native Americans. The most important one is for educators to realize Native Americans are all very diverse. Hundreds of tribes have thousands of different languages, ceremonies, songs, religions, etc. People sometimes come up to me and ask "Can you speak Indian?" There are over 600 tribes and even more languages, so of course I cannot speak "Indian." We need to address these issues as soon as possible. We need to protect children of Native American descent as well as others of all races from negative and inaccurate information. We can end the ripple effect of the traumas experienced by their ancestors.

Physical abuse has become very popular among all teenagers, and particularly in Native American students. We need to show them that things can and will get better. We can give you alternative lesson plans and resources, but you need to use them and take interest in them. Native youth have the right to know the truth. We need to work on decreasing the number of gasps in the room when an audience hears that Native women were raped by priests and soldiers. This is not merely Native history, it is American history and should be common knowledge. We need to communicate a factual history even if it is not complimentary to those who wrote it. Communication will help us address the issues together. "Action may not always bring happiness, but there is no happiness without action." (Agnes Rappilier)

Needless to say, as an educator and I parent, I was proud to see that she was able to use her writing skills to express her frustrations. She was recognized by her teachers, peers, and the native community. It was not the first time she had addressed these issues but it was the first time she had received positive reinforcement for her positions. Unfortunately, most California Native youth share her frustrations, but few receive positive feedback for their expression of these concerns. During roundtable discussions California Indian youth indicate that racism and bias are often the norm in their schools.

> Young people, especially those in urban Indian communities, have also expressed they often feel a target of racism at school because of being Native American. They encounter non-Native peers within their schools and communities who negatively stereotype them because of their race. The youth feel there is a lack of education about Native American history, culture and general awareness of cultural diversity in their schools. Students say they want help in educating their peers about Native American cultures and traditions to help address and demystify any stereotypes made against tribal youth. (Voices of Native Youth Report 2012, Center for Native American Youth, The Aspen Institute, p. 11)

Thus, there is a longstanding tradition and permissive culture in elementary and high schools that appropriates Native American identities (Figure 7.1). How do native educators, advocates and students counteract the impacts of this reality? Over the years we have employed various political, institutional, and grassroots strategies. Third time is the charm, as they say, with finally passing legislation that would end the use of "Redskins" as a school team name or mascot (California Racial Mascots Act, 2015). The California Racial Mascots Act would require California schools to phase out "Redskins" as a team name and mascot by Jan. 1, 2019. Similar legislation failed to pass the state Legislature in 2002, but did win approval in 2003, only to be vetoed by then Governor Arnold Schwarzenegger, who said it was up to local communities to decide on team names and mascots. However, research clearly shows that these team names and mascots can establish a hostile and unwelcoming learning environment for AI/AN students. Furthermore, evidence for this is found in numerous studies, including "Missing the Point:

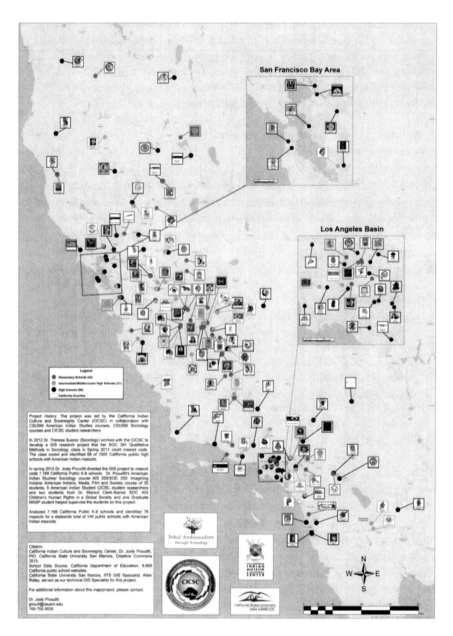

Figure 7.1 Cultural appropriation in California public K–12 schools: Tribal mascots and stereotypes.

The Real Impact of Native Mascots and Team Names on American Indian and Alaska Native Youth" (Stegman & Phillips, 2014).

This reveals that the presence of AI/AN mascots directly results in lower self-esteem and mental health for AI/AN adolescents and young adults. Numerous studies show that these mascots negatively impact the educational experience of all students, especially students with little or no contact with AI/AN people. More often than not, these stereotypical representations are believed as factual representations and support the development of cultural biases and prejudices.

AB 30, Alejo. School or athletic team names: California Racial Mascots Act.

Existing law provides that it is the policy of this state to afford all persons in public schools equal rights and opportunities in the educational institutions of the state, as specified, and further prohibits, and provides remedies for, acts that are contrary to that policy.

This bill would establish the California Racial Mascots Act, which would prohibit public schools from using the term Redskins as a school or athletic team name, mascot, or nickname beginning January 1, 2017, subject to specified exceptions. The bill would also provide that this prohibition may not be waived by the State Board of Education. To the extent that this prohibition would impose additional duties on public schools, the bill would impose a state-mandated local program.

The California Constitution requires the state to reimburse local agencies and school districts for certain costs mandated by the state. Statutory provisions establish procedures for making that reimbursement.

This bill would provide that, if the Commission on State Mandates determines that the bill contains costs mandated by the state, reimbursement for those costs shall be made pursuant to these statutory provisions.

http://leginfo.legislature.ca.gov/faces/billNavClient.xhtml?bill_id=2015 20160AB30

AB 30 was approved by Governor Jerry Brown on October 11, 2015.

The people of the State of California do enact as follows:

SECTION 1.

Article 3.5 (commencing with Section 221.2) is added to Chapter 2 of Part 1 of Division 1 of Title 1 of the Education Code, to read:

Article 3.5. The California Racial Mascots Act

221.2.

The Legislature finds and declares all of the following:

(a) The use of racially derogatory or discriminatory school or athletic team names, mascots, or nicknames in California public schools is antithetical to the California school mission of providing an equal education to all.

(b) Certain athletic team names, mascots, and nicknames that have been used and remain in use by other teams, including school teams, in other parts of the nation are discriminatory in singling out the Native American community for the derision to which mascots or nicknames are often subjected.

(c) Many individuals and organizations interested and experienced in human relations, including the United States Commission on Civil Rights, have concluded that the use of Native American images and names in school sports is a barrier to equality and understanding, and that all residents of the United States would benefit from the discontinuance of their use.

(d) No individual or school has a cognizable interest in retaining a racially derogatory or discriminatory school or athletic team name, mascot, or nickname.

221.3.

(a) Beginning January 1, 2017, all public schools are prohibited from using the term Redskins for school or athletic team names, mascots, or nicknames.

(b) Notwithstanding this section, a public school may continue to use uniforms or other materials bearing the term Redskins as a school or athletic team name, mascot, or nickname that were purchased before January 1, 2017, if all of the following requirements are met:

(1) The school selects a new school or athletic team name, mascot, or nickname.

(2) (A) Except as provided in subparagraph (B), the school refrains from purchasing or acquiring, for the purpose of distribution or sale to pupils or school employees, any uniform that includes or bears the term Redskins.

(B) Notwithstanding subparagraph (A), prior to January 1, 2019, a school using uniforms that bear the term Redskins may purchase or acquire a number of uniforms equal to up to 20 percent of the total number of uniforms used by a team or band at that school during the 2016–17 school year for the purposes of replacing damaged or lost uniforms.

(3) The school refrains from purchasing or acquiring, for the purpose of distribution or sale to pupils or school employees, any yearbook, newspaper, program, or other similar material that includes or bears the prohibited school or athletic team name, mascot, or nickname in its logo or cover title.

(4) The school refrains from purchasing or constructing a marquee, sign, or other new or replacement fixture that includes or bears the prohibited school or athletic team name, mascot, or nickname. This paragraph ap-

plies to facilities that bear the prohibited school or athletic team name, mascot, or nickname, in which case the school shall remove the prohibited name no later than the next time the associated part of the facility is replaced in the normal course of maintenance.

(c) It is the intent of the Legislature that implementation of a new school or athletic team name, mascot, or nickname does not result in a requirement to immediately purchase or replace materials or fixtures until they would have needed to be purchased or replaced without the enactment of this article.

(d) This section is not subject to waiver by the state board pursuant to Section 33050, except as specified in this section.

SEC. 2.

If the Commission on State Mandates determines that this act contains costs mandated by the state, reimbursement to local agencies and school districts for those costs shall be made pursuant to Part 7 (commencing with Section 17500) of Division 4 of Title 2 of the Government Code.

This has been a nearly half century battle in our state. Over the years many have fought long and hard to make changes on behalf of our AIAN student population. In recent years however we could not be happier about the work of AIAN students from the k-16 who have engaged successful in this effort and have helped to change legislation. From Dahkota Brown a then 16 year old Miwok junior at Argonaut High School in Jackson, California addressing the California State Assembly Education Committee.

As a sophomore lineman for the Argonaut football team, Brown said he dreaded game day against the Calaveras High School "Redskins" because it included war cries from fans, sports announcers announcing "a wild party of Redskins!" and even his own friends shouting "Kill the Redskins! Send them on the Trail of Tears!" He recalled his cousin crying after a football game during which a female student dressed up as "Pocahottie" while other students pretended to prepare to burn her at the stake.

"I do not blame those students, the school or staff for any of these things," Brown said in an email interview. "I do not think they knew better or considered what they were doing as wrong." But, he said, "I will blame people for hearing the facts and then not caring enough to stop the harm." http://edsource.org/2015/california-bill-would-be-first-in-the-nation-to-ban-redskins-school-mascot/77867

Dahkota Brown's testimony and efforts were impactful he along with many others in the state have assisted to make the change. Brown was recently appointed by President Obama to serve as the youngest member ever of the National Advisory Council on Indian Education (NACIE). I am very proud to serve alongside this young man and excited about the contributions he will make as he continues his education.

COLLEGE STUDENTS, GIS,
CULTURALLY RELEVANT RESEARCH

Each day when I arrive at the California Indian Culture and Sovereignty Center (CICSC), we are focused on how we can work with our college students to honor our mission, which is, "We foster collaborative research and community service relationships between the faculty, staff, and students of CSU San Marcos and members of Tribal communities, for the purpose of developing and conducting research projects that support the maintenance of sovereignty and culture within those communities" (https://www.csusm.edu/cicsc/index.html). Furthermore, we are governed by our four guiding principles:

Responsibility—To support political and economic development, education, health and wellness, media and film, language preservation, and natural resource management

Reciprocity—To reinforce collaborative research, fostering indigenous research methods

Respect—To champion sovereignty and cultural preservation

Relationships—To create and sustain communication between tribes and scholars

The CICSC believes that our research must provide useful knowledge for creating future public policy, and fosters productive discussions about tribal educational needs. Our goal is to make American Indian education resources a priority for Native students, tribes, and families in California. Therefore, working with our American Indian Studies classes, CICSC student researchers, and our American Indian Student Alliance, we have engaged a few research projects which we believe have both impacted legislative changes and served as agents for change.

Project Title: Cultural Appropriation in California Public K–12 Schools: Tribal Mascots and Stereotypes

Project History: The project was led by the CICSC in collaboration with CSUSM American Indian Studies Courses, CSUSM sociology courses, and CICSC student researchers.

In 2012, Dr. Theresa Suarez (sociology) worked with the CICSC to develop a GIS research project that her SOC 361 Qualitative Methods in Sociology, class in spring 2013 could mascot code. The class coded and identified 68 of 1500 California public high schools with American Indian mascots.

In spring 2015 Dr. Joely Proudfit directed the GIS project to mascot code 7,169 California public K–8 schools. Dr. Proudfit's American Indian Studies/

Sociology course AIS 350/SOC 350: Imagining Indians: American Indians, Media, Film and Society course of 35 students, 6 American Indian Student CICSC student researchers and two students from Dr. Marisol Clark-Ibanez SOC 403 Children's Human Rights in a Global Society and one Graduate Masters of Sociological Practice MASP student helped supervise the students on this project. Our students analyzed 7,169 California Public K–8 schools and identified 78 mascots for a statewide total of 146 public schools with American Indian mascots. The maps (42" x 58") were printed and presented to Assemblyman Alejo at the Democratic State Convention in Spring 2015, at the annual ESRI conference and to representatives of Governor Brown's office. The map powerfully visualizes those data and in real time showed how impactful our students can be in working together to impact a legislative change.

UNIVERSITIES, STEREOTYPES, AND MEDIA & FILM

While we have only recently seen some successes with our efforts to make some changes to mascots in the K–12 arena. We know that the real work is still ahead of us. We found through our GIS mapping project that students in some areas in the state can go from kindergarten to college being exposed to American Indian mascots through their entire public education. The impact of these images, whether they are called warriors, chiefs, Indians, redskins, braves, Aztecs, or Apaches, has been felt and carried over into the college arena. This is evident in the numerous instances of college cultural misappropriation parties and events. One such example is in a Cowboys and Indians themed party held off campus by California State University–San Marcos (CSUSM) anthropology graduates the spring of 2013.

On a Monday afternoon in early June, I [Proudfit] was contacted by several individuals asking what was happening at CSUSM and what would I be doing about it? Although I do not personally engage in social media platforms like Facebook, Instagram, and Twitter, a few recent CSUSM anthropology graduates do and posted via various forms of social media the following:

#CowboysAndIndians
#AnthropologyGrads
#TooManyDrinks
#StillHaveAHeadache
#GraduatonParty
#CSUSMclassof2013

Those hashtags and messages couples with numerous photos of girls dressed as Indians (elaborate headdresses and all) with their party cups in tow made their rounds. By the time the conversation came to me, some of the Facebook postings from tribal elected leaders, community members, and others read, "This is what a degree from CSUSM gets you?"

You can imagine my horror, frustration, embarrassment, and concerns. That this was only a few months after a recent "Chola"-themed sorority party students from our campus held just proceeded to add insult to injury, but this was felt severely by our Native students and tribal communities. I crafted a response to have posted on our California Indian Culture and Sovereignty Center website and asked that our students and staff not respond. We agreed to post my message as an open letter on our Facebook page and keep it up for through Friday at 4:00 p.m. so that we did not focus our efforts and conversation on this frustrating and painful subject. The following is the statement I posted:

> As the Director of Native Studies and American Indian Academic Strategic Planning at CSUSM struggling to grow a culturally sensitive and relevant native studies program and curriculum I am disappointed that students from this campus would deem this appropriate.
>
> The fact that anyone would think it is ok to appropriate, stereotype and fetishize American Indian culture is disturbing particularly in light of the efforts American Indians have made at CSUSM.
>
> Vine Deloria, Jr. was a critic of the field of anthropology and provided much evidence to support his criticism. This is why he valued American Indians gearing up for battle in the intellectual arena.
>
> "The problems of Indians have always been ideological rather than social, political or economic.... [I]t is vitally important that the Indian people pick the intellectual arena as the one in which to wage war."—Vine Deloria, Jr.
>
> The actions of these CSUSM graduates set back the progress this field has made.
>
> His words have never been more significant.
>
> I would encourage these students to return to the CSUSM campus and take a Native Studies course, engage with our American Indian Student Alliance, visit the California Indian Culture and Sovereignty Center and dialogue with our Office of Tribal Liaison. Perhaps now the powers that be will understand that a major in Native Studies is required and courses in American Indian studies should be required by all of our students to graduate.
>
> I hope that the entire CSUSM community understands how truly offensive and inexcusable this party was especially in light of recent racist antics by others on campus against the Latino community.

The reaction was quick, aggressive, and abhorrent. By the morning, I had walked into what would normally be a quiet summer morning at our campus center to an environment of fear and worry from our summer student employees and researchers. They had already received threatening phone calls, and our Facebook page was overcome with numerous angry, hateful, and outright ignorant Facebook messages, not by anonymous strangers but by individuals who were either related to or friends of the CSUSM women adult graduates who had publicly shared their images and postings all over the internet. The point is that in many of these scenarios, social media respondents are either anonymous or hide behind pseudonyms. In this situation, not only did they identify themselves, but many responded from their work emails to personally attack me. This attack was definitely a coordinated effort. Those who opposed my statement and attacked me refrained from addressing me as Dr. Proudfit but instead referred to me as Ms. Proudfit. Somehow they believed if they ignored my credentials they would simply go away. This kind of attack and disrespect was not just directed at me but our entire American Indian communities and culture. Nor did they stop with insults and threats, but the family of one of the girls in the photo hired an attorney who contacted our system-wide chancellor's office. I was asked to meet with my supervisor, who asked me to take down the Facebook and Instagram photos but that my open letter could stay up. You can imagine my shock—now these women feel as they are the victims and sought to infringe on my first amendment rights and go after a tenured American Indian professor for writing a thoughtful and restrained open letter which, by the way, is appropriate for me to do as the Director of the California Indian and Cultural Center! These individuals tried to defend their behavior, they made excuses, and even the parents chimed in with how much money they spent on the party to authenticate and—wait for it—they even dared to say that there were "real" Indians present at the party. Now, can you imagine any other group being treated that way when they dare to speak out in a calm, educated way? Can you imagine for one minute those at UCSD only a few years earlier who held the "Compton cookout" party having the nerve to say, we played music sung by African American rappers, we wore clothes that African Americans wear...? Instead the cowboys and Indians party proponents made statements: "state-funded professor trolling the internet to attack these young girls"; "Ms. Proudfit should be sued for copyright infringement"; "Ms. Proudfit should be fired."

As a three-time tenured professor in the California State University system, I could have never imagined this kind of attack. There could be no stronger lesson for how isolated and alone American Indians students, staff, and faculty feel when the face these types of issues that unfortunately happen on a regular basis. What we need is a unified front from all different groups—in particular those who have also been marginalized, culturally attacked, or mimicked—to stand with us and address these issues head on. Why are American Indians often left alone in their fight to protect their culture?

Do a simple web search of my name along with cowboys and Indians and you will find a full array of images and comments. I am proud to say that many individuals from around the country responded with articulate responses to those trying to defend their right to be offensive toward Native peoples. It was difficult not to want to further engage in the dialogue, but as I shared with our students and staff, we made our statement; we would only post to our Facebook for the next few days books and video links to educate individuals. We allowed the conversation to continue via our Facebook for four days. We felt that was plenty of time in which to showcase the amount of ignorance and racism there is out there targeted at American Indians. We hit the proverbial gold mind of ignorance and what I was counting on for research material. This was a painful and scary situation for our center and students, but it clearly underscored how much work we need to do in the area. Since then we have done numerous presentations, we created a poster campaign that is being used globally against stereotypes and cultural misappropriation, and I have a forthcoming textbook due in 2017 entitled *Beyond the American Indian Stereotype* that will address these types of issues and provides the instructor and students with components and activities for resolution to address these issues.

In an effort to bring others into the discussion and address these concerns collectively, the CICSC began a dialogue with Arturo Ocampo, Associate Vice President for Diversity for CSUSM. He was a true champion of diversity and equity and eager to work with us on developing a campaign to address these issues across campus. After a series of racially offensive events perpetrated by CSUSM students "celebrating" Halloween, graduation, and other campus events by wearing various costumes that parodied other racial/political groups, I decided to create a teachable moment by challenging students in my class to think outside the box and to think "beyond the stereotypes" to create an emotional, ethical, and moral response to the incidents. The result of this effort was a campus-wide collaboration and the creation of the "There is More to Me than What You See. Beyond the Stereotype There is History" campaign.

The intentionally developed the project as part of a wider cross-cultural, campus-wide effort. I wanted to share what I teach in all my courses and encourage students to question "how they know what they know" and "where they learned it from." While typically my focus is solely on American Indians and Native American representational issues, because of several campus events and the student outrage, the campaign quickly grew beyond redressing the affront experienced by any one particular group. A coalition of collaborators formed between students, faculty members, administration, student organizations, and staff at CSUSM with the California Indian Culture and Sovereignty Center taking the lead role for the project.

The group met throughout the spring semester in 2014 in a coordinated effort with American Indian Studies courses, graphic design, and photography class to design the campaign. To combat the negative imagery, current CSUSM students, men and women, volunteered from my classes to present a contrasting image—an image of confident, empowered, and triumphant individuals who know their cultural heritage, ancestry, and the way in which this knowledge impacts their contemporary identity. Behind each contemporary student pictured tearing up the offensive stereotypical images are silhouettes of historical figures who have played a significant role in that student's community and personal identity formation. The historical role models include Sitting Bull, LaDonna Harris, Maya Angelo, Emiliano Zapata, Senator Daniele Inouye, and Representative (now Senator) Tammy Duckworth.

That spring the product was not the quality we had hoped for, so we shelved the project. However, that summer I decided to invest my own time and money into creating a professional campaign geared and wide distribution. I hired Megan Doughty, a CSUSM visual performing arts graduate to help me fine-tune the campaign images, layout, and message; I hired professional models to dress up in costumes that were purchased from on-line party retailers. Female and male models donned the costumes, which included scantily clad Native American maidens, Mexican bandits, and African-American men represented by the model wearing an "afro" wig in "blackface" to show the offensive behavior perpetrated by some groups and clubs at CSUSM, in order to have these images torn up and the stereotype literally torn apart. It was important to own the stereotyped images so that we could make the poster available for public use.

The CICSC agreed to have this work licensed under Creative Commons Attribution-Noncommercial-No Derivatives 4.0 International License. These posters may be downloaded and reproduced for nonprofit and/ or educational purposes. Neither the images or text may be changed or altered in any way.

The Beyond the Stereotype campaign features CSUSM students in eight posters to help educate and facilitate conversations on cultural appropriation, stereotypes, and microaggressions. The campaign is designed to educate the public and campus community about cultural appropriation, often defined as the adoption of elements, such as traditional clothing, of one culture by members of a different culture, particularly when the source culture is a minority group that has been oppressed or exploited. Because cultural appropriation often enlists the use of stereotypes, part of the aim of the project is to also understand stereotypes and the harm they cause.

In addition to the poster campaign we had them on exhibit for three months in spring 2015 in the university student union, which has an average of 40,000 people monthly walk through it. The exhibit included an interactive component in which participants could share personal stories of cultural appropriation they have experienced, watch a rotating loop of related video clips, and sign a diversity and civility pledge. CSUSM sponsored workshops, activities, and discussions around the topics raised by the posters. We will also be providing curriculum, resources, readings, and other information on cultural appropriation, stereotypes, and microaggressions which can be found at the Beyond the Stereotype Resource page (www.csusm.edu/cicsc/projects/beyond-the-stereotype.html) for the campus and on our CICSC website. Many of the posters are permanently displayed around campus in a very large format.

We initially created 10 posters; the two that were not included in this first release were Arab Americans. Although we felt they should have been exhibited, the administration felt that those two should be released in a second round of posters that will address stereotypes of other marginalized groups, which would include, but not be limited to, sex, sexual orientation, disability, class, and religious and cultural groups.

We are proud of our students and the courage they displayed in working with the California Indian Culture and Sovereignty Center. The result of their frustration and pain was a proactive campaign now being used around the globe in Germany and Brazil, to name but a few places.

While there are many instances of these types of racist, ignorant efforts happening in our schools on a regular basis, I am proud of the fact that we were able to inspire and empower our students to combat the negatives by having them engage in social justice efforts, thereby impacting the social, political, cultural, and legal environments around them for long-lasting substantive change. That is a victory.

In an effort to continue addressing these issues, the W. M. Keck Foundation has awarded a $250,000 grant to the CICSC to develop a program on American Indian digital media and culture. This is the first grant that CSUSM has been awarded from the Keck Foundation.

Keck's Undergraduate Education Program promotes distinctive learning and research experiences in science, engineering, and the liberal arts at 4-year undergraduate colleges in states designated by the foundation. The funding from this award will support a joint project between the California Indian Culture & Sovereignty Center (CICSC) and the Video in the Community program titled The American Indian Digital Media & Culture Project (AIDM&C). Over the next three years, we will work with undergraduate students to create, research, design and produce digital media arts products and projects with the assistance of tribal community subject and digital media matter experts to incorporate American Indian epistemology in digital media making. I am thrilled by this opportunity to connect the institution and the tribal nations, communities and individuals to 21st century storytelling and media making. The overall goals are to create an international model for the presentation of tribal cultural knowledge through the delivery of interdisciplinary undergraduate media arts-based projects and to provide tribal community members, students, and faculty the instruction, support, and resources needed to create community responsive media projects.

Lastly, public institutions must work with their tribal nations and surrounding tribal communities to education and serve as agents of change. For the past several years, the California Indian Culture and Sovereignty Center (CICSC) at California State University–San Marcos (CSUSM) has held an annual California's American Indian and Indigenous Film Festival (CAIIFF). Screenings take place at CSUSM and at the Pechanga Resort and Casino in Temecula, CA, in late November.

The festival, formally known as the San Diego American Indian Film Festival, is a grassroots community event organized by the CICSC in collaboration with its tribal and university partners. The CAIIFF is delighted to strengthen tribal cultural sovereignty in film, media, and the arts by providing an accessible, fun, engaging, and unique platform to showcase American Indian life, culture, history, and stories about the lived realities American Indians face both past and present. Located in the heart of southern California's Indian country, the California Indian Culture and Sovereignty Center at Cal State–San Marcos is the nexus for innovating partnerships between American Indians, academics, and the regional community. The CAIIFF is a product of this innovation and has become a regional "don't miss" event. Screenings are scheduled each year both at CSUSM and at the Pechanga Resort and Casino to literally bring the movies and moviegoers "home" to American Indian communities.

We offer each year an eclectic lineup of 20-plus films, shorts, and documentaries, and we work closely with some of Indian country's most notable native media makers, such as Peabody- and Emmy-award winning director/producer Chris Eyre, filmmaker Blackhorse Lowe, actress/producer/voice artist Irene Bedard, Sterlin Harjo, and artist/writer/director/humanitarian Steven Paul Judd, to name but a few. Additionally, we include our tribal leaders and professionals from the region who serve as advisors and moderators at many of the Q&A sessions.

Our efforts are proof positive of how academic institutions can work hand in hand with our tribal faculty, staff, students, and community to collectively and positively impact the communities in which they are intended to serve.

REFERENCES

Alejo, L. (2015, October 11). *AB-30 School or athletic team names: California Racial Mascots Act.* Retrieved from https://leginfo.legislature.ca.gov/faces/billNav-Client.xhtml?bill_id=201520160AB30

The Aspen Institute, Center for Native American Youth. (2012). *Voices of Native Youth Report*. Retrieved from https://assets.aspeninstitute.org/content/uploads/files/content/upload/Youth_Report_Vol.%202_2012.pdf

California Racial Mascots Act, AB30, authored by Assemblyman Luis Alejo, D-Salinas (2015).

Proudfit, J. (Forthcoming). *Beyond the American Indian Stereotype: There's More to me than what you see, beyond the stereotype, there's history*. Santa Barbara, CA: ABC-Clio.

Stegman, E., & Phillips, V. (2014, July 22). *Missing the point: The real impact of Native mascots and team names on American Indian and Alaska Native youth*. Retrieved from https://www.americanprogress.org/issues/race/reports/2014/07/22/94214/missing-the-point/

CHAPTER 8

REVITALIZING CRITICALLY ENDANGERED LANGUAGES IN CALIFORNIA

Case Study and Promising Practices

Theresa L. Gregor
California State University, Long Beach

Stanley Rodriguez
California State University, San Marcos
University of California, San Diego

"Matmir onyaow tiipay askay peruwii nyapum myum hiiku, milchish wiiyu askay kiitu, wakain! Nyawait ewuu yechesh owak nyapum nyawait mat, askay wakain tawa nyapum askay nymit wechow."

"Our culture and language was like a clay pot that held all that was important to us. When the outsiders invaded they took that pot and threw it to the ground and destroyed it. All that was left were shards. It broke our hearts but we took the shards and ground it with new clay. The temper from the ground shards makes the new pot. This new pot is stronger than before because it has both the old and new."

—Gloria Castaneda, Cultural Chief of San Jose De La Zorra
(Personal communication with Stan Rodriguez)

On Indian Ground: California, pages 101–120
Copyright © 2017 by Information Age Publishing

101

Language is the vehicle that drives a culture. The expression and interpretation of one's unique society, spirituality, and view of one's universe is expressed through language. Despite efforts to destroy American Indian cultures and languages, as Gloria Castaneda explains above, the tools to revitalize California Native languages (Figure 8.1) are all around us, fragmented yet available to gather and combine with new materials to build a "stronger" vessel than before. The rate of language regression for many California tribal communities is diminishing, thanks to language revitalization efforts, and cultural activisim across the state.

Figure 8.1 California Indians root languages. Source: Hinton, L. *Flutes of Fire: Essays on California Indian Languages.* Berkeley, CA: Heyday Books, 1994.

In this chapter, the authors set out to highlight the work of members from the Living Language Circle started by the Yocha Dehe Wintun and Santa Ynez Chumash to bring together California Native Language Teachers for annual forums (Yocha Dehe Wintun Nation, n.d.b). The language and culture of a people is like a library filled with an invaluable store of knowledge that is irreplaceable, and when the language is eliminated, the effect is like a library burning down. This chapter highlights methods, strategies, and promising practices to rebuild that library. The authors sent a survey to various community members working in language revitalization throughout the state. The UC Berkeley linguistics department hosts an interactive map of California Indian languages and states that, linguistically speaking, "California is... the most diverse area of North America" (Berkeley Linguistics, n.d.). There are over 20 different Native language families in California, and prior to Euro-American contact and disruption, "between 80 and 90 different languages were spoken within the boundaries of what is now the state of California" (Berkeley Linguistics, n.d.). The map in Figure 8.2 is from Leanne Hinton's work on California Indian languages and identifies the major California Indian language groups, and Figure 8.3 is a screenshot of the UC Berkeley interactive language family map on the linguistics department website.

The survey consisted of 20 questions about the state of their tribe's native language fluency and efforts to revitalize. The following tribal language programs are examples of the work from Northern, Central, and Southern California:

- Northern California: Hoopa Valley Tribe
- Central California: Yocha de he Wintun Nation
- Central California: Tuolumne Mewuk Band of Mewuks
- Southern California: Iipay/Tiipay Language Immersion at Kumey-aay Community College.

J. Martins is a Hupa language teacher with a clear credential; Leland Kinter is the Cultural Resources Committee chairman for the Yocha Dehe Wintun Nation; Carlos Geisdorff is learning the Tuolumne Mewuk language and works with Candra Neff in the Tuolummne Me-wuk language program; Mr. Stan Rodriguez is a master language teacher at the Kumeyaay Community College Iipay/Tipay language program. Stan Rodriguez contributed the Case Study section that begins the chapter to highlight the pedagogy he employs in the Iipay/Tiipay language immersion program at Kumeyaay Community College located on the Sycuan Indian Reservation.

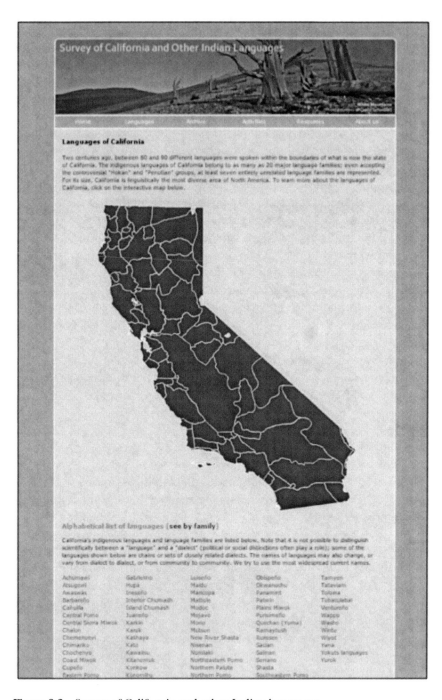

Figure 8.2 Survey of California and other Indian languages.

Survey of California Indian Language Programs

1) Name of Teacher/Speaker/Program Director

2) Tribe(s) and Tribal Location

3) Name of Language Group and Language Program

4) # of Speakers

5) # of Students

6) What methods are you using to teach the language?

7) Who is involved in the program design/delivery?

8) What resources are you using to teach the language?

9) Are you using digital platforms to teach the language? If so, please describe which one and its impact on the user/learner.

10) What obstacles have you had to overcome to teach the language? How did you overcome these?

11) How are you "testing" a learner's ability?

12) Does your program teach a specific form of writing the language?

13) What is your favorite language lesson to teach?

14) What is your least favorite language lesson to teach?

15) How are you recruiting speakers/learners?

16) What outside resources do you use to enhance your program (linguistic materials, conferences/trainings, etc.)?

17) How are your language classes offered to the community? What is the frequency of the classes?

18) How has teaching the language impacted your life?

19) What aspects of your program are still in need of development?

20) If money was not an obstacle, what would you do to enhance your language program that you are not already doing?

Figure 8.3 Survey questions for California Indian language programs.

CASE STUDY: STAN RODRIGUEZ AND KUMEYAAY LANGUAGE REVITALIZATION THROUGH LANGUAGE IMMERSION

Of the 6,000 indigenous languages that are spoken today, it is estimated that 3,000 of those are endangered to go extinct by the end of the 21st century (Hinton & Hale, 2008; Rivenburgh, 2011). The primary reasons for language extinction are globalization and neocolonization of Indigenous people. As more people rely on the dominant-settler languages, native languages will remain at risk. Tribal heritage languages were endangered through both overt and covert practices that forbade the use of native languages and instead replaced them with an invasive language and culture. This practice occurs throughout the world as one group attempts to exert its control over another group, such as the English over the Irish, the Japanese over the Koreans, and the United States government over American Indians.

The vibrancy of a language is measured by the amount of children speaking it. In many instances the loss of one's own language leads to the loss of culture, which puts the affected culture in crisis and allows it to become susceptible to abuses from within and from without (see Nettle & Romaine, 2000). The loss of one's identity is an attribute of a number of interpersonal social issues associated with intergenerational trauma such as violence, addiction, depression, and suicide (Duran & Duran, 1995). This chapter will give a history of my people, our cultural practices, our traditional territory, and how contact with Europeans led to the repression of our language and how the Kumeyaay community is addressing language loss and revitalization.

The language and culture of a people is like a library filled with an invaluable store of knowledge that is irreplaceable, and when the language is eliminated the effect is like a library burning down. This case study addresses strategies on how to rebuild that library for Iipay/Tiipay speakers.

The Kumeyaay People

The Kumeyaay people of the San Diego area are broken down to Iipay for the north and Tipay for the south and Kumiai for the desert. The Kumeyaay people occupied the area from the north to present-day Camp Pendleton in Oceanside all the way to San Vicente, south of Ensenada Baja California Mexico, and from the west coastal area going east through Imperial Valley and sharing land on the Colorado River with the Quechan people on the Ft. Yuma Indian reservation. The Kumeyaay are a people of the coast, valleys, mountains, and the desert. The people had extensive trade routes and had a migratory cycle. This cycle occurred during the springtime by the coast, during the summer and fall in the mountains, and during the wintertime in the desert. Evidence of Kumeyaay inhabitation, such as the rock snake pictograph in Ocotillo, has been dated to be over 10,000 years old. In Imperial County, in ancient times, there existed an immense lake that was fed by the Colorado River. Evidence of inhabitance is still found by the ancient shoreline with stone fish traps left behind and through the various song cycles that are sung today.

Today there are 12 reservations that are Kumeyaay in San Diego County. They are San Pasqual, Santa Ysabel, Mesa Grande, Cosmit/Iñaja, Barona, Viejas, Sycuan, Jamul, Cuayapay, La Posta, Manzanita, and Campo. Pala is a combination of Cupeño and Iipay, and the Fort Yuma Reservation has

Kumiai along with Quechan. Across the Mexican border, the Kumeyaay communities are San Jose de Tecate, Neji, Huaje de las tunas, Pena Blanca, la Necua, San Jose de la Zorra, la Huerta, and part of Santa Catarina.

The Social Structure

The native people of the San Diego area were broken up into the clan or *shumulq* system. The clans maintained the area they lived in and the resources in the environment, such as the health of the oak trees, in order to nurture the production of food sources, like acorns, which were a dietary staple for the Kumeyaay. Encroachment by other clans without permission was forbidden. Exceptions to this were if a hunter was pursuing a wounded animal and the animal crossed into another s*humulq's* territory; then the hunter was permitted to proceed without having to ask for permission. There were open areas that would be areas of food and social gathering such as Torrey Pines for pine nut gathering, the base of Point Loma for gathering abalone, Pacific beach for the grunion run, and the agave fields by Ocotillo for baking. Groups would make alliances for food distribution and self-protection.

Political Structure

The chiefs or leaders were more like advisors, and their power came from persuasion. When the time came for the group to move to another location, the individuals would decide whether or not they would go. Another leader came from a special group of individuals who were trained since childhood to settle disputes. They were placed in communities to whom they were not related. The reason for this is that this individual would be unbiased and would render judgments that were for the benefit of the community.

Spirituality

The people were connected to the land by our creation story. This land is our holy land, and every place has a lesson to teach us. Our creation story takes six days to be told in its entirety, and it is told to the youth during the puberty ceremony. The songs from the 22 different song cycles, along with the stories, teach my people the reason for the universe, and the role that we play, and the way that we should conduct ourselves. Rather than chants, the songs are in the language, and each song tells a story. If one does not understand Kumeyaay, one will lose key points in a ceremony. The language is filled with metaphors, and there is a deeper meaning to the actual word. In order for the youth to continue to carry on the traditions, they must learn and communicate in the language.

The Protocol with Neighboring Tribes

To the north of the Kumeyaay people live the Luiseno Cupeño Juanano and Cahuilla people. They speak a different language, which is Uto Aztecan. To the east live the Quechan and Cocopah people. To the south are the Paipai, Kiliwa, and the Cochimi people. It was common for people to speak more than one language. The cultural protocol was that if one group entered another group's area, then the immigrant group spoke the indigenous group's language.

The Kumeyaay Language

The Kumeyaay language is a Yuman language, which is the name given for the dozen or so languages that are closely related. The territory of the Yuman language groups are Southern California; Southern Nevada; Western Arizona; and in Mexico in Baja California, Baja Sur, and Sonora. Of these groups, they are broken down to Cochimi (Northern and Southern in Baja California Mexico), Delta California Yuman (Iipay, Tipay, Kumiai, and Cocopah), River Yuman (Quechan, Mojave, Maricopa, and Halchidhoma), Pai (Yavapai, Walapai, Havasupai, and Paipai), and Kiliwa.

Despite the intact land base and thriving population of the Cochimi community, their language was listed as extinct during the beginning of the 20th century due to the isolation of the reservation, the lack of resources, and the need to find gainful employment, which drove many to leave their homeland.

History of Oppression and Resistance

The world of the Kumeyaay changed on the date of September 28, 1542 when Juan de Cabrillo Rodriguez landed in San Diego and stayed for one week. There was friction and a confrontation when a group of Spaniards attempted to go hunting and fishing without permission. The Kumeyaay referred to the Spaniards as *guacamal*, which meant "the enemy who comes." Later the encroachments continued with their return 200 years later to set up missions up and down the California peninsula. The missions trained the Indian to perform menial labor in anticipation of Spanish colonists' arrival. The priests discouraged the use of Kumeyaay and attempted to replace it with Spanish. Therefore, the natives were colonized as a servant class. Many Kumeyaay resisted. The atrocities committed to subjugate the Kumeyaay people led to the missions being attacked and the priest Father Jayme to be murdered in 1775 (Engelhardt, 1920). "The Kumeyaay," Richard Carrico writes, "were a people who could and would resist threats to their religion, culture, and life ways" (Carrico, 1997, para. 10).

The Mexican Encroachment

After Mexico gained independence from Spain, the Mexican government promised to secularize the mission lands and return them back to the native people; however, in practice the social elite gave the land to friends and relatives. Although the Spaniards were no longer in power, their descendants were, and they attempted to continue with the social cast system that the Spanish used to subjugate the native population. The responses from the Kumeyaay were continued uprisings and better coordinated raids on ranches and towns. The raids became so successful that San Diego almost fell three times to Kumeyaay forces.

THE MEXICAN AMERICAN WAR AND THE AFTERMATH

Friction between the Mexican and American government continued until hostilities erupted and started the Mexican American War. Both sides attempted to exploit the Kumeyaay with false promises of autonomy and the preservation of Indigenous land and culture. The Americans attempted to attack San Diego and were surrounded by Mexican forces. It was Kumeyaay who were able to help the Americans escape. The battle of San Pasqual was the only battle of the Mexican American War in California. This took place in San Diego County at San Pasqual, and it lasted two days. The Mexicans won the battle. The Mexican military approached the Kumeyaay and asked the Kumeyaay for help. If they defeated the Americans, then the Mexican government would give San Diego back to the Kumeyaay. The Americans approached the Kumeyaay and said that if the Natives assisted the Americans defeat the Mexicans, then the government would give the people back San Diego.

When the Americans won the war, California was going through a transition that would prove disastrous for the native California people. Gold was discovered at Sutter's Mill in Sacramento, California, and wave after wave of prospectors and settlers poured into California. The northern and central California tribes bore the brunt of the onslaught, with whole tribes massacred. Men, women, children, and infants were slaughtered. Of the

251 tribes that were present in California prior to the gold rush, there were only 51 tribes left three years after the start of the gold rush. The Kumeyaay struggled with the invasion, and although there was friction, the bands continued to press the government to honor the promises that were made.

The Treaty of Santa Ysabel

On January 2, 1852, the Treaty of Santa Ysabel was signed to establish a reservation. The boundaries of the reservation encompassed territory east of present-day El Cajon to Ocotillo in Imperial County and from the Mexican border north to the Riverside County line. This treaty was one of 18 treaties that were made with the surviving California tribes. Although these treaties were made in good faith by California Indian leaders, the ratification of the treaties was met with immediate opposition from many non-Indians who were residing in California and who wanted the lands that were designated for Indian use. Many settlers who came were from the south and had Confederate leanings. A group petitioned the federal government stating that if these treaties were ratified, then they would side with the fledgling Confederacy (Richards, 2007).

This was on the eve of the Civil War, and the government decided that rather than set up the possibility of California joining the Confederacy, they would cede to the protests of the settlers, and the treaties were sealed and never ratified. The impact on the Kumeyaay was disastrous, resulting in the loss of most of their tribal land. Today San Diego has 18 federal Indian reservations, more reservations per capita than any other county in the country, and it is also home to the smallest reservation, the Jamul Indian Village, which has only six acres of land.

Life Under the American Government

The Bureau of Indian Affairs (BIA) was set up to address the welfare of the native people. The BIA was initially set up under the war department, then later under the department of the interior. The native people were put under the care of this, and our status was wards of the government. The reservations were set up, and the mobility of the people who resided in the reservations was severely restricted. One could not leave without permission. Although the government promised to address the needs of the people, corruption in the system meant theft of food and supplies, and therefore, the land within the reservation could not sustain the population. Soon the resources were depleted. Many Kumeyaay attempted to leave in order to search for food and for employment. The San Diego sheriff arrested many for vagrancy and the police harassment continued for many years.

The youth were also targeted due to the government policy of "kill the Indian, save the man." The native religion was suppressed and the children were forcibly taken to missionary and BIA boarding schools. Their hair was cut, and when the children spoke their languages, they were severely admonished. Corporal punishment was widespread, and the impact of this was the loss of many youth who were able to speak the Kumeyaay language.

The vibrancy of a language is not measured by how many of the adults speak, but by how many of the youth speak the language. Also, a language's use and sophistication is dependent upon one's stage in life. This is demonstrated by the woven belt that is on the babies cradles. There are seven stars on the belt, and each represents a stage in the life of an individual: infancy, toddler, youth, adolescence, adulthood, senior, and elder. Each stage had a language that was used that was appropriate for that group. When many of the youth were kept from speaking their language, the result is many stayed at the stage that they were in when they stopped learning. As a result, today many Kumeyaay speakers will talk what is called "baby or child talk" because their language use was stunted.

The Loss of the Kumeyaay Language in Mexico

In Mexico, the Kumeyaay lived in more isolated areas, and due to the sparsely populated area, the people were left alone from the 1950s through the 1960s, and the language and culture was intact and the surviving culture was much more vibrant. The Mexican government in an attempt to stop the use of the language created *Escuela Bilingues* (bilingual schools)— in name only—the Mexican teachers would not allow the children to speak the Kumeyaay language in order to promote Spanish use. The result is that the Kumeyaay youth in Baja do not speak the native language.

The Revival

As our people continue to grow, our concern for the state of the language and what can be done to reverse this trend is also intensifying. The search for speakers was made in the communities, and some of the problems that arose were dialect differences and the lack of knowing how to teach a language. Also, with fewer Kumeyaay teachers and larger groups of students, the students tend to go towards the easier path of communication, which is going back to speaking English or Spanish. Many techniques used to teach the language were met with mixed results. The degree of success was also dependent on the number of individuals who spoke the language and whether or not the speaker was able to teach.

Looking for Speakers

A survey was conducted identifying speakers on the various reservations and found that there was a considerable cross section from fluent speakers to semi fluent speakers to passive speakers to non-speakers. For the purpose of this paper the definition of speaker is one who can convey their message in the Kumeyaay language.

The following indicates the approximate number of fluent Kumeyaay speakers:

- Santa Ysabel—12
- San Pasqual— 4
- Mesa Grande—Unknown
- Inaja—0
- Barona—7
- Viejas—4
- Sycuan—1
- Jamul—2
- Ewiiaapaayp—0
- La Posta—0
- Manzanita—0
- Campo—6
- Mexico bands:
  - San Jose de Tecate—2
  - Neji—5
  - Peña Blanca—5
  - Huaje de las Tunas—1
  - La Necua—2
  - San Jose de la Zorra—20
  - La Huerta—5
  - Santa Catarina—4

Types of Programs Used to Teach Language

Kumeyaay Community College (KCC) was developed to teach courses focusing on Kumeyaay language, history, and ethnobiology, as well as cultural arts such as basket making, pottery, and tool making. KCC has an MOU (memorandum of understanding) with Cuyamaca College and offers classes for credit. The language classes are 5-unit courses and are offered at KCC on the Sycuan Reservation. The instructors are Stanley Rodriguez and Ana Gloria Rodriguez. The Barona Reservation classes are offered through the Barona Museum and have been taught most recently by Pat Curo and occasionally by Stan Rodriguez; past instructors at the Barona Museum include the late Herman Osuna. The San Pasqual Reservation classes are taught through the cultural department once a week by Stanley Rodriguez. It was formally taught on the Viejas Reservation twice a week by instructors Tom Hyde and Stanley Rodriguez. Manzanita Reservation classes were taught by the late tribal chairman and by Stanley Rodriguez. Santa Ysabel Reservation classes have been taught through the youth department by instructors Herman Osuna, Nancy Nagel, and Stanley Rodriguez. Mesa Grande Reservation classes were formerly taught one night a week by instructors Paul Gonzalez and Stanley Rodriguez. Campo Reservation classes were taught on the reservation by various local speakers.

In Mexico, the Neji Reservation classes were taught in conjunction with the Tecate Museum by instructors Norma, Aurora, and Karla Mesa. San Jose de la Zorra Reservation classes were taught through the Secretaria de Educacion Publica (SEP) by various community members and at UABC Universidad Autonoma de Baja California by Gregorio Montes.

The Methods Utilized to Teach Language

Following are examples of the various methods used:

- *Situational fluency training:* This involves breaking down a situation into the verbiage that is needed for successful completion of the situation didactic then the practicum phase in which the students role-play the situation, and as the individual continues to gain proficiency, other situations are taught. The premise is that the student will be able to incorporate the information and will be able to free talk, but this must be reinforced repeatedly or students will forget what they have learned.
- *Visual identification and recall:* This technique involves placing pictures of people, animals, objects, and actions. The words to be learned are given, and then pictures of the topic taught are attached to a wall; the instructor will then stand behind the student and point to various pictures. The student will say the word in Kumeyaay. If the student is correct, then the instructor will move on to the next picture; if not, then the instructor will continue to point at the picture until the student says the correct answer. When the student gains proficiency, the instructor will increase the speed and

vary the repetition. As the students recall consistently, a new set is prepared and the process is repeated. The student develops vocabulary and recall is consistent, but although the student develops vocabulary, it is third party and not conversational.

- *Language pods:* As students gain proficiency, this method utilizes the group when they have vocabulary proficiency. The group will sit in a circle and various topics are written on cards and each individual will take turns picking a card and the group then discusses the topic. After an allotted amount of time (approximately 15 minutes), the next individual will take a flash card and the process will repeat itself. This gives individuals an opportunity to develop proficiency as a speaker and to be able to speak to a variety of topics, but the participants need to have some vocabulary in order for this to be successful.
- *Games:* The use of games, both traditional and contemporary, allows the student the opportunity to develop vocabulary through repetition. First the verbiage is given, and the rules are that the students utilize the language only. The game proceeds and, through the game, the language is reinforced.

California Language Program Profiles: Promising Practices

Northern California: Hupa

The Hoopa Valley Tribe root language group is Athabaskan. "Athabaskan languages are highly distinctive, unlike any other languages in the world" (Baldy, 1996, p. ii). Athabaskan speaking peoples in California stretch along the Pacific North Coast to Alaska. The Hupa language is spoken along the southern parts of Humboldt County, the northern section of Mendocino County, and the southwestern edges of Trinity County. The Hupa language is comprised of mainly "classificatory verbs" that are "modified and inflected with verbal prefixes" to create almost all the words in the Hupa language, including nouns (Baldy, 1996, p. iii).

J. Martins is the Hupa language teacher who is Clear Credentialed. A California clear credential refers to having a preliminary single or preliminary multiple credential. The Hoopa Valley Tribe is located in Hoopa, California in Humboldt County. The Hoopa Valley tribe supports and authorizes all credentialing. The Census 2000 reported 64 speakers of the language (U.S. Census, 2000). There are 487 students enrolled in Hoopa Valley Elementary School. Martins uses a combination of methods for language instruction including content-based instruction (CBI), total physical response (TPR), language domain reclamation, and games.

Content-based instruction is a five-step lesson that involves total immersion. The steps in each lesson are:

Step 1. Setting the stage, which can include role playing
Step 2. Comprehensible input through the introduction of vocabulary
Step 3. Guided practice through activities such as language games
Step 4. Independent practice, which places the student at the center of
the lesson to demonstrate knowledge
Step 5. Assessment (Hinton & Hale, 2013, pp. 196–197)

The total physical response method encourages students "to respond physically to simply requests by the teacher. The physical aspect of responding to the teacher's instructions as the teacher models the expected behavior helps students learn new vocabulary and even some basic grammatical patterns" (Francis & Reyhner, 2002, p. 115). The language reclamation method "as a linguistic process begins with identifying and locating sources of the language" (Amery, 2000, pp. 28–29). The challenge with the language reclamation method is in reconstructing an often dormant language with little to no extant sound recordings. Advocates of this method recognize the difficulty in reconstructing a language from historical records and caution teachers to carefully analyze all sources for consistency and accuracy, which can be a lengthy and complex process.

At the Hoopa Valley tribe, Martins creates original lessons for instruction of the language that he typically teaches to groups of 25 students three times per day. Over 88% of the residents at Hoopa Valley are American Indian. At present, Martins does not rely on digital platforms to teach the language. Martins uses assessments from the CBI method to evaluate students' language acquisition and retention. Martins' favorite lessons to teach are numbers, kinship, and songs and the least favorite lesson to teach is the section on verbs. Martins uses the International Phonetic Alphabet to write the language for students.

The Hupa language classes are taught at the public schools, so the recruitment of language learners is not a challenge since instruction is built into the educational system. Martins has spent a third of his life at Hoopa Valley tribe teaching language, and when asked what resources he would like to enhance the language program if money were not an obstacle, Martins writes, "Buy computers, pay for language games and curriculum, stories, and interactive lessons. Pay elders and language coordinator for curriculum development" (Language survey submission, 2015).

Central California: Yocah Dehe Wintun Nation
The Yocha Dehe Wintun Nation's root language stems from the Penutian language family. "Yocha Dehe—pronounced 'YO-cha DEE-hee'—means 'home by the spring water' in our native Patwin language, and it takes us back to our origins, our roots, our land. As the historical inhabitants of California's Capay Valley, our homeland is at the heart of our culture and heritage"

(Yocha Dehe Wintun Nation, n.d.a, para. 1). Wintun languages fall into two groups: Wintu and Nomlaki. There are two dialects in the language: Hill Patwin and Patwin Tewe (. Alfred Kroeber (1932) noted that before Euro-American colonization, there were over 12,000 Wintu, Patwin, and Nomlaki speakers. The cultural resource committee chairman is Leland Kinter, who is a language teacher and works alongside Bertha Mitchell, Patwin language manager, to prepare and deliver curriculum in Patwin language.

Language instruction at Yocha Dehe is provided through direct instruction, games, conversation, technology, and sequential spatial curriculum, which involves using visual aids and imagery to facilitate language acquisition. The tribe offers 16 classes per week: 2 high school, 2 adult classes, and 12 children's classes three times per week. Kinter states that his language learners, "love gameshows, slideshows, and activities," but he reminds us that, "direct instruction/conversation is best" method for practicing language (Language survey submission, 2015). Assessments and evaluation of student progress is "constant" at Yocha Dehe and involves two formal assessments per year to allow the teachers to determine what needs to be further developed to enhance student learning. Written language instruction is taught using a simple orthography using Spanish and Hawaiian vowels.

The greatest obstacle Kinter overcame to teach the Patwin language was teaching while still learning the language himself. Kinter does not have a favorite lesson that he teaches but says that he likes the students' overall enthusiasm in learning the language. To continually develop and share language resources, Yocha Dehe hosts an annual California Language Teacher's Conference; he and Mitchell try to attend others during the year, and they regularly consult with a linguist from UC Davis. While the language program at Yocha Dehe is thriving, Kinter yearns for all tribal members to participate in the language program. If money were no obstacle, to enhance the current program, Kinter says that he would continue to produce a video of one traditional story in Patwin each year and develop a Patwin language immersion camp for the students.

Tuolumne Me-Wuk Band of Me-Wuk Indians

Like its western neighbors at Yocha Dehe Wintu Nation, the Tuolumne Me-Wuk Band of Me-Wuk Indians' language family is Miwokan, which is part of the Penutian language family and is hypothesized to be a subgroup with the Ohlone languages. Central Sierra Miwokan language is spoken along the foothills of the Sierra Nevada, Stanislaus, and Tuolumne Rivers. Levy (1978) believed that before Euro-American colonization there were nearly 20,000 speakers of Miwokan languages. The Tuolumen Me-Wuk are located in Tuolumne, California. According to their tribal history:

> The first known contact on record of Native perspective of the Spanish Explorers was the Moraga Second Expedition to Central California through Tu-

olumne County in 1806. However Me-Wuk peoples have a very long and rich history dating back for thousands of years. The Me-Wuk have always been knowledgeable about the resources of the land, and hunted and gathered what they needed. If the resources were not readily available on their land, Me-Wuk would migrate in order to trade with others. The primary food staples were fish, acorns, and deer meat. The diet was also supplemented with various wild berries, seeds and nuts. The typical village consisted of umachas (cedar bark homes), chakkas (acorn granaries) and a hangi (ceremonial roundhouse). The ceremonial roundhouse was the epicenter of village life and should be respected as would any place of worship. The roundhouse was used for a variety of purposes by different groups. It is typically 30 to 40 feet in diameter and is covered by earth, bark, or shingles. Dances are still held in the roundhouse as a way of giving thanks and respect for all that the Earth Mother gave to the people. (Tuolumne Me-Wuk Tribal Council, n.d., para. 3)

Language revitalization efforts at Tuolumne began in earnest in 2004 when Sonny Hendricks began working on the Native Language Preservation Project. He was assisted by Debbie Colston and Candra Neff. Carlos Geizdorff is the teacher and program director for the Tuolumne Me-Wuk Language Program. Hendrick's language activism resulted in the creation of the first draft of a tribal dictionary in 2007, the employment of over a dozen elders as language consultants, and the creation of the current language program. Today, Carlos Geisdorff along with Candra Neff and others continue Hendricks' work. Although Geisdorff is still learning the Miwokan language, he is an advocate and teacher. Neff is involved in the program design and delivery and works with linguist Sheri Tatsch, who helps with curriculum development.

Today there are approximately 30 children and 10 adults actively participating in the Tuolumne Me-Wuk language program. The language classes are offered after school to children and during the day for adults. The program developed its own orthography but does not teach a singular writing style. Recruitment for adult learners is done through the tribal newsletter advertising the classes and via posters placed around the community. Neff states that adult classes are offered on a weekly basis while the children's classes are offered four times per week. Assessment of language acquisition is informal, as the goal is to gain more community interest and participation.

Neff's favorite lessons are playing games with the children, and she believes that teaching the language is the most important thing the tribe can do for its people (Language survey submission, 2015). The program staff attended the Breath of Life Conference at UC Berkeley in 2014, which helped them locate archival recordings of fluent Miwokan speakers. Many resources are still needed to strengthen the Tuolumne Me-Wuk language program, including funding for adult classes in the evenings, finalizing the dictionary, and developing more learning materials using technology.

Legislative Support of American Indian Languages in California

State Assembly Bill 163, the American Indian Language-Culture Credential, which was introduced by Assemblyman Das Williams (D-Carpinteria) and supported by the Santa Ynez Band of Chumash Indians, was signed into law on Monday, July 13, 2015. Under the American Indian Language-Culture Credential created by this bill, applicants can be authorized to teach courses in American Indian language, American Indian culture, or both in California public schools.

> This bill would instead require the commission, upon recommendation by a tribal government of a federally recognized Indian tribe in California, to issue an American Indian language-culture credential with an American Indian language authorization, or an American Indian culture authorization, or both, to a candidate who has met specified requirements. The bill would authorize the holder of an American Indian language-culture credential to teach the American Indian language, or culture, or both, for which the credential was issued in California public schools in preschool, kindergarten, grades 1 to 12, inclusive, and in adult education courses, and would make the holder of that credential eligible for a clear teaching credential after 5 years, upon application and the recommendation of the tribal government, as specified. The bill would encourage each federally recognized American Indian tribe to develop a written and oral assessment that should be successfully completed before an applicant is recommended for an American Indian language-culture credential with an American Indian language authorization, American Indian culture authorization, or both, as provided. (American Indian Language-Culture Credential, 2015, para. 2)

Writers of the bill acknowledge that American Indian language proficiency is "essential" to American Indian children and that the preservation of American Indian languages and cultures is "important part of our national heritage" that is of significant value to all Americans. In addition, the AB 163 stipulates that a "language and cultural assessment" be created by the tribe to establish standards regarding assessment for a successful teacher-candidate. For the language assessment, a tribe must consider and establish guidelines regarding (a) the dialects of the language to be included in a candidate's assessment, (b) whether a writing/literacy component will be standardized and assessed, and (c) what the baseline will be for knowledge of fluency to qualify as a speaker of that tribal language as well as what methods are considered most effective for teaching the language in the classroom. Tribes will also create a cultural competency assessment for teacher-candidates based on the standards to assess a candidate's knowledge of the tribe's culture and its practices including "ceremonies, traditions, social institutions and relationships, holidays and festivals, health practices and traditions, patterns of work and leisure, and culinary traditions and practices." Tribes will now have the authority to establish the standards for appropriate teaching methods and determine the requirements to evaluate Native language instruction in the classroom. Tribes will also administer the assessment at an "appropriate location" to avoid creating a hardship on tribal members to travel to a university campus.

Finally, the bill sets guidelines regarding teachers for the language and credential program to be authorized and certified or recertified according to the new guidelines established by the tribe.

CONCLUSION: REBUILDING THE CLAY POT

Native languages have been assaulted for over five-hundred years and today's language advocates will do well to remember that it will take time to fan to life the embers barely burning the remnants of California Indian languages. California Indian people have endured multiple invasions and we still have our land, culture and our language. With the efforts of many individuals working independently and collaboratively, the revitalization of California Indian languages is increasing each and every day. With legislative support at the state level, policies and practices that begin at the tribal initiative can be reinforced in public schools and colleges. This is a major victory for language and cultural activists.

The goal of these programs is to develop speakers who can teach others. Evidence of future speakers is heard in the sound of the students speaking the language in their day-to-day affairs; this is the most rewarding and inspiring part of language revitalization work. When the youth are talking in their Native languages, it honors the elders, their teachings, and their experience of intergenerational survival. While for some California Indian communities the road to complete language recovery is longer and full of unexpected roadblocks, language practitioners are fully aware that patience is the key to revitalization practices. Heritage languages tie us to the land and to the universe. When American Indians reconnect these relationships and concepts through language, then healing begins.

Although language activists have a long road ahead to increase fluency and literacy, California Indian communities are empowering themselves. We are rebuilding our clay pot.

The efforts of the individuals profiled here are a testimony to the resilience and persistence of California Indian languages. Their work and collective efforts put out the fire destroying our tribal cultures and their work is strengthening the long term recovery of Indian language use in California. We owe them an enormous debt of gratitude and we wish them continued success in their efforts to revitalize their native languages.

REFERENCES

Amery, R. (2000). *Warrabarna Kaurna! Reclaiming an Australian language.* Boca Raton, FL: CRC Press.

American Indian Language-Culture Credential. (2015). Retrieved from http://leginfo.legislature.ca.gov/faces/billNavClient.xhtml?bill_id=201520160AB163

Baldy, R., Badgely, L., Beck, R., Carpenter, C., Carpenter, W., Golla, V., . . . Sherman, H. (Eds.). (1996). *Hupa Language Dictionary, 2nd edition.* Na:tinixwe Mixine:whe'. Hoopa, CA: Hoopa Valley Tribal Council. Retrieved from http://scholarworks.calstate.edu/bitstream/handle/2148/48/HupaLanguageDictionary.pdf;sequence=1

Berkeley Linguistics. (n.d.). *Survey of California and other Indian languages.* Retrieved from http://linguistics.berkeley.edu/~survey/languages/california-languages.php

Carrico, R. (1997). Sociopolitical aspects of the 1775 revolt at Mission San Diego de Alcala: An ethnohistorical approach. *The Journal of San Diego History: San Diego Historical Society Quarterly, 43*(3). Retrieved from http://www.sandiegohistory.org/journal/1997/july/missionrevolt/

Duran, E., & Duran, B. (1995). *Native American Postcolonial Psychology.* New York, NY: SUNY UP.

Engelhardt, Z. (1920). *San Diego mission.* San Francisco, CA: James H. Barry.

Francis, N., & Reyhner, J. A. (2002). *Language and literacy teaching for Indigenous education: A bilingual approach.* Bristol, England: Multilingual Matters.

Hinton, L., & Hale, K. (Eds.). (2013). *The Green book of language revitalization in practice.* Leiden, The Netherlands: Brill Books.

Kroeber, A. L. (1932). The Patwin and their neighbors. *University of California Publications in American Archaeology and Ethnology, 29,* 253–423.

Levy, R. (1978). Eastern Miwok. In R. F. Heizer (Ed.), *Handbook of North American Indians* (vol. 8, pp. 398–413). Washington, DC: Smithsonian Institution.

Nettle, D., & Romaine, S. (2000). *Vanishing Voices: The Extinction of the World's Languages.* Oxford, England: Oxford University Press.

Richards, L. L. (2007). *The California gold rush and the coming of the Civil War.* New York, NY: Alfred A. Knopf.

Rivenburgh, N. K. (2011). Media framing of complex issues: The case of endangered languages. *Public Understanding of Science 22*(6), 707.

Tuolumne Me-Wuk Tribal Council. (n.d.). *History.* Retrieved from https://mewuk.com/cultural/history/

United States Census. (2000). *American Indian and Alaska Native: Census 2000 data for 539 tribes.* Retrieved from http://www.census.gov/aian/census_2000/census_2000_data_for_539_tribes.html

Yocha Dehe Wintun Nation. (n.d.a). *Heritage.* Retrieved from http://www.yochadehe.org/heritage

Yocha Dehe Wintun Nation. (n.d.b). *Living language circle.* Retrieved from http://www.yochadehe.org/cultural-resources/language/living-language-circle

CHAPTER 9

HIGHER EDUCATION IN CALIFORNIA

Joely Proudfit and Linda Sue Warner
California Indian Culture & Sovereignty Center

With 723,225 American Indians/Alaska Natives (AIANs), California has the largest AIAN population of any other state—a 15.2% increase from the 2000 census. Two of the nation's largest off-reservation communities reside in California—54,236 AIANs in Los Angeles and 17,855 in San Diego. Historically, AIAN students have been underserved and neglected by the state's education system. This neglect impacts the future of tribal communities and their ability to deal with an ever-changing world.

Furthermore, AIAN students deal with challenges that are unique compared to other marginalized communities. AIAN student enrollment is often the smallest at the various public institutions throughout the state. This leads to further marginalization when comparing the data to other racialized groups; often AIAN students' educational needs become invisible and less important. These circumstances dictate that there is an urgent need to provide data on the engagement of AIAN students in California's higher education systems.

On Indian Ground: California, pages 121–135
Copyright © 2017 by Information Age Publishing
All rights of reproduction in any form reserved.

The California Indian Culture and Sovereignty Center (CICSC) at California State University–San Marcos (CSUSM) has authored three reports (n.d.a., n.d.b., n.d.c.) that compiles publicly available data to provide much needed information about AIANs in K–12, community college, California State University and University of California systems. The data includes: enrollment, graduation rates, dropout rates, degrees conferred and personnel by race/ethnicity. It is important to note here that this series of three reports from 2012–2016 was made possible by financial support from the San Manuel Band of Mission Indians. The San Manuel Band of Mission Indians has been an invaluable tribal partner and has made an "investment change" in public policy reporting about the educational attainments, roadblocks, gaps, and achievements of American Indians and Alaska Natives in the State. Without their progressive investment this work would not be possible. It is from these three years of reports that we offer a comprehensive overview of higher education California.

In the report on *The state of American Indian and Alaska Native: Education in California 2012* (CICSC, n.d.a.) the California Indian Culture and Sovereignty Center at CSUSM documented the gaps in education for American Indian and Alaska Native peoples in California. In the 2014 report on *The state of American Indian and Alaska Native: Education in California* (CICSC, n.d.b.) we highlighted promising practices to help bridge some of these gaps. These practices include (a) formalizing institutional–tribal partnerships; (b) creating a kinship network of support for AIAN recruitment, retention, and graduation; (c) building and designating AIAN gathering grounds on campus in the form of dedicated meeting space, study space, and place for social interaction; (d) developing and delivering curriculum that meets tribal educational needs; and (e) creating pathways for persistence through college for AIAN students that focus on educational strengths (and are linked to culture and identity). To effectively implement these practices, public institutions must develop American Indian studies programs that include the hiring of AIAN faculty and staff to build and sustain relationships with tribal nations and communities.

From the day our doors officially opened at the California Indian Culture and Sovereignty Center (CICSC), we have been committed to providing useful tools, research, and curriculum for American Indian education in California. *The State of American Indian and Alaska Native: Education in California* reports (CICSC, n.d.a, n.d.b., n.d.c.) provide timely, necessary, and important data revealing gaps, highlighting successes, and pointing to areas in need of further research and improvement. The research at the CICSC originates from real community needs and we are determined to find solutions for these needs.

CALIFORNIA'S MASTER PLAN

California's Master Plan for Education (Coons et al., 1960) was passed by the California legislature in the spring of 1960 as the Donahoe Higher Education Act. The Donahoe Act enumerated many of the components for the future of public higher education in California. The Master Plan has four major dimensions:

1. It created a system that combined quality higher education with access.
2. It transformed the public colleges and universities of California into a coherent system.
3. It established a framework that allowed each of the three higher education segments to focus on creating this unique form of excellence along with its own responsibilities.
4. It acknowledged the role that independent colleges and universities played in California's higher education structure.

The Donahoe Act was highly instrumental in the development and expansion of the post-secondary opportunities in California. By 2016, all of California's postsecondary institutions experienced declines and various levels of rebounds in AIAN enrollment since 2010. The California Community Colleges (CCCs) seem to be recovering at a greater pace than the mainstream 4-year institutions in the California State University (CSU) and the University of California (UC) systems. According to the UC Accountability Report 2014, UC transfer admissions have doubled in the past 20 years with 30% of its admissions from California Community Colleges (Annual Accountability Report, 2014, p. iii).

After presenting data from previous reports and engaging representatives from the UC/CSU in a discussion about the decline in AIAN enrollment trends at the CSU, two contributing factors emerged. The first and most significant explanation for the drop-off and decline of AIAN enrollment in the CSU is due to changes for *maintaining, collecting, and reporting racial and ethnic data to the U.S. Department of Education*. This change in collecting and reporting was meant to align with the results of the Census 2000, which utilized revised standards from the Office of Management and Budget (OMB) from 1997 to allow respondents to select one or more racial categories for identification. This was the first time the U.S. Census captured multiracial/ethnic data about individuals. The revision added two additional categories for reporting: "Hispanic/Latino" and "two or more races" in addition to the original five aggregate reporting categories: American Indian and Alaska Native, Asian, Black or African American, Native Hawaiian or Other Pacific Islander, White.

The Federal Registry (2007) published the comments regarding each of the changes to the Department of Education's reporting and data collection. Section III. B. "Two or More Races Category Reporting" (p. 59270, Section III.B.1) notes that the addition of the two or more races category will change the population counts in single race categories. Commenters responded to this claim by pointing out that long-term data will not accurately depict the demographics in single-race categories such as Black, White, American Indian, and Asian depending on the population density in a particular state. They argued that "using the two or more races category will result in longitudinal data falsely showing declining minority populations in current single race categories" (Federal Registry, 2007, p. 59270, Section III.B.1). In its response to the comments, the Department of Education acknowledges that there will be changes but that these changes "will not be large enough to cause significant shifts in student demographics" and that the change in categories will produce "more accurate data." They also state that they will "monitor the data trends reported" and "[i]f necessary, we will request access to the specific racial and ethnic data provided in response to the two-part question by the individual" (Federal Registry, 2007, p. 59270, Section III.B.1).

This is extremely problematic for several reasons and should be a major area of concern for tribal leaders and educators. First and foremost, American Indian and Alaska Native people are a political group with multiple heritages not any single racial/ethnic group. As a political group, American Indian/Alaska Native identification should be counted so that our numbers rise to the top instead of being erased in a generic mixed-race category that is invisible and uncounted. Second, it is clear that the U.S. Department of Education's process is failing to accurately report the actual numbers of AIAN students in California; we know from the U.S. Census that California is second only to Oklahoma as having the highest number of people identifying as American Indian and Alaska Native. Furthermore, California ranks highest for all census respondents who identified as American Indian or Alaska Native alone or in combination with another race. A recently released Pew Study (Taylor, Passel, & Wang, 2010) on multiracial identity of approximately 1,600 individuals between February and April 2015 shows that 6.9% of those surveyed claimed a mixed-heritage and that the largest biracial group (50%) reported was White and American Indian/Alaska Native. The study diverged from the Census Bureau's data collection methods to account for the parents' and grandparents' racial identification of the adults in addition to the information that was self-reported. Given the unique political distinction of American Indian/Alaska Native people, it seems logical and necessary now more than ever that we advocate for changes to these data reporting policies—our numbers are small but they are not insignificant—and every one of our students identifying as AIAN should be counted on their own and then in conjunction with one or more races if that is what is reported.

The call for change is needed sooner rather than later because the data counts justify and determine the level and amount of federal aid for AIAN education in the state. The corollary outcome is that our low numbers correspond to the lack of or low educational funding for AIAN students in the state. Tribal leaders and educators also need to educate parents and students about the reporting guidelines and how AIAN and mixed-race identity is counted so that individuals can more accurately be counted when they primarily identify as AIAN people. The data that follow show the drop-off and plateau in AIAN student enrollment for both full-time freshmen and transfer students beginning around 2008, right about the time when the new reporting requirements were being implemented.

In the 2014 report, we provided a side-by-side comparison of the enrollment rates for AIANs at the UC and CSU. We have updated these charts with data from 2002–2014 for freshmen and transfer students. In the CSU system, the decline is drastically sharp from 2007 with 355 AIAN full-time freshmen (FTF) and 137 in 2008, and as of 2014, this decline never rebounds for the CSU. The UC numbers show an uptick in AIAN enrollment since the implementation of the plus factor, which gives AIAN applicants additional consideration as a political classification, not an ethnic/racial minority when they apply for admission to the UC.

THE CALIFORNIA COMMUNITY COLLEGE SYSTEM

The California Community College System is an integral part of California's Master Plan for Education. The primary mission of CCCS is to provide academic and vocation instruction to a diverse population of students. California Community Colleges also offer students and opportunity to complete lower-division course work or the first two years of their undergraduate work. Additionally, CCCS provides remedial instruction. English as a second language (ESL) courses, adult noncredit courses, community service courses, and workforce training. Importantly, California Community Colleges offer admittance to all students who would benefit from instruction. Additionally, these students have the ability to transfer to the UC or CSU system, originally based on a 1:2 ration for every incoming freshman straight from high school.

CCC: AIAN Enrollment

California's Community College system is the largest education system in the nation consisting of about 2.6 million students and 112 colleges throughout the state. The CCC was established in 1967 as part of California's three-tier system of public education along with the California State

University system and the University of California system. The community colleges in California have the highest enrollment of self-identified AIANs of any of the institutions of public higher education in California. High AIAN enrollment at the community college level is due in large part to the fact that AIAN high school students qualify to attend the CSU or the UC at a lower rate than any other ethnic group in California (CSUSM, 2012). The statewide enrollment of AIANs at CCC was 7,430 (0.47%) in fall 2012 and the AIAN enrollment in spring 2013 was 7,296 (0.46%) (CCC Chancellor's Office, n.d.). The California Community Colleges offer a broad range of academic programs for the general student population, but there are also programs at various community colleges throughout the state designed to specifically serve the unique educational and cultural needs of AIAN students and communities.

AIAN students comprised 0.45% of the student body across the 113 California Community Colleges in fall 2014; there was a 5.02% increase (495 AIAN students) in enrollment from fall 2013–fall 2014. Overall, AIAN enrollment from fall 2011 to fall 2014 has decreased by 4.81% (523 students). AIAN enrollment from fall 2011 for AIAN at CCC has increased by 1,532 students in the past 4 years.

CALIFORNIA STATE UNIVERSITY AND UNIVERSITY OF CALIFORNIA SYSTEMS

California's public 4-year university system is a two-part system that includes the California State University (CSU) system and the University of California (UC) system. The CSU system has 23 campuses, and the UC system has 10. In 2011, these 33 campuses enrolled 3,451 AIAN students at both the undergraduate and graduate level. The CSU system is the largest university system in the nation and considers itself the "gateway institution for the great majority of students seeking a baccalaureate education in California, and for those who seek professional training as teachers, nurses, social workers, and engineers" (California State University, n.d., para 1). The University of California is also a publicly funded state university system with an emphasis on research. Added to the accessibility and abundance of community colleges in the state, the three-tier system in California ensures that higher education is available and attainable for everybody.

CSU: AIAN Enrollment and Achievement

There were 1,440 AIAN students enrolled in the California State University system in fall 2014. The top three academic programs AIAN students enroll in are business management, social sciences, and psychology. The number of degrees awarded to AIAN undergraduate and graduate students in the CSU continued to decrease from 470 undergraduate degrees awarded in 2011–2012 to 414 awarded in 2012–2013. At the same time, the number of AIAN graduate degrees awarded also declined in the same 3-year time span with 71 AIAN graduate degrees awarded in 2011–2012 and 2012–2013 compared to 67 in 2013–2014. Graduate and undergraduate degrees awarded to AIAN students at the CSU decreased by 10.26% between 2013–2014 and 2014–2015. The AIAN student enrollment in the CSU for fall 2014 was 1,442 (0.3%). There are 1,230 American Indian undergraduate and 212 AIAN graduate and postbaccalaureate students.

University of California System

The UC system and its 10 campuses focus on academic research providing education at the undergraduate, graduate, and professional levels. According to the Master Plan on Public Higher Education (Coons et al., 1960), the UC system has the exclusive authority to offer doctoral degrees, as well as instruction in law and medicine. Access to the UC system was directed at the top one-eighth of the high school graduating class.

UC: AIAN Enrollment and Achievement

The UC system enrolled 1,699 AIAN students in fall 2014. AIAN undergraduates make up 1,250 students and AIAN graduate students number 449 for fall 2014. The UC system granted 8% more AIAN undergraduate degrees and 13% more master's degrees than the CSU. The UC awarded 363 bachelor's degrees versus the CSU's 336 to AIAN undergraduate students. For fall 2013, the UC system also awarded more masters degrees to AIAN students, with 76 degrees granted versus the CSU's 67.

High School Graduation and College Readiness

The largest AIAN graduating class from high school was in 2009–2010, with 3,169 graduates.

- The AIAN college completion rate of "A-G" requirements in high school for college entry increased by 1.4% between 2009 and 2014.
- There was a 5.2% increase in high school graduation rate from 67.3% in 2009–2010 to 70.8% in 2013–2014.

California's largest cohort of high school graduates was the class of 2010 with 3,169 AIAN across the state earning a high school diploma. All post-secondary institutions have experienced declines and slight rebounds in AIAN enrollment since 2011. The CCCs are rebounding at a greater pace than the CSU and UC systems. For example, compared to data reported in 2014 from Fall 2011, the enrollment rate for AIAN at CCC has increased by 1,037 students in the past four years. Additionally during this time, CSU enrolled more AIAN first-time freshmen (FTF) than UC in 8 out of the last 12 years. Beginning in 2008, the UC AIAN enrollment of FTF began to increase over the CSU. CSU AIAN enrollment of FTF in 2008 declined sharply from an average of 300 FTF per year to fewer than 150 FTF per year for the past 6 years.

In 2014, UC enrolled more transfer students than CSU who reported an almost 50% decline in transfer enrollment from 2002 cohort to 2014 cohort. The UC transfer enrollment increased 43% from 2002 cohort to 2014 cohort. Although AIAN transfer rates for admission remained relatively steady for the CSU, the UC began closing the gap in 2010, and in 2014 more AIAN transferred to UC campuses than CSU campuses. All of these statistics confirm that AIAN students are underserved in the three systems.

HIGHER EDUCATION AND AMERICAN INDIAN COMMUNITIES IN CALIFORNIA

For the state with the largest American Indian population in the nation, there are currently no postsecondary institutions designated as Native American Serving Non-Tribal Institutions (NASNTIs), which require a minimum of 10% of the total enrollment to be American Indian. This would suggest that while California has one of the most extensive networks for postsecondary education, the tribal populations are spread across wide geographic regions so that enrollment numbers are low in any one institution. Few institutions in the state provide either the access or ability to retain American Indian students in significant numbers. The current postsecondary efforts in California are housed in various academic departments and centers across college campuses. Some programs are located within departments with a diversity mission and share resources with other minority programs; few resources are available to these programs, which work in semi-isolation from each other.

Examples of programs within the state that encourage students to connect with tribal communities through study of Native history and culture are as follows:

- American River College (www.arc.losrios.edu): The Native American Resource Center on this 2-year campus offers a wide variety of support services for American Indian/Alaska Native students.
- California State University–Chico (www.csuchico.edu): The college offers a minor in American Indian studies within the multicultural and gender studies department. The minor focuses on the history, literature, worldviews, social practices, and legal issues of Indian tribes.
- California State University–Long Beach (www.csulb.edu). The American Indian studies program, founded in 1969 offers a certificate and a minor program in American Indian studies with an emphasis on four major areas: American Indian history, ethnic diversity in the United States, contemporary issues (such as American Indian philosophy and federal Indian law) and American Indian traditional material culture (with a focus on arts and crafts).
- California State University–Sacramento (www.csus.edu): The Native American studies program functions within the department of ethnic studies at California State University at Sacramento. It offers a Bachelor of Arts degree in ethnic studies with a concentration in Native American studies. The focus of the program is on three primary areas: teaching, research, and community service. A variety of course offerings include California Indian history, ethno-history, and culture (American Indian films and literature), traditions (Native American oral tradition and storytelling), and law (Native American tribal governments).
- California State University–San Marcos—California Indian Culture and Sovereignty Center (www.csusm.edu/cicsc): The University's commitment to California tribes can be seen in outreach across the state, as well as through direct services to students on campus. The America Indian Studies Department CSUSM currently offers a minor and began to offer a major in Fall 2016. The new AIS Department was approved for Fall 2017. The American Indian studies minor and soon to be major is a research-based interactive program grounded in culture-based higher learning. The American Indian studies department offers students an integrated knowledge platform to understand the diverse needs and interests of American Indian communities in California and beyond.
- College of the Redwoods (www.redwoods.edu): Courses in Native American Studies in this two-year institution provide certificates and degrees.
- Humboldt State University (www.humboldt.edu/nativeprograms): Humboldt State offers a Bachelor of Arts and a minor in Native American Studies. Resources at Humboldt State include projects in Indian Natural Resource, Science and Engineering Program, Indian

Tribal Education and Personnel Program, Native American Studies, and the HS Library Collections on North American Indians.

- Palomar College (www2.palomar.edu): American Indian studies is housed in the department of American Studies and provides a certificate in American Indian studies. The certificate in American Indian studies provides cultural knowledge and insight recognized by prospective employers such as state, federal, and tribal government agencies.

- San Diego State University—Department of American Indian Studies (www.sdsu.edu): The American Indian studies program at SDSU offers a major in American Indian studies and a minor to provide students with a liberal arts focus. The American Indian studies program focuses on individual elements that comprise the Native American cultures.

- Stanford University (www.stanford.edu): The Native American studies program at Stanford began offering classes in 1992 and was established as part of the Center for Comparative Studies and Ethnicity in 1997. The purpose of the Native American studies major and minor is to introduce students to a broad range of approaches to the academic study of Native American people, history, and culture.

- University of California–Davis (www.ucdavis.edu): Native American studies at UC Davis was created in 1969. Native American studies received departmental status in 1993. The designated emphasis (DE) in Native American Studies was also established that same year. The DE in Native American studies is affiliated with the graduate programs in anthropology, comparative literature, history, performance studies, psychology, sociology, and Spanish. The graduate program in Native American studies was approved in 1998, making UC Davis only the second university in the nation to offer a PhD in Native American studies.

- University of California–Los Angeles (www.ucla.edu): The American Indian Studies Center was formed in 1969 when students, faculty, and community members pressed UCLA to create a curriculum and research center concentrating on Native American history and culture. In 1982, the center faculty created the interdepartmental program's (IDP) master's degree in American Indian studies and developed a series of core courses. Since that time, the center has provided administrative and resource support to the IDP, including a student lounge and computer work area. Students study and often work in the Center where the IDP's academic coordinator is also housed. In the mid-1990s, the Center and IDP faculty created a minor, BA, and JD/MA in American Indian studies, which was approved in 2002.

- University of California–Santa Cruz (www.ucsc.edu): The university is home to the American Indian Resource Center. The center is dedicated to increasing native visibility both nationally and internationally, and work in the areas of Indigenous paradigm shifts, traditional knowledge, intergenerational leadership and activities, Indigenous justice, and sustainable communities.

These programs are representative only and do not reflect the total list of coursework that may be available to students in postsecondary education in California. There is no evidence that general education coursework reflects or emphasizes Native ways of knowing. Coursework that emphasizes American Indian history or literature or art may be available to students in institutions that do not have an academic department or a center dedicated to American Indian studies. In these instances, outreach to tribal students and communities is often linked to the individual instructor and may prove transitory.

The state of California was home to DQ University from 1971 to 2005. The Yocha Dehe Wintun Nation spearheaded an initiative to develop a tribal college in California. Tribal colleges are proven successes with greater student retention, graduation rates, and workforce development than those achieved by Native students attending mainstream postsecondary institutions. The California Tribal College seeks to address critical issues by offering an important opportunity to bridge the achievement gap that stands in the way of student success. The development of the California Tribal College can and will meet the unique needs of Native students and improve success within and well beyond Indian Country.

The California Tribal College (CTC) offered its inaugural certificate program in tribal leadership and governance, elected the first slate of board of regents, completed a feasibility study, and held a successful fundraiser where Governor Brown offered a keynote address in support of the CTC in 2015. Plans continue to emerge.

LACK OF ACCESS BY TRIBAL COMMUNITIES

In California, 1.9% of the total population self-identified as American Indian/Alaska Native in 2010. Overall enrollment rates for American Indians in fall 2011 and fall 2012 decreased in both the California Community College system and California State University system and a slight increase in the enrollment in the University of California system (CICSC, n.d.a.). The trend line for rates of retention and success of enrollment in transferable courses at California Community Colleges in 2011 and 2012 indicates that American Indian/ Alaska Natives are below all other race/ethnicity groups except African Americans. These retention rates are critical when determining a student's access to a 4-year institution because they need to be able to provide evidence of academic success if they are to continue. A critical recent decrease in transfer and admissions shows a 30% decline. Additionally, the number of American Indian students enrolled in California community colleges who transferred to a 4-year institution is minimal. With the decline of overall enrollment, we anticipate a decline in retention and graduation rates.

Interview data suggest that outreach to California tribal members coupled with the addition of more stringent admission requirements and budget cuts for tribal programming at state institutions have affected the pipeline (the ability of students to enroll and maintain enrollment in post-secondary education) as students have fewer resources. Lack of clear role models who can identify with the constraints found by American Indians/Alaska Natives in postsecondary institutions was also cited (CICSC, n.d.a.).

These localized findings are similar to national data on the American Indian/Alaska Native enrollments, transfers, and retention. However, the Institution of Education Sciences forecasts an increase in enrollment by 15% in the next eight years (U.S. Department of Education, 2008). This projection will continue to widen the ever-increasing gap in American Indian/Alaska Native completion and will continue to affect the workforce development and economic opportunities for tribes.

The AIAN Postsecondary Educational Workforce

The AIAN postsecondary educational workforce remains marginal across all three systems, in particular in academic (temporary, non-tenure track, and tenured and tenure-track positions). The CSU increased AIAN faculty members by 4 in 2013, but the UC experienced a decrease of 14 AIAN faculty members in the same period, despite a growth in AIAN student enrollment during the same period. There is also a general and overall decline in the AIAN workforce for non-academic jobs, such as administrative and support staff positions. There are 651 AIAN personnel working in California Community College, 210 AIAN personnel working in the CSU and 890 AIAN personnel working the UC. For a detailed breakdown by system and between non-academic and academic positions please see the *2016 The State of American Indian & Alaskan Native Education in California Report.*

Promising High-Impact Practices for AIAN Education

The needs we have highlighted here are addressed across the state with promising practices that include such initiatives as:

- Formalizing educational relationships that support tribal sovereignty and self-determination through tribal–university memorandums of understanding or other means using place-based tribal community needs, regional needs, and Native Ways of Knowing.
- Tailoring coursework for AIAN students based on the student's specific educational strengths and areas in need of assistance, such as earlier intervention in the K–12 system to spell out the A-G requirements for college entry—for example, a "4-3-2-1 Go To College" campaign—to educate tribal students and parents that four years of English, three years of math, two years of language, and two years of lab science, plus one college elective is needed to get into college in California.
- Creating a sense of "kinship" to strengthen communication between faculty, staff (advisors), and students, again by assessing the local, regional, and tribal community needs (place-based).
- Building specific AIAN "gathering grounds" for students and the community (on and off campus) to meet, study, and network, and plan around the dynamic and vibrant community events happening on local tribal lands.
- Designing, offering, and delivering courses to directly serve the needs of the AIAN community (at tribal sites when and if possible). Create a tribal advisory board that provides consultation on overarching administrative or fundraising plans, but also listen to this group's needs and advice for curricular plans for academic master planning.

ACTIONS FOR ADVOCACY

There are 109 federally recognized tribes in California and numerous others waiting recognition. These tribal groups must be consulted and included in all educational plans and policies. Tribes are unique political entities, sovereigns that should be treated on a government-to-government basis. California has long been a leader in American Indian education, but our vigilance and attention to the changing needs of American Indian education is a constant requirement. Building on the findings from our 2014 *State of American Indian and Alaska Native Education in California Report*, the CICSC's recommends the following practices to increase American Indian educational achievement rates from K–16:

- Advocating to change policy for data collection and reporting with the Department of Education to designate AIAN as political entity not solely a racial/ethnic group/minority. To accomplish this, an

Figure 9.1 California tribes map.

investigation into the funding that been diverted and divested in AIAN education in California as a result of homogenizing and normalizing reporting policies by the Department of Education should be conducted and presented in a comprehensive report.
- Mirroring student AIAN demographics at an institutional and systemic level with AIAN faculty (and staff when possible). To accom-

plish this, cluster hires for AIAN faculty and staff should become a high-impact practice for public institutions for education.

We recognize that higher education demographics are reflective of the work and efforts of the PK–12 community of educators and, as such, it is important that parents of American Indian students and tribal communities engage school administrators and college officials as they create policies and practices that impact American Indian/Alaska Native youth in California.

REFERENCES

Annual Accountability Report: University of California. (2014). Retrieved from www.universityofcalifornia.edu/accountability

California Community Colleges Chancellor's Office. (n.d.). *Management information systems data mart.* Retrieved from http://datamart.cccco.edu/Students/Student_Term_Annual_Count.aspx

California Indian Culture & Sovereignty Center. (n.d.a.). *The state of American Indian and Alaska Native: Education in California 2012.* San Marcos, CA: Author. Retrieved from https://www.csusm.edu/cicsc/projects/projects_docs_images/the.state.of.aian.education.in.ca.report.pdf

California Indian Culture & Sovereignty Center. (n.d.b.). *The state of American Indian and Alaska Native: Education in California 2014.* San Marcos, CA: Author. Retrieved from https://www.csusm.edu/cicsc/projects/projects_docs_images/cicsc_2014_education_report_download.pdf

California Indian Culture & Sovereignty Center. (n.d.c.). *The state of American Indian and Alaska Native: Education in California 2016.* San Marcos, CA: Author. Retrieved from https://www.csusm.edu/cicsc/projects/projects_docs_images/2016saianec_final1.pdf

California State University. (n.d.). *Explore the system.* Retrieved from http://www.calstate.edu/explore/?source=homepage

Coons, A. G., Browne, A. D., Campion, H., Dumke, G., Holy, T., & McHenry, D. (1960). *A master plan for higher education in California, 1960–1975.* Sacramento, CA: California State Department of Education.

U.S. Department of Education. (2008). *Status and Trends in the Education of American Indians and Alaska Natives: 2008.* NCES 2008-084. Retrieved from https://nces.ed.gov/pubs2008/2008084.pdf

Federal Registry. (2007). *Two or More Races Category Reporting.* Retrieved from https://www.gpo.gov/fdsys/pkg/FR-2007-10-19/pdf/E7-20613.pdf

Taylor, P., Passel, J. S., & Wang, W. (2010). *Marrying out: One-in-seven new U.S. marriages is interracial or interethnic.* Washington, DC: Pew Research Center.

CHAPTER 10

A MULTILOGICAL APPROACH TO GIFTEDNESS

Creating a Space for Indigenous Knowledge

Kishan Lara-Cooper
Humboldt State University

Historically, the classroom has not been a safe or nurturing environment for community members of the Hoopa Valley Indian Reservation (HVIR), located in northern California. Since the time of contact in 1846, education was imposed on the Indigenous people of the HVIR. From 1893 to 1932, children were required by the federal government to attend boarding school in the Hoopa Valley. Their traditional upbringing and cultural beliefs were invalidated, while they were forced to adopt the values of mainstream society. Despite the history of genocide, relocation, colonial education, and constantly shifting legislation, the HVIR community has sustained their ways of knowing and understanding; their relationships with the human, natural, and spiritual realms; and their methods of transferring

On Indian Ground: California, pages 137–156
Copyright © 2017 by Information Age Publishing
All rights of reproduction in any form reserved.

knowledge. In addition, they have maintained their own form of education and concepts of giftedness.

Yet, in spite of their resilience, the HVIR community suffers from alarming social indicators:

- 92% of HVIR students scored below proficient in mathematics and 67% scored below proficient in language arts on standardized tests (California Department of Education, 2014).
- There is a 60 percent high school dropout rate (Crosbie, 1993).
- 89 percent of HVIR students are socioeconomically disadvantaged (Oliveira, 2006).

Research suggests that the subjugation of Indigenous knowledge manifests itself in disturbing statistics such as these (Cajete, 1994; Calderon, 2001; Crosbie, 1993; Daniels, 1988). Native American students consistently rank below average in high school completion, standardized test scores, grade point average, college admittance, and representation in gifted and talented programs (United States Department of Education, 1990). These statistics are indicative of the incongruent nature of educational paradigms of the community and the school system. The mainstream school system is founded on a monological epistemology; Western concepts are the sole informant. Students who master these Western concepts (i.e., sitting in front of the class, asking multiple questions, appearing engaged, excelling on tests, etc.) are deemed "intelligent" or "gifted." One of the first federal definitions of giftedness was determined by Terman (1926), who defined giftedness as intellectual ability demonstrated by those who score high on intelligence and academic achievement tests. Since the educational paradigm revolves around the notion of giftedness, it is imperative to create a space for Indigenous knowledge by defining giftedness from a community context.

Consequently, this qualitative study1 examines the concept of giftedness as defined and practiced by the HVIR community. The exploration of giftedness from an Indigenous community context provides an opportunity to think multilogically not only in terms of giftedness but also in terms of educational paradigms. What are students expected to learn in school? How is their success evaluated? And how do these concepts relate to community expectations and evaluations? This study opens a discussion of how these definitions of giftedness influence a child's self-concept, self-esteem, and social identity by asking the following questions:

- What is giftedness as defined by the HVIR community?
- What characteristics do HVIR community members identify as indicative of giftedness?

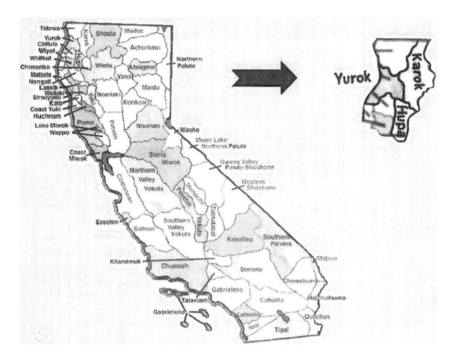

Figure 10.1 Map of indigenous California. Map showing Indigenous California peoples, including those of the Hoopa Valley Indian Reservation.

HVIR is known to its first inhabitants as Na-tin-xw, meaning "where the trails return" (Nelson, 1978). Na-tin-xw was established as the Hoopa Valley Indian Reservation in 1864. Throughout this chapter, I will use HVIR to refer to the Hoopa Valley Indian Reservation and Hupa to refer to the people of the Hoopa Valley. The HVIR, located 40 miles inland from the north Pacific coast, has a population of 3,000. The HVIR is the largest reservation in the state of California, measuring 12 square miles or 84,000 acres (Crosbie, 1993; see Figure 10.1). Participants in this research consisted of Hupa, Yurok, or Karuk tribal members who reside and/or attend school on the Hoopa Valley Indian Reservation. Careful measures have been made to ensure research methods that were sensitive to the needs of the research community, including cultural sensitivity, protection of identity, and clarity of participants' rights.

FINDINGS

Giftedness can be defined through *k'winya'nya:nma-awhiniw2* ("the human way"), meaning to live in balance and harmony with the world by having honor and respect for community members, the environment, self, ancestors, and creation. The human way is guided by language and culture and is characterized by honor, humility, patience, gratitude, discipline, compassion, a good heart, generosity, responsibility, and respect; maintaining relationships with the human, natural, and spiritual realms; understanding and valuing the HVIR worldview; and making a contribution to the HVIR community.

An important aspect of *k'winya'nya:n-ma'awhiniw3* is that everything is connected, like the weaving in a basket. A 19-year-old Hupa/Yurok college student illustrates the importance of recognizing multiple gifts and acknowledging that each gift is of equal value:

> You have to know respect . . . culture . . . language . . . where you come from . . . everything that I have been taught I want to pass it down to my children. . . . There is no number one or number two. I can't say that language is more important than basket making. I can't say that fishing is more important than jumping in the middle [a ceremonial dance movement] because everything has its own place. Everything has its own importance. . . . Nothing in our world has more importance than the other. They are all connected. (student interview 2, May 13, 2008)

The 19-year-old eloquently expresses the essence of giftedness when she explains, "Nothing in our world has more importance than the other." Within the community context, giftedness is holistic in nature. The HVIR concept of giftedness is not defined by the most beautiful singer, the prettiest dancer, the greatest regalia-maker, or the most skilled fishermen. Rather, singing, dancing, regalia-making, and fishing are expressions of *k'winya'nya:n-ma'awhiniw*. Contrary to mainstream concepts of giftedness, the HVIR definition of giftedness embraces contributions made by the entire community. Hence, community members believe that everyone has a gift. However, to truly be gifted, one must recognize, develop, and utilize the gift to contribute to the community concept of *k'winya'nya:n-ma'awhiniw*. A 40-year-old community member argues that "all children are gifted" (Community Survey 309, August 2008). Likewise, a 24-year-old community member states, "Hupa people are all gifted in their own way" (Community Survey 301, August 2008), and a 43-year-old community member emphasizes, "Everyone is gifted with a special talent. We all have to find it. Some are artists, singers, cooks, leaders, dancers, etc." (Community Survey 68, August 2008). The principle that everyone has a gift is significant because it acknowledges the importance of recognizing gifts, as well as contributing to the greater community.

Characteristics of Giftedness

Kawagley's (1995) tetrahedral framework (see Figure 10.2) illustrates the Yupiaq worldview and its connection with the human, natural, and spiritual

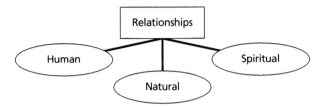

Figure 10.2 Diagram of relationships. Diagram of the human, natural, and spiritual relationships as a foundation in defining giftedness.

realms of life. I utilize this framework to explore the HVIR characteristics of giftedness. Kawagley's (1995) framework, a tripod replica of a Yupiaq hunting tool used to dry meat, exemplifies a harmonious existence between the worldview and human, natural, and spiritual realms. In this model, the worldview sits like a globe on top of the tripod, each leg representing a different realm. Because equal emphasis rests on each leg, the worldview remains constant. However, without equal representation and emphasis on all three realms, the worldview is out of balance. Kawagley (1995) states, "It illustrates that the Yupiaq worldview is based on the alliance and alignment of all elements and that there must be constant communication between the three constituent realms to maintain this delicate balance" (p. 16). I will build on Kawagley's (1995) diagram to illustrate the HVIR concept of giftedness:

Three constituent realms are used in this study to describe relationships with the human, natural, and spiritual realms of the world. Of 220 surveys, "relationships" and related terms appeared 2,019 times. For instance, when asked to define giftedness from a tribal perspective, an 18-year-old high school student responded, "Someone who has a love, respect, and passion for culture and our way of life. Someone who cares and loves the people" (Community Survey 312, August 2008). Similarly, a teacher and community member defines giftedness as "understanding their connection and their responsibility to this place and to each other" (Community Survey 72, August 2008). A 27-year-old graduate student adds that the gifted "respect[s] how to live in a good way with balance. Understands our traditional values like harmony with nature" (Community Survey 216, August 2008). These survey responses demonstrate the significance of relationships with community, ceremony, and nature.

Human Relationships

Human relationships and camaraderie are an integral part of the HVIR philosophy. Members of the community believe that individuals are a representation of their entire community. A Hupa community member emphasizes the significance of building and maintaining human relationships:

> What we do today has a long range of feelings for other people, even people that are gone, our family, extended family, all the people that have ever left foot prints here, you are affecting them... so, they say when you do something it reaches a long way. (Community member interview 11, July 2, 2008)

Therefore, each individual must be responsible and accountable for their decisions, actions, and behavior. Even more important, when an individual struggles, the entire community struggles. A Yurok community member says, "[E]veryone's eyes are watching one another and we are accountable for one another. That's why I said, if I see someone struggling, I am just as responsible as anyone else" (Community member interview 2, May 4, 2008).

Another aspect of human relationships is respect and value for elders. *Natinixwe*, the term used to refer to Hupa people, was translated by a Hupa language student as "a spirit people on a human journey." Some believe that when the goal of *k'winya'nya:n-ma'awhiniw* is achieved, the journey is completed here on earth and a new journey will begin. In other words, it is a lifelong journey to truly live in balance and harmony with the world. Likewise, elders who live in this manner are treated with the ultimate honor, respect, and admiration.

A Hupa/Yurok/Karuk community member defines giftedness as one who "respects themselves, others, and especially elders" (Community Survey 195, August 2008). Children are taught at a young age to value the knowledge and experiences of their elders. Elders are sought for their guidance and expertise. At ceremonies or cultural events, young children assist their grandparents or greet elders as they arrive at the event. A Hupa elder shared a story of a young Yurok man who would sing to her every time that she saw him. She identified this young man as gifted because he was not only a gifted traditional singer, but it was evident to her that he cherished his relationships with elders (Community member interview 12, February 7, 2008).

It should be noted that elders and grandparents also value relationships with the young. An elder and grandparent articulated how special her grandchildren are because they always visit her. She identified "care-taking grandparents" as a characteristic of giftedness (Community member interview 12, February 7, 2008). In a related example, a teacher shares a story of an elderly Hupa language teacher who identified gifted students according to the respect they demonstrated in the community. He says:

> Even people that were not very good language students, when they would see my elder in the store or something they would tell him "*he:yung, dixwe:di 'a:nt'e*" [hello, how are you?], his impression was that was the best kid in the whole class! (Teacher interview 4, May 23, 2008)

An important aspect of maintaining relationships with elders, family, and community members is to visit them. It is not uncommon on the Hoopa Valley Indian Reservation to travel to an elder's home to visit or help with chores. An individual who takes the time to visit, listen, and maintain human relationships often is identified by community members as gifted.

Traditionally, valuing community relationships also is an integral component to the HVIR ways. Food often is used to maintain relationships. At the conclusion of a ceremony, when company arrives, or at a community gathering, the sharing of food exemplifies the camaraderie and generosity of the people. A Yurok student relates his first cultural teaching from his grandparents when he learned to fish and share his catch with the community:

> You hear stories about a long time ago that people would go and take care of everyone, that is what we did, take care of everyone. If we got more than we needed, well we would call everybody and none went to waste.... It just makes you feel so happy.... Every time you see those people, they never forget it. They come up to you and they always have a big smile, they say, "oh I am so glad to see you" and it makes you feel real good...you have got to take care of your elders...your family and everybody around you. (Student interview 3, May 19, 2008)

The student clearly loves to build and maintain relationships with his family, elders, and community by sharing food with them.

Not only are human relationships with community, elders, and family important, but also maintaining relationships with one's inner self. A Yurok community member states:

> I think it's being honest with themselves...when we sing and we hear these songs, it's those songs that are in us. And we are tuning into ourselves and it's sometimes hard to hear ourselves because we have so much noise going on that we have to quiet ourselves or find that place by the water or someplace that we can hear ourselves, our inner selves. It's where the truth is, where it is the most beautiful. 'Cause if we are honest to ourselves, there is no way that we can't be honest to other people. (Community member interview 2, May 4, 2008)

Community members have voiced the significance of building and maintaining relationships with family, community members, elders, grandparents, and self. Participants of this study contend that these relationships can be sustained through visiting, listening, generosity, and honesty. Figure 10.3 illustrates characteristics of giftedness as reflected by the three constituent realms of human, natural, and spiritual relationships. Human relationships are an attribute of giftedness that can be characterized by relationships with elders, family, community, and self.

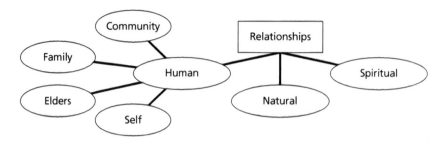

Figure 10.3 Human relationships. Human relationships can be characterized by relationships with community, family, elders, and self.

Natural Relationships

Traditionally, HVIR people have always had a natural relationship of respect and reverence with the environment, homelands, ceremonial sites, prayer sites, gathering sites, and wildlife. At the time of contact, U.S. soldiers attempted to relocate the people away from the valley. Captain John, a spiritual leader of the HVIR, led the people in a fight to maintain their tribal lands. He argued that because *Natinixwe*, the people of the valley, came into being at *Natiniwh*, they had a spiritual connection to the land and would die before they abandoned their home (Nelson, 1978). The community also believes that those who leave the valley will always return. In the Hupa language, this relationship with place can be referred to as *ninis'a:n-whoLts'it*, meaning "the world/the land knows me." This translation emphasizes the relationship between land and human beings. A high school teacher describes his connection to "place" when he shares his greatest reward as a teacher: "My greatest reward? Just knowing that I can make a difference in a community that I love" (Teacher interview 3, May 12, 2008). Similarly, another high school teacher expresses his connection to community:

> It is an incredible thing to live where your family has lived forever. And to teach in a classroom full of kids that have the same specialness about them. To appreciate that in the kids is like you are appreciating yourself. That's pretty rare; there is not anywhere else where you would get that. (Teacher interview 4, May 23, 2008)

Likewise, when a community member was asked to define a gifted person, he responded, "I would think that they were raised with respect and raised with the familiarity of their surroundings...a connection to the land" (Community member interview 11, July 2, 2008). This connection can be demonstrated through relationships with the environment, gathering sites, ceremonial sites, and prayer sites. Before gathering basket materials, food, or materials to make regalia, a prayer is recited, and often the gatherer has fasted and purified so that she can enter the gathering grounds with a pure heart. Once she has arrived at the gathering site, she will introduce herself to the *mita:n* ("spirit keepers of the forest") and show that she has come in a good way. In many circumstances s/he may bring a gift or an offering. She will then gather only what she needs, making sure to leave plenty for the health and survival of the plant and for future gatherers. While on the gathering grounds, she behaves with sincerity, respect, care, and gratitude.

Ceremonial sites and prayer sites are treated with similar respect. The HVIR tribes share two sacred sites, Doctor Rock and Chimney Rock. The ceremonies of all three tribes originate from these sites. At the beginning of the ceremony, the medicine person or Indian doctor will train and fast for several days. After, the medicine person will "borrow" the medicine, bring it to the village, and begin the ceremony (Alderman & Kennedy, 1991). Only those who are of a spiritual capacity travel to the sacred sites. Ceremonial sites and prayer sites were identified thousands of years ago. Creation stories describe the uniqueness and purpose of each site. Generation after generation has followed this intricate formula.

A Hupa elder remembers the first time she participated in a ceremony. She was nearly 8 years old and participated by serving people, helping to cook, and setting tables. At 85 years old, she observes her great-grandchildren participating in the same manner. She states, "[My] experience is a testimony to the fact that in ritual, we walk in the footsteps of our ancestors" (Community member interview 12, February 2, 2008). Because ceremonial and prayer sites have been determined and utilized for centuries, there are often markers that identify the exact location of the site. As such, one may be dancing in the exact place that his great-great-great grandparents had danced years before—hence the term "*whichwo ayadin, whichwing ayadin,*" which translated from the Hupa language means, "my grandmother's fathers walked here before me, my grandmother's mothers walked here before me." Figure 10.4 illustrates the connection and respect for prayer sites, wildlife, environment, homeland (place), gathering sites, and ceremonial sites.

Spiritual Relationships

Relationships with ancestors, the creator, regalia, song, and ceremony create a spiritual foundation that is crucial to achieving *k'winya'nya:n-ma'awhiniw* ("the human way"). A community member explains the importance of song to the HVIR community, saying, "The ways of our people grow in our hearts. And that which grows in our heart, is difficult to express in words" (Community member interview 16, January 5, 2009). Correspondingly, a Hupa teacher shares, "It is a community value; it is a Hupa value, to

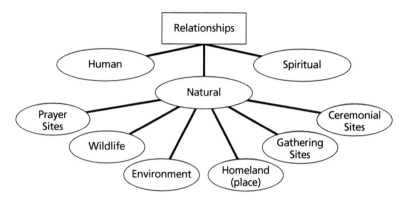

Figure 10. 4 Natural relationships. Natural relationships can be characterized by relationships with prayer sites, wildlife, homeland (place), gathering sites, and ceremonial sites.

be able to sing and express yourself in a prayer format" (Teacher interview 1, May 10, 2008). A student says, "I think it [song] is what let me express myself. I am not too good with words, so when I sing I can let the people feel what I am feeling" (Student interview 5, June 27, 2008). A Hupa/Yurok community member attests to this spiritual connection when he describes the sanctity of song and ceremony:

> That is a true gift when a person makes that connection... you can feel the spirits or you can feel a greater power than yourself come into the dance. You can just feel it when there are certain people that can sing, that it just kind of raises the back of my hair, like a warm sensation that your body will go through. (Community member interview 5, May 16, 2008)

There are many types of songs in the HVIR community, including songs of healing, world renewal, love, transition, continuity, or gratitude. These prayers are handed down from generation to generation. Songs are taught to children at a young age. Through this process, parents, grandparents, aunts, or uncles will explain the meaning of each song, as well as the purpose of the song. As the young person grows, so does their love and spiritual connection with their song. A Hupa/Yurok community member shares his story of learning to sing from his grandfather:

> I wanted to sing just like my grandpa, how he rolled his voice. When he talked to me he said, 'you know, there are no two singers that sing alike. Everybody sings their own way. You can sing another person's song but it will never sound the same because no singers sing alike.' ... [H]e kind of gave me this whole history of singing in the deerskin dance. Even to this day, every time the deerskin dance comes up, he will tell me the same story, this is what you got to do,

this is how you do it. I can mouth exactly what he is going to say now. I understand that now because it is something that is really important to him that he wants to leave for me. (Community member interview 5, May 16, 2008)

In this statement, the grandfather shares that "there are no two singers that sing alike," not only because their voices sound different, but also because each song is a prayer and no two prayers are exactly the same.

Each song has its own spiritual life that must be treated with honor and respect. It is a common belief that songs have their own spiritual life and rest in the aura by creeks, rivers, or the ocean. It is believed that songs come to those individuals that are spiritually connected, in tune with their natural environment, and can recognize and hear a song when it comes to her/him. A singer who is gifted with a song demonstrates a spiritual connection, and is therefore identified as gifted from a community perspective. Another Hupa/Yurok community member describes the characteristics of a gifted singer:

> He was very reverent and I don't think he did it to be showy or to be sounding good. I think he was praying. He was like praying on behalf of all of us.... That probably is a characteristic [of giftedness.... I think you can feel it when somebody is praying. When they are pulling all of your prayers in and sending them all out to the world. I think that's a gift. (Community member interview 1, May 4, 2008)

As illustrated in the above statement, HVIR community members believe that a singer is a representation of the entire community. In ceremony, there may only be one singer who prays on behalf of everyone. Therefore, a singer who can extract the prayers from all of the participants and send them out to the world through song is considered gifted.

A spiritual connection with regalia or prayer items is also a characteristic of giftedness. Regalia, like songs, has a spiritual life. Creation stories describe spirit animals that sacrificed their lives for the purpose of prayer. This spiritual life of regalia is treated with deep and sincere respect. Therefore, children are taught at a young age how to care for regalia and how to behave in its presence. Creation stories and oral traditions explain the history, purpose, and meaning of each prayer item used in ceremony. A Hupa community leader elaborates on the significance of regalia:

> I have been asked that a lot, why do we use certain ones [regalia items]? And I would say well to me, most people always look to the Bible or Christianity, some form of Christianity, so to me, when I am sitting at that medicine fire and I look up and see that line of dancers and I look at all of the regalia that they have on. To me, I can look at that regalia and it is just like an open scripture. Just looking at that line because every piece of thing, every feather,

every color, every different item, has a purpose and that is what we maintain
our balance with. That is what they are showing us is to maintain that balance.
(Community member interview 11, July 2, 2008)

Likewise, an elder shares a lesson that he was taught by his grandmother
about the importance of taking regalia to participate and contribute to
ceremony:

When I was a little boy, my grandmother told me, she says, "If you can't get
these Indian things [regalia] over there to the ceremony, hang them up on
the fence, and their spirits will still be involved in our ceremony." (Community member interview 9, January 21, 2005)

Giftedness may be identified by how a person takes care of, handles,
or creates regalia. Community members who demonstrate reverence, patience, and humility while caring for regalia, handling regalia, or making
regalia are identified as gifted.

While creating regalia, it is important to have a positive attitude and
good feelings. It is believed that all of your thoughts and prayers become
a part of the regalia as you make it. A student describes making regalia as
"therapy for his soul." He says that he would like his children to learn the
art of regalia-making so that they can feel connected to their culture and
feel good about themselves (Student interview 3, May 19, 2008).

Finally, spiritual connections with ceremony are demonstrative of giftedness. There are ceremonies for the continuance of humankind, world
renewal, healing, and rites of passage. A community member shares:

Whenever I went to brush dances, I always thought of people that were gifted.
The little kids that would go in there and that would dance ... would just be so
outstanding and I would think in my mind, how could they only be six years
old. (Community member interview 1, May 4, 2008)

A parent and community member believes that young people have such a
love for ceremony because it validates their teachings from home and acknowledges their Indigenous identity. He states:

When you are at the dances, you are seeing who you are, you are seeing the regalia, its within arms' reach and every single Hupa tribal member, Yurok tribal
member, Karuk tribal member can relate to that because we all have grass
roots in that stuff (regalia/ceremony), no matter how far we get off from
ourselves, we all get back down to reality when we hear Indian songs and are
in the presence of regalia. (Community member interview 6, May 26, 2008)

A community member elaborates on dance participants who love and
cherish ceremony, "They love it [ceremony] and they want to be there ...

how many kids get to do something that involves their grandparents, their parents, their siblings, their aunts, all in the same event" (Community member interview 1, May 4, 2008). This community member identifies the following student as one of those children that loves ceremony and has a strong spiritual connection. The student shares her thoughts on ceremony:

> The first time that I got to dance all night (11 years old)... I remember in the morning round, I looked up and I saw people with smiles on.... [T] hey were proud of me. That was one of my first experiences knowing that I was doing something right.... [T]hose moments have been influential in my life.... There are no words to express how I felt. It was just such a spiritual feeling. (Student interview 2, May 13, 2008)

According to the HVIR definition of giftedness, this student would be a prime example of demonstrating a connection to family, community, elders, homeland and spirituality. In addition, community members who have an understanding of the purpose of ceremony, as well as a spiritual bond with ceremony, are considered gifted. Not only is having an understanding of ceremony important to defining giftedness, but also valuing the significance of understanding ceremony. Another community member highlights the importance of perceiving this concept, stating:

> The rules mainly teach respect.... I always ask them, do you know why you are dancing? Did your mom or your dad tell you why you are dancing?... You are showing me that you understand why you are doing this because this whole dance is prayer. It's prayer. All of the prayer items, all of the regalia that you use, that is a part of the prayer and your motion when you dance is a part of the prayer. So, you are actually praying. When you dance, you are praying. You are not out there seeing who is out there seeing you dance. You are thinking about prayer and when you can understand that, you are ready to dance. (Community member interview 11, July 2, 2008)

Figure 10.5 illustrates attributes of giftedness as it relates to the human, natural, and spiritual realms of relationships. Spiritual relationships are exemplified by relationships with the creator, ancestors, ceremony, regalia, and song. The diagram in Figure 10.5 is a section of a larger diagram. The complete diagram includes characteristics of giftedness, including cultural skills, such as regalia-making, traditional games, gathering, basket-making, fishing, hunting, auditory, oratory, and observatory; values, such as honor, respect, generosity, sincerity, discipline, "a good heart," compassion, patience, gratitude, and humility; human relationships with community, elders, family, and self; natural relationships with prayer sites, wildlife, the environment, homeland (place), gathering sites, and ceremonial sites; and spiritual relationships with the creators, ceremony, song, ancestors, and

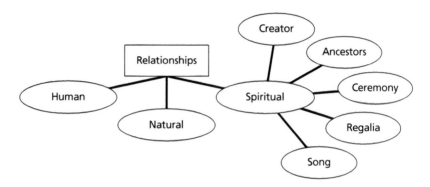

Figure 10.5 Spiritual relationships. Spiritual relationships are portrayed by relationships with the creators, ancestors, ceremony, regalia, and song.

regalia. The connecting line represents language and culture. Characteristics of giftedness are guided and connected to each other through language and culture.

Illustrations of Giftedness

Three key concepts illustrate giftedness: *nilts'it* (inherent gifts), *xoL-diniL'ay* (learned gifts), and contribution. *Nilts'it* translates in the Hupa language as "it comes as a gift" or "it passes on through him/her." This definition reflects the Hupa philosophy that humans are "spirit beings on a human journey." A Hupa elder contends that "singers are born with a natural gift in them. A singer that makes you cry out of loneliness for the ancient ones is born with a gift" (Community Surveys 320/335, August 2008). It is believed that some people are "born old," meaning that a spirit is working through them. For example, when the Hupa elders share that a singer makes them cry out of loneliness for the "ancient ones," it is because the ancestors, the *kixina:y* (meaning "angel" or "those that have come before"), are using that person as a tool to carry on the "human way." As stated by a community member when he described the gift of singing, "I am just a person, it's like I am a middle man. . . . [S]ometime I will just open my mouth and a song will come out" (Community member interview 5, May 16, 2008).

Similarly, dreams/visions are gifts given by the *kixina:y*. These types of gifts cannot be learned nor taught. This illustration of *nilts'it* is validated by the Hupa word for the powers of an Indian doctor, *xwa:'a:neh*, meaning "through her it speaks."

XoL-diniL'ay means "he knows it, he has learned how to do it, and he understands it." *XoL-diniL'ay* exemplifies an individual who recognizes the beauty of *k'winya'nya:nma-'awhiniw*, is a good listener, a hard worker, has a good heart, and a desire to learn and to understand. These individuals recognize the importance of learning about language, culture, and ceremony and demonstrate their love and values for this knowledge by being active learners. In addition to learned skills and characteristics, *xoL-diniL'ay* can be illustrated by individuals who have a desire to learn. A community member comments that they have "a thirst for knowledge, the desire to always continue learning" (Community Survey 201, August 2008).

Traditionally, there was only one way in which giftedness was illustrated, through *nilts'it*, meaning that an individual was born with a gift from the Creators. These gifts may include visions/dreams, possessing a "good heart," the ability to heal (medicine people or Indian doctors), or artistry or singing. Today, there is another manner in which giftedness is illustrated through *xoL-diniL'ay*, meaning that a gift is learned. These gifts are illustrated by those who demonstrate an appreciation, understanding, and love for *k'winya'nya:n-ma'awhiniw*. These individuals strive to learn, to protect, and to contribute to the preservation of the "human way." They strive to live in balance and harmony with the world and maintain relationships with the community, nature, and spirituality. This form of giftedness is considered contemporary, since traditionally it was expected or natural behavior. Due to the history of genocide, colonization, and colonial education of HVIR people, this once natural way of living is now viewed as a gift. A community member agrees:

> Long ago, they didn't have to recognize it as a tool, it was just taught to them as a tool, that is all that they knew and it was a choice to do it or not. You weren't considered gifted if you did it and was that good person, you were just considered Hupa. That was the way it was done. But in this day and age, if you can do that, that is a gift. (Community member interview 16, January 5, 2009)

In this generation, both illustrations of giftedness are of equal importance, particularly in child-rearing and educational practices.

Community members have contended that a gift is meaningless unless it is shared with the community. Therefore, despite the illustration of giftedness, it must be in conjunction with making a contribution to the community. A student states that "everyone has a gift, but if you don't do anything with it, then it might not benefit the people that much" (Student interview 4, May 21, 2008). The contribution of each person is like a piece of a puzzle. All the puzzle pieces are needed in order to see the larger picture. If a person's contribution is missing, a piece of the puzzle is missing. For example, in ceremony, there is room for the contributions of many. A community member shared his experiences of reviving ceremony, stating, "You have two or three of those old fellas there . . . you had to have all of them there because they all have their bit of knowledge" (Community member interview 3, April 28, 2005). It is important in the HVIR community to acknowledge community roles and contributions. If one person knew how to perform each role, the ceremony would lack the camaraderie and relationship that is so important to the HVIR community.

In mainstream society and education, there is a notion that "everyone shall be created equal." In the HVIR community, the goal is that "everyone shall live in harmony." Each individual is gifted in a different area, and when all their knowledge and expertise is joined together, they create a whole. From an HVIR perspective, if everyone were created equal, it would eliminate uniqueness and contribution of each person. In other words, it would create individuals, rather than a community.

DISCUSSION

In this study, giftedness has been defined as those who strive to live *K'winya'nya:n-ma'awhiniw* by maintaining relationships with the human, natural, and spiritual realms of the world; understanding and valuing the HVIR worldview, and making a contribution to the HVIR community. HVIR concepts of giftedness are harmonious with attributes of giftedness that have been identified by other Indigenous communities, scholars in gifted education, psychologists, educators, and neuroscientists (Cajete, 1994; Martin, 1996; Renzulli, 2002; Reynolds, 1991; Romero, 1994; Sternberg, 2005; Subotnik & Jarvin, 2005). Despite the congruency of HVIR attributes of giftedness with contemporary definitions of giftedness, many school districts continue to operate under Terman's (1926) definition. The National Excellence Report (1993) says, "In one recent survey...most [school districts] mainly use tests and teacher recommendations to admit students to gifted and talented programs" (p. 1). More specifically, in the HVIR school system, giftedness is characterized by an individual who demonstrates a mastery of core concepts such as reading, writing and arithmetic. The school district has adopted the following definition:

> A 'highly gifted pupil' means a gifted and talented pupil who has achieved a measured intelligence quotient of 150 or more on an assessment of intelligence...or has demonstrated extraordinary aptitude in language arts, mathematics, science, or other academic subjects. (California Department of Education, 2005, p. 9)

It should be noted that the HVIR community did not identify intellectual ability, IQ, or individualism as characteristics of giftedness. The risk of identifying gifted students solely from test scores, referral, and academic achievement is that it promotes a monological epistemology, invalidates the students' concept of giftedness, and ultimately eliminates a space for student connection to the classroom. This disconnect can influence a child's self-concept, sense of industry, self-esteem, construction of social identity, and formation of "out-groups."

From a developmental perspective, a child develops her or his values, beliefs, and self-concept in the first five years of life. This is significant because it acknowledges that children have already established their worldview before they ever set foot in a "formal" classroom. For example, children of the HVIR community enter the classroom with an appreciation and understanding of the expressions of *K'winya'nya:n-ma'awhiniw*.

In middle childhood, ages 6 to 12, children develop self-esteem. In this psychosocial stage of "industry versus inferiority," children build a sense of industry when feeling success. However, "inferiority develops when negative experiences at home or school lead to feelings of incompetence" (Berk, 2012, p. 16). At the same time, children are establishing personal and social identity. Turner, Brown, and Tajfel's (1979) social identity theory outlines three stages of development: social categorization, where a child places himself and others into categories; social identification, where a child adopts the identity of a group; and social comparison, where a child establishes in-groups and out-groups. When a child does not feel a sense of belonging or connection to the classroom, the classroom may be deemed as an out-group.

In the HVIR community, an educator shared, "Something happens over the summer before the kids get to the sixth grade . . . they just seem to lose interest" (Community member interview 13, April 30, 2007). Simultaneously, standardized test scores demonstrate a decline from the 5th to the 6th grade (Oliveira, 2006). Could this lack of interest, motivation, and decline in test scores be indicators of the school's induction to an out-group? If so, what influenced this social comparison? Was the child feeling a sense of industry or inferiority in the classroom?

Developmental theory argues that a child's social and cultural experiences influence her or his learning experiences (Vygotsky, 1978). In order for children to learn new information, they must be able to relate it to prior personal, behavioral, and environmental experiences (Bandura, 1986) and interactions between children and their environment including home, school, and society directly impact their development (Bronfenbrenner & Morris, 2006). Therefore, it is critical to create a safe and nurturing environment that embraces diversity, validates students' contributions, and promotes healthy development. By creating a space for Indigenous knowledge in the classroom, an opportunity is provided for children to see how the classroom fits into their experiences and worldview.

Although this Indigenous research project focused on the HVIR community, the findings are applicable in education settings throughout the world. This study provides a knowledge base for teacher preparation programs, tribal education programs, public and private school systems, gifted and talented programs, school site councils, researchers, and curriculum developers to shift the paradigm of education. The intent of this research is not to encourage teachers to attempt to teach Indigenous culture. This research emphasizes the significance of acknowledging and validating Indigenous knowledge, embracing diversity, and thinking multilogically. Furthermore, this research promotes a multilogical epistemology, whereby Indigenous knowledge is recognized, validated, and most importantly approached through its own theoretical lens. In closing, the following quote further illustrates the need to shift the paradigm of education from a monological epistemology to a multilogical epistemology:

> Being gifted or talented means, to me, to just be normal. Everyone has a special gift or talent, even if it is not visible. Everyone can contribute in some way to make this a better world. . . . Every second someone's talents are wasted is a second in which the world gets a little worse. So, the next time you see someone whose is down and out, don't feel sorry for that person, feel sorry for the world. (Ulrey, 1991, p. 25)

NOTES

1. This chapter is a reproduction of an article published in the *Journal of American Indian Education*. Permission has been given by the *Journal of American Indian Education* to include all or part of this work in this book series. Furthermore, information shared in this article is part of a larger work that will be published at a future date.
2. *K'winya'nya:n-ma'awhiniw* directly translates as "the way of the *k'winya'nya:n*" in the Hupa language. *K'winya'nya:n* translates as "acorn eater." Human beings, from a Hupa perspective, are acorn eaters. Therefore *k'winya'nya:n-ma'awhiniw* is "the acorn eater way" or the "the human way." Despite its seeming simplicity, the implications of "the human way" are very complex. Some community members believe it describes a way of life, while others consider it a philosophy or a goal of how to live.
3. Words in the Hupa language will appear in italics.

REFERENCES

Alderman, E., & Kennedy, C. (1991). *In our defense: The bill of rights in action*. New York, NY: Harper Collins.

Bandura, A. (1986). *Social foundations of thought and action: A social cognitive theory*. Englewood Cliffs, NJ: Prentice-Hall.

Berk, L. E. (2012). *Infants, children, and adolescents* (7th ed.). Boston, MA: Allyn & Bacon.

Bronfenbrenner, U., & Morris, P. A. (2006). *The bioecological model of human development*. In R. M. Lerner (Ed.), *Handbook of child psychology: Vol. 1. Theoretical models of human development* (6th ed., pp. 793–828). Hoboken, NJ: Wiley.

Cajete, G. (1994). *Look to the mountain: An ecology of Indigenous education*. Durango, CO: Kivaki Press.

Calderon, L. (2001). *A holistic approach for addressing the social/emotional needs of the Hoopa Valley children*. Hoopa, CA: Klamath-Trinity School District.

California Department of Education. (2005). *Gifted and talented education resource guide*. Retrieved from http://www.ktjusd.k12.ca.us/ourpages/auto/2012/5/30/39049078/California%20Dept_%20of%20Ed%20GATE%20Programs.pdf

California Department of Education. (2014). *2013 STAR test results*. Retrieved from http://star.cde.ca.gov/star2013/SearchPanel.aspx?lstTestYear=2013&lstTestType=C&lstCounty=12&lstDistrict=62901-000&lstSchool=1234004&lstGroup=1&lstSubGroup=1

Crosbie, P. (1993). *Educational needs assessment of the Hoopa Valley Reservation*. Arcata, CA: Humboldt State University.

Daniels, R. R. (1988). American Indians: Gifted, talented, creative or forgotten? *Roeper Review, 10*(4), 241–244.

Kawagley, A. (1995). A Yupiaq worldview: a pathway to ecology and spirit. Long Grove, IL: Waveland Press.

Martin, D. E. (1996). *Towards an understanding of the Native Hawaiian concept and manifestation of giftedness* (Unpublished doctoral dissertation). University of Georgia, Athens, GA.

Nelson, B. (1978). *Our home forever: The Hupa Indians of northern California*. Hoopa, CA: Hupa Tribe.

Oliveira, D. (2006). *Klamath-Trinity Joint Unified School District: Impact Aid reports to tribes and community members 2005–2006 school year*. Hoopa, CA: Klamath-Trinity Joint Unified School District.

Renzulli, J. (2002). Emerging concepts of giftedness: Building a bridge to the new century. *Exceptionality, 10*(2), 67–75.

Reynolds, K. J. (1991). *Native conceptions of giftedness* (Unpublished doctoral dissertation). Lakehead University, Ontario, Canada.

Romero, M. E. (1994). Identifying giftedness among Keresan Pueblo Indians: The Keres study. *Journal of American Indian Education, 34*(1), 35–58.

Sternberg, R. J. (2005). The WICS model of giftedness. In R. Sternberg & J. E. Davidson (Eds.), *Conceptions of giftedness* (2nd ed., pp. 327–342). New York, NY: Cambridge University Press.

Subotnik, R. F., & Jarvin, L. (2005). Beyond expertise: Conceptions of giftedness as great performance. In R. Sternberg & J. E. Davidson (Eds.), *Conceptions of giftedness* (pp. 343–357). New York, NY: Cambridge University Press.

Terman, L. M. (1926). *Genius studies of genius: Mental and physical traits of a thousand gifted children*. Stanford, CA: Stanford University Press.

Turner, J. C., Brown, R. J., & Tajfel, H. (1979). Social comparison and group interest in in-group favouritism. *European Journal of Social Psychology, 9*(2), 187–204.

Ulrey, C. (1991). On being gifted and talented. *Journal of American Indian Education, 31*, 25.

United States Department of Education, Office of Educational Research and Improvement. (1990). *National Education Longitudinal Study of 1988.* (NCES 90-464). Retrieved from http://nces.ed.gov/pubs90/90464.pdf

Vygotsky, L. S. (1978). *Mind in society: The development of higher psychological processes.* Cambridge, MA: Harvard University Press.

CHAPTER 11

ASSESSING CALIFORNIA STATE CURRICULUM AND ITS IMPACTS ON K–12 STUDENTS

Nicole Quinderro Myers-Lim
National Indian Justice Center
and California Indian Museum and Cultural Center

My daughter entered the 4th grade 4 years ago. I remember feeling anxious about how her educators might present California Mission history to her and her classmates. When the assignments began coming home, I soon realized that the angst I had felt was grounded in the fact that materials hadn't progressed much since I was in school. The traumas that I experienced as a 4th grade student came rushing back, and a realization set in that during the last 30 years, nothing had changed. For many individuals, this issue seems inconsequential. The majority of the population of California does not view the presentation of California Indians in history as an issue that needs to be addressed. Many believe that the diversity of our state fosters tolerance and acceptance of differences in beliefs and cultures. More often than not, Native parents and students who complain about these representations are labeled as overly sensitive and preoccupied with a history

On Indian Ground: California, pages 157–169
Copyright © 2017 by Information Age Publishing
All rights of reproduction in any form reserved.

that is no longer relevant to our modern lives. How often have we heard the phrase, "Can't we just all get along?" However, these issues are much more than an unfortunate experience for Native Americans, who represent a small percentage of the general U.S. population. These issues are integral to a cycle of genocide that continues to be perpetrated towards Indigenous peoples across the globe.

The representation of native perspectives in the teaching of our histories is a matter of civil rights. Dr. Martin Luther King, Jr., said, "Nothing in the world is more dangerous than a sincere ignorance and conscientious stupidity." Specifically in reference to the treatment of Native Americans, he went on to describe,

> Our nation was born in genocide when it embraced the doctrine that the original American, the Indian, was an inferior race. Even before there were large numbers of Negroes on our shores, the scar of racial hatred had already disfigured colonial society. From the sixteenth century forward, blood flowed in battles of racial supremacy. We are perhaps the only nation which tried as a matter of national policy to wipe out its indigenous population. Moreover, we elevated that tragic experience into a noble crusade. Indeed, even today we have not permitted ourselves to reject or to feel remorse for this shameful episode. Our literature, our films, our drama, our folklore all exalt it. (as quoted in National Congress of American Indians, 2013, p. 4)

Silent or institutional racism is difficult to combat, because you must first get people to acknowledge that it exists. In a society that believes its members are educated, progressive and integrated, disavowal fuels the perpetuation of injustice. Dr. King was referring to a cycle of genocide that is implemented in eight stages. These stages include classification, symbolization, dehumanization, organization, polarization, preparation, extermination, and denial (Stanton, 1988). When looked at with California Indian historical experiences, the stages become very clear. Stage one, classification, begins by distinguishing the perpetrator and the victim. It can be as simple as "us" versus "them." Stage two is symbolization, clearly evidenced by the labeling of native peoples as "savages," "uncivilized," "diggers," and "redskins." Stage three, dehumanization, is where the victims of genocide are equated with animals, insects, and diseases. Stage four becomes sanctioned organized violence against these groups. California is rich in this history, beginning with Spanish soldiers and continuing through statehood. During this era, militia organizations were sent out to hunt "unruly" Indians. They were reimbursed by the state of California 50 cents to 5 dollars per Indian that was killed. Stage five is polarization; here, further division is driven between the two groups through propaganda, laws, and social interaction. Examples of this can be highlighted throughout the mission system and well into the 20th century. We can look to physical segregation in mission quarters, to the indentured servitude of the 1860s to demonstrate this phase. Stage six is preparation. During this stage, the victims are segregated. Boarding schools, reservations, and Rancherias clearly evidence this stage. Stage seven is extermination. While clearly, a more than 90% reduction of the California Indian population post missions and gold rush periods demonstrates extermination, we can also argue that this stage reaches further. The stereotype of the "Vanishing Redman" has been a longstanding ideal set by the dominant society. During the mission era, the padres often sought to label Native people as the "last full-blooded Indian"—evidenced by the story of "Old Gabriel," who is honored in the Vatican as the "oldest living full blood Indian of the New World" (A. Galvan, personal interview; see https://calisphere.org/item/ark:/13030/c8xk8ckz/), and also by Ishi, who in 1911, became famous as "the last of his tribe." While it is true that in order to survive a post-gold rush California, Ishi lived in hiding for 30 years, today there are at least five tribes that claim him as their ancestor.

The eighth and final stage of genocide is denial. In this stage, the perpetrators of genocide do not admit that they committed any crimes. Moreover, the victims are often blamed for what happened. When we continue to present history in the light most favorable to the victors, we are continuing the stage of denial. In *Points of View vs. Historical Bias*, Sarah Supahan (1999) discusses the creation of elementary textbook content. She states that many textbooks are developed according to standards set forth by the American Legion in 1925. There are four guiding principles: the content "must inspire the children with patriotism, be careful to tell the truth optimistically, only dwell on failure only for its value as a moral lesson, and speak chiefly of success" (Supahan, 1999, p. 1). A factual understanding the history of California Indians or Native American history in general is virtually impossible under these guidelines. Thus, the framework of genocide remains in full effect. History is subjective and for Americans it is often told in a romantic, optimistic and patriotic fashion. I often find that highly educated and well-intentioned academics fall into the familiar pattern of romanticizing or justifying the facts. When explaining the past, there is often a "they were men of their time" excuse offered with the historical record. When children are appalled to hear that Native people were slaughtered or beaten and forced into servitude, their educators often attempt to lessen the impact by adding commentary. Common examples include teacher or docents saying, "we can't judge the past," or "despite the atrocities of the Spanish, the Indians were treated much better in the missions than they were during the Gold Rush." I challenge educators to just present the facts and let the students explore the moral implications. History is clearly full of mistakes, and if you are teaching California Indian history there are many lessons to be learned. To overcome denial, we must revise the record to reflect the facts and integrate native perspectives. Native voices will conflict with those that are commonly accepted; however, it will challenge the "sincere ignorance and conscientious stupidity" that Dr. King warns us of.

Sarah Supahan goes on to explain how we can prepare ourselves to examine bias in educational materials. She challenges educators to ask, "Who is writing the excerpt, what kind of point of view is being presented and for what purpose?" (1999, p. 15). A couple of years ago, I came across a book on the history of California at a yard sale. I glanced at the date and found that it was published in 1866. I purchased it knowing that it would be a great resource for examining historical bias. As I read it, I thought through these questions. When describing California Indians, author Franklin Tuthill states,

> The Indians of California were the farthest fallen below the average Indian type. They were neither brave nor bold, nor generous nor spirited. They seem to have possessed none of the noble characteristics that, with a slight coloring of romance, make heroes of the red men of the Atlantic slopes, and win for them our ready sympathy. We hear of no orators among them, no bold braves terribly resenting and contesting to the last usurpations of the whites. They were "diggers," filthy and cowardly, succumbing without a blow to the rule of foreign masters. (1866, pp. 88–89)[5]

From the description it is clear that the author's opinion was biased. The Indians of California are depicted as "uncivilized" and "undeserving of pity." We don't have biographical information about this author. However, the 1860s were during the infancy of California statehood. Laws were passed by the legislature to eradicate and indenture California Indians. In his 1852 address to the legislature, Governor Burnett called for "the war of extermination" to continue until California Indians became "extinct" (Lindsay, 2012). Given this climate, it is reasonable to conclude that the violence against Indians needed to be justified, and an effective means to this end was to create propaganda that painted them as less than human. While it is easy to recognize the bias of the 1860s, it is harder to assess the impact that this publication has had on what is accepted as historical record today. It is safe to say that the impact of this bias was far-reaching. *The History of California*, has been cited in many subsequent texts. Author Robert Cowan (1914) stated in his *A Bibliography of the History of California and the Pacific West 1510–1906*, that Tuthill's work was "scholarly and written in a readable style" (p. 234). He went on to commend the book by saying that the "lapse of time has not impaired its general usefulness" (p. 234). If we examined how many times during the last 150 years Tuthill's has work been relied upon as a primary resource for understanding and summarizing this era of history, we would find many examples of bias being cycled into new educational materials. How do we begin the daunting task of correcting the record? We must practice our skill of recognizing and reframing bias if we are going to combat denial.

When 4th graders across the state of California are presented with units on the missions and the gold rush, they are presented with bias. Bias emerges in many forms, such as loaded words, stereotypes, misinformation, lack of information, myths, lies, inappropriate justifications, and culturally insensitive lesson plans, songs, and projects. The issues have to be addressed on multiple levels. When we examine curricula, we often find that bias begins in the standards. For example, section 4.1 of the standards states, "Students demonstrate an understanding of the physical and human geographic features that define places and regions in California" (California State Board of Education, 2000, p. 12). Section 4.3 says, "Students explain the economic, social, and political life in California from the establishment of the Bear Flag Republic through the Mexican-American War, the Gold Rush, and the granting of statehood" (California State Board of Education, 2000, p. 13). Thus, the emphasis on California Native experiences in the classroom falls under 4.1 rather than 4.3 of the standards. Most 4th graders are presented with anthropological theories, also often biased, of precontact populations rather than historical facts of atrocities that occurred post contact. When presented with a complete picture of California mission history, many 4th grade teachers face the challenge of how to present massacres, abuses, and sexual crimes to a classroom of nine-year-olds. Keeping this unit under the requirement of 4th grade social studies standards is an inherent problem. A full analysis of this period is likely more suited for upper school students. However, continuing to perpetuate myths and romantic fantasies is a dual injustice. Where educators are proactive and reframe the curricula they run into issues when it comes to identifying resources that provide native perspectives. Where can they find the truth in a format that is digestible for their students? The majority of field trips to the 21 missions do not offer Native displays or docents. California Native educators and advocates are working to address these issues, from calling for curriculum standard reform to creating educational websites and exhibits (californiamissionsnativehistory.org) and integrating Native perspectives into mission displays. Educators can contribute to these efforts by recognizing bias and calling existing interpretations of history into question. Examine these issues with your students and explain how some of the prevailing myths have evolved.

Given the current emphasis on precontact California tribal cultures, most 4th grade students are directed toward the belief that California "history" began with the arrival of the Spanish and establishment of the missions. There is physical evidence and written accounts of California Indians thousands of years before the Spanish arrived. Tools have been found in various parts of California that date back centuries before European contact. There are also accounts by European explorers and pirates, like Sir Francis Drake, who made contact with Indians before the first mission was established. California Indian oral history dates back since time immemorial.

We do not have any census data that indicates an exact number of Indians living in California during the mission era. Missionaries only documented how many Indians were in the missions and speculated about how many Indians lived in the villages surrounding the missions. Many tribes in the north or interior regions of California were indirectly impacted by the missions. Thus, the missionaries did not factor these populations into their calculations. The people who settled in those regions during the gold rush did not keep accurate records of the native populations that they decimated in search of gold. As a result of these two occupations, native populations were weakened, but neither the Spanish nor the countless gold miners kept track of how many Indians lived in California at any one time. Some scientists estimate that there were over 300,000 Indians living in California before the missions were established. Other scientists argue that the 300,000 figure is low, and it was more likely closer to 1,000,000 people (Paddison, 2016, p. 1). Regardless, we know that California was a place rich in cultures and resources. Native populations thrived prior to contact, which brought disease, violence, and environmental degradation. California history began and continues with indigenous people, who remain connected to their ancestral territories and cultural resources.

Another commonly stated misconception is that California Indian people were welcoming and did not resist missionary arrival. Some accounts by Spanish missionaries suggest that Indians were welcoming and willingly entered the missions; however, these accounts were highly biased and usually false. In letters to their superiors or to each other, missionaries would have been inclined to make each other believe that Indians had willingly come to the missions in order to make their missions appear to be running smoothly. Missionaries may have also tried to cover up the atrocities that occurred in the missions. By contrast, the personal diaries and private accounts of the missionaries suggest that Indians were resistant to mission authorities. Missionaries forbade California Indians from practicing their religions, speaking in their traditional languages, and eating their traditional foods. Many Indians forced into the missions attempted to keep their cultures alive and were punished for doing so. The accounts of Indians being punished by the missionaries tell us that Indians resisted Spanish rule and did not welcome it.

The Spanish and others had been coming and going in California for over 150 years. From accounts of some European explorers, we know that Indians traded with Europeans, but we do not know how much communication occurred and whether Indians were informed of their plans. When the Spanish established the first mission in San Diego, the surrounding tribal villages organized a defense upon the encampment within one month of their arrival. This is usually characterized as a "revolt" or an "uprising" in historical texts. However, it is more accurate to describe this event as a defense. The Kumeyaay were defending their homeland and people by attempting to drive the Spanish invaders out of their territories. Under these circumstances, to say they "revolted" would presume they were rising up against a recognized authority. This was not the case and is a good example of how the selection of terms can lead to the mischaracterization of history.

Much of the focus of mission curricular resources are on the daily life of Indians in the mission. Many lessons are based on the theme of agriculture, music, food, and skills that the padres were said to have taught to the Indians. This material fosters a misconception that "California Indians were docile and happily accepted mission life" (Supahan, 1997, p. 4). Most accounts of daily life in the missions suggests that Indians were unhappy in the missions because they were mistreated by the priests, were restricted from practicing their religious ceremonies, were separated from their families, and suffered high rates of mortalities. After the first mission broke ground, the Kumeyaay defended their communities within one month of the Spanish encampment being established. The padres did not record a baptism for at least two years. This demonstrates that the Spanish were not very successful in getting the natives to "accept" mission life. The term "accept" suggests that native people in the missions had a choice in the matter.

Records reflect very few baptisms during the first years of the missions (Carrico, 1997). The low number of baptisms during the first few years of many missions can be understood as resistance from the tribes around the missions. Many tribes refused to live in the missions and resisted the Spanish attempts to force them there. The small number of baptisms performed during this time may have generated an increased effort by the soldiers who came with the missionaries to round up Indians and take them captive. Without these numbers, the missions would not have been able to function. This information serves to debunk the idea that Indians "willingly joined" the missions or were "curious" about them. There is an underlying theme that with change" or the altering of native life ways, came "progress," or the path for the creation of a "new and better" society. It is the way that genocidal practices are justified throughout the historical record.

Another justification often offered to justify the treatment of Native Americans is that they were "uncivilized." Elementary students are taught that civilization is a product of the dominant society and that the status of Native people was elevated by their willingness to learn the ways of Europeans. In the eyes of the padres, California Indians were considered "uncivilized" because they looked different, had different religious beliefs and languages, and did not appear to have building structures, governing authorities, and agricultural practices. Many of these elements were integrated into California Indian societies; however, they were in forms unfamiliar to

Europeans. California Indians were different from Europeans, but this does not mean that they were "uncivilized." Europeans failed to recognized or acknowledge many of these existing practices. California Indians did make permanent dwellings, practiced (and continue to practice) their own religions, used their languages, cultivated and harvested foods and medicines from their environments, and had governance and political organizations. California Indians were far from uncivilized. Ironically, many government agencies are looking to Indigenous practices of environmental stewardship, restorative justice, medicine, and food sovereignty to address contemporary issues resulting from failing environmental, justice, and health systems.

Europeans also had specific motives in labeling native people as "uncivilized." Under European laws, "uncivilized natives" and "uncultivated lands" satisfied the elements of the Doctrine of Discovery. This doctrine empowered European explorers to claim "newly discovered" lands for their crowns (Morales, 2012). These laws began appearing as early as 1095, when Pope Urban II issued the Papal Bull Terra Nullius, which translates to "empty land." Thus, the Vatican sanctioned European powers to seize lands in all non-Christian parts of the world. This essentially enabled the practice of war and conquest of all peoples considered non-Christian. These practices were justified by the labeling of indigenous people as "uncivilized and less than human" in contrast to the European powers who were depicted as "entrepreneurs" engaged in setting forth a "God-ordained" purpose (Morales, 2012).

Many 4th grade textbooks begin a discussion of California missions by stating that Indians wandered to or joined the missions. Unfortunately the two words most commonly used to describe Indian contact with the missions are misleading. The term wander implies that the Indians casually arrived at the missions without purpose. Furthermore, it also implies that California Indians existed without purpose prior to the missions being created. This was not the case. Indians lived in societies and practiced cultures where every day had purpose in providing for families and community members. They knew the intricate natures of their homelands and did not get lost or wander around. The second term joined implies that Indians became members of, or enlisted in, the mission system. This suggests that it was a voluntary process. The mission was created under a "feudal manorial labor system" Indians were intended to be "absorbed into Spanish colonial society at the lowest level." They were forced to labor for Spain for the "good of the Spanish crown and its citizens" (Sturtevant, 1978, p. 101).

Based on the low number of baptisms during the first few years in missions, Indians likely resisted the missions and the padres rather than "wandering" over. This idea is often used in romanticized accounts of mission life or to avoid talking about kidnapping and forced labor, which were tactics used by the padres to bring Indians into the missions as laborers. Missionaries banned Indians from using their traditional languages, practicing religious ceremonies, and eating traditional foods; these were a few reasons why Indians did not want to be forced into the missions. Although it is often ignored, California Indians traded with tribes across vast regions and passed on stories about the poor treatment they were subjected to in the missions. Indians were beaten for small crimes within the missions, and they experienced excessive punishment and cruelty by the padres. Both physical and psychological punishments were crafted and carried out by the priests. Even if Indians had come willingly to the missions, they would not have stayed, nor wanted to stay because of these harsh practices.

As 4th graders move out of the mission era and on to the gold rush and early California statehood, California Indians are often absent from the instructional material. The assumption that results from this lack of information is that as the missions ended, the native populations concurrently disappeared. At the California Indian Museum and Cultural Center, the first permanent exhibition created by the museum was on the topic of Ishi. While Ishi is a popular historical figure, museum staff realized that his story spoke for the thousands of Indians who did not survive into the 20th century. Ishi survived until 1916, but his survival was based on the fact that he lived in hiding for 30 years. Instead of discussing the atrocities that occurred in Ishi's lifetime, he is often romanticized as "the last wild Indian of California." Elementary school children often read a romanticized and anthropological account of Ishi's life and come to the museum to ask, "Are there any Indians today that live like Ishi did?" They lack an understanding that Ishi lived alone, not out of a nostalgic desire to hold onto the past, but out of necessity for survival. He lived in fear and hiding during a time when he would have been murdered by militia groups seeking $5.00 payments from the state of California. He lived in a time where his children would have been sold into indentured servitude. He lived in a time when he would not have had the ability to testify against a non-Indian in a court of law. He lived at a time when he would have been rounded up and sent to work in the gold mines with hundreds of other Indian men, most of whom would die because they were not provided food or water. He lived at a time when he was imprisoned simply because he came out of the wilderness and into town. This is the history of California. A history too often ignored. The denial of these facts does an injustice to every student who graduates from K–12 schools in our state. They grow up and into adulthood never knowing the whole story.

How can we invoke the most effective change? The answer is simple: learn the truth and share it. It is time we all participated in the responsibility of correcting the record; we owe it to our ancestors and our children. The task at hand can be overwhelming, given the imminent need to overhaul the education standards and resource materials. However, there are working models we can follow in creating change. The Montana Office of Public Instruction has been successful in creating change for educators and students. They have developed seven "Essential Understandings" for which each state educator receives training (Juneau, 2001, 2010, 2012). These understandings can be readily adapted to a California construct. Making sure that each educator is grounded in and develops the capacity to convey to their students seven basic concepts about California Indians would go far in correcting the record and counteracting existing bias. For example, the seven basic understandings (adapted from Montana Office of Public Instruction) for California could include the following:

ESSENTIAL UNDERSTANDING 1

There is great diversity among the 150 (plus) tribes of California. There is diversity in their languages, cultures, histories, and governments. Each tribe has a distinct and unique cultural heritage that contributes to modern California.

This discussion should include how federally recognized and federally unrecognized tribes are distinguished and the historical factors that contributed to the large numbers of federally unrecognized tribes in California. Additional instruction could be given on contemporary issues of tribal governance from cultural resources protection to economic development.

ESSENTIAL UNDERSTANDING 2

There is great diversity among individual American Indians as identity is developed, defined, and redefined by many entities, organizations, and people. There is a continuum of Indian identity ranging from assimilated to traditional and is unique to each individual. There is no generic American Indian.

This discussion should include the diverse populations of Indians in California, including the large numbers of tribes, geographic regions, and urban Indian centers created by federal relocation programs.

ESSENTIAL UNDERSTANDING 3

The ideologies of Native traditional beliefs and spirituality persist into modern day life as tribal cultures, traditions, and languages, are still practiced by many American Indian people, and are incorporated into how tribes govern and manage their affairs. Additionally, each tribe has its own oral history beginning with its genesis that is as valid as written histories. These histories predate the "discovery" of North America.

Here the discussion should recognize the cosmologies of California tribes. Oral history should be offered and analyzed. If there is a discussion of the Bering Strait, additional migration theories should be offered up for analysis.

ESSENTIAL UNDERSTANDING 4

There were many foreign, state, and federal policies put into place throughout American history that have impacted California Indian people and that shape who they are today. Much of Indian history can be related through several major policy periods.

Here students should examine the mission period, the gold rush, the allotment period, boarding school era, termination, and self-determination. While the current California 3rd grade standards call for students to "describe the ways in which California, the other states, and Sovereign American Indian tribes contribute to the making of our nation and participate in the federal system of government" (California State Board of Education, 2000, p. 12), students must develop knowledge of the definition of sovereignty. A comprehensive understanding of sovereignty must be accompanied by the historical context that has impacted it over time.

ESSENTIAL UNDERSTANDING 5

Reservations are land that have been reserved by the tribes for their own use through treaties and was not land that was "given" to them. The principle that land should be acquired from the Indians only through their consent with treaties involved three assumptions:

1. That both parties to treaties were sovereign powers.
2. That Indian tribes had some form of transferable title to the land.
3. That acquisition of Indian lands was solely a government matter not to be left to individual colonists.

Understanding the 7.5 million acres of land that was set aside under the unratified treaties of California and how the injunction of secrecy caused many California Indian tribes and families to become landless is critical to understanding both history and contemporary issues for California natives. The dispossession of land has had rippling impacts on the ability to maintain cultural resources, languages, employment, health, political stability, and many other issues.

ESSENTIAL UNDERSTANDING 6

History is a story most often related through the subjective experience of the teller. Histories are being rediscovered and revised. History told from an Indian perspective conflicts with what most of mainstream history tells us.

Just because Native American history conflicts with mainstream or dominant society's history does not mean that it is untrue or undeserving of discussion. Often when California Indians attempt to correct the record, they are accused of having "liberal agendas" or dismissed as wanting "too much political correctness." This attitude reflects the culture of genocide and centuries of denial of Native American experiences. It is time we change the record and move forward with knowledge of past injustice.

ESSENTIAL UNDERSTANDING 7

Under the American legal system, Indian tribes have sovereign powers, separate and independent from the federal and state governments. However, the extent and breadth of tribal sovereignty is not the same for each tribe.

Tribal sovereignty is complex and ever-changing. Student must explore concepts of inherent sovereignty, external and internal sovereignty powers, and the evolution of legal fictions that have eroded federal recognition of sovereignty over time. These are upper division concepts, and while they may be introduced in lower grades, a comprehensive understanding of "tribal sovereignty" and where it fits within the system of local, state, and federal governments is not possible in the third grade.

As educators we have far to go in the journey of combatting the legacy of genocide and overhauling the educational system's presentation of California Indians. Many of us have worked for decades to make small advancements in a slow-moving machine. Beginning on common ground and adopting skills in the evaluation of bias and the advancement of common principles for all educators is a critical step in the right direction.

REFERENCES

California State Board of Education. (2000). *History social science content standards for California public schools, kindergarten through twelve.* Sacramento, CA: Author.

Carrico, R. L. (1997). Sociopolitical aspects of the 1775 revolt at Mission San Diego De Alcala. *San Diego History Society Quarterly, 43*(3). Retrieved from http://sandiegohistory.org/journal/1997/july/missionrevolt/

Cowan, R. E. (1914). *A bibliography of the history of California and the Pacific Northwest 1510–1906.* San Francisco, CA: San Francisco Book Club.

Juneau, D. (2001). *Montana Office of Public Instruction state superintendent, essential understandings regarding Montana Indians.* Helena, MT: Montana Office of Public Instructions.

Juneau, D. (2010). *Montana Office of Public Instruction state superintendent, essential understandings regarding Montana Indians.* Helena, MT: Montana Office of Public Instructions.

Juneau, D. (2012). *Montana Office of Public Instruction state superintendent, essential understandings regarding Montana Indians.* Helena, MT: Montana Office of Public Instructions.

Lindsay, B. C. (2012). *Murder state: California's Native American genocide, 1846–1873.* Lincoln, NE: University of Nebraska Press.

Morales, R. (2012). *Debunking the doctrine of discovery: Colonial excuse for the seizure of land and the oppression of people.* Vancouver Public Library Presentation. Retrieved from http://vancouver.mediacoop.ca/fr/video/robert-morales-debunking -doctrine-discovery/16402

National Congress of American Indians (NCAI). (2013). *Ending the legacy of racism in sports and the harmful "Indian" sports mascots.* Washington, DC: Author.

Paddison, J. (2016). *California cultures: Before 1768, pre-Columbian California.* Berkeley, CA: University of California Press.

Stanton, G. H. (1998). *The eight stages of genocide.* New Haven, CT: Yale Program on Genocidal Studies.

Sturtevant, W. C. (1978). *The handbook of North American Indians: California.* Sacramento, CA: Government Printing Office.

Supahan, S. (1997). *A Time of Resistance: California Indians During the Mission Period: 1769–1848.* Eureka, CA: Klamath-Trinity Joint Unified School District Indian Education Program (California Humboldt County Office of Education).

Supahan, S. (1999). *Points of view versus historical bias.* Hoopa, CA: Klamath-Trinity Joint Unified School District Indian Education Program (California Humboldt County Office of Education).

Tuthill, F. (1866). *The history of California.* San Franciso, CA: H. H. Bancroft and Company.

CHAPTER 12

COUNSELING

Cultural Components to Counseling and Advising

André P. Cramblit
Northern California Indian Development Council

This chapter will highlight counseling and advising in a historical context as well as current implications for those in the field, including a look at best practices and an examination of different programs showing success in working with Native students in California, including related personal anecdotes and reflections and guidance given to us by Native Elders who are our first and most important advisors. If counselors of American Indian students do not consider the unique cultural and linguistic needs of their pupils, they will ultimately be pushed out of school. Many Native American students drop out or are shunted by counselors to "alternative education programs" such as home study, continuation schools, and so on. By allowing this to occur, we are relieving the system of their primary duty of educating our students. We are placing the burden of finding a pathway through the maze of education upon the people most unprepared to accomplish that task, the students and their families. We must work to break down the

On Indian Ground: California, pages 171–180
Copyright © 2017 by Information Age Publishing
All rights of reproduction in any form reserved.

artificial barriers that impede development and alienate students and families from the system and give them the guidance that will enable them to successfully navigate what is already a disconcerting process. If working diligently with the school system does not result in tangible changes that benefit your students, then perhaps a charter school is something to consider, but that is a whole other article to discuss the possibilities for Native students. It is important to listen to students and families and temper that with your own experience to change the overall system to best serve the needs of your community.

School counseling is a lost art. In the past, schools had multiple counselors to maintain a smaller caseload so they had time to know the students they worked with on a more personal level and where able to dedicate time to working with them individually. "Gone are the days of school counselors sitting in their office simply handing out college applications, making schedule changes for students who want to drop a class or meeting with the troublemakers in the school" (American School Counselor Association, n.d.b, para 1). Due to ever dwindling budgets, and changing school environments the role of the school counselor has transformed into a hodge-podge of additional duties that reduce the time they can spend with students individually. Moreover, mandated curriculum and testing such as Common Core State Standards (CCSS) and the Smarter Balance assessment have placed added burdens on the already heavy workload of the school counselor. The role of the counselor has fundamentally changed over these and has gotten away from the original intention of what services and skills they could provide to influence the students they work with.

> School counselors are certified/licensed educators with a minimum of a master's degree in school counseling, making them uniquely qualified to address all students' academic, career and personal/ social development needs by designing, implementing, evaluating and enhancing a comprehensive school counseling program that promotes and enhances student success. (American School Counselor Association, n.d.a, para 1)

HISTORICAL CONSIDERATIONS

American Indians have had a long and tragic history with formal western education. Upon military subjugation, it became commonplace to send Native students to distant boarding schools that removed students from their tribes physically, spiritually, culturally, and linguistically. (In California that school was and still is Sherman Indian School in Riverside, CA.) Before issues such as educational reform can be addressed for this student population, it is critical to acknowledge this reality. For decades, federal educational policy intended to acculturate Native students. Dealing with formal education issues brings up painful reminders to all Natives of how the education system has been abusive, almost beyond comprehension, to Indian people.

> The removal of children from their families is considered one of the most devastating traumas that occurred to the Native American people because it resulted in the disruption of the family structure, forced assimilation of children, and a disruption in the Native American community. This situation is considered the crucial precursor to many of the existing problems for some Native Americans. (Brave Heart & Debruyn, 1998)

For both counselors and Native families it is important to be aware of this history and how that continues to have an impact on American Indian students. In terms of counseling and advising, the lingering effects of long-past damage caused by formal schooling in relation to the concept of intergenerational grief and historical trauma is best fully addressed as a separate issue (Brave Heart & Chase, 2014).

By and large, the counseling and advising of American Indian students in government-operated schools has been limited to categorizing and funneling them into vocational paths or perhaps military service. The types of vocational trades were mostly limited to service-oriented fields such as barbering, domestic servitude, farming, manufacturing, and so on. This has led to this type of school being more of a warehousing and processing organization rather than an academic/educational institution.

As America's student bodies become more ethnically and culturally diverse, Bruce and Brigland (2012) report that school counselors, for the most part, continue to be mostly White (77%) women (78%). This serves to further distance already alienated American Indian students from a Western-based school system and will only serve to widen the achievement gap and limit their academic success. For example, many California tribes provide instruction and guidance primarily from an adult member of the same sex and in many instances from a family member. Native students themselves identify the seven most important traits of an ideal counselor. According to Bransford (1982), the counselor would be:

1. Indian
2. A friend and available
3. Open-minded
4. Patient
5. Knowledgeable about tribal culture and values
6. Professionally competent
7. A good listener

—although Trimble (1976) added that "trustworthiness and understanding were valued by American Indian students over any other counselor attribute."

BEST PRACTICES

Throughout California Native communities, counseling and or advising has been more of a tribal or village responsibility. This is typically a collective effort of a variety of individuals who could share their own strengths and skills with the younger generation. It is important for these youth to know, see, and emulate those who have walked a similar path in addition to the more routine duties of counselors such as advising, filling out class schedules, and overseeing testing. The utilization of counselors as part of a comprehensive group has the potential for positively impacting American Indian students, as it comprises a traditional format they are familiar with. The power of collaborations cannot be underestimated. Much like student study teams (sometimes referred to as student success teams), cooperative relationships between Indian education programs (Title VII, Johnson O'Malley and California's American Indian Education Centers), school district personnel, parents, tribes, and community agencies will guide the growth and potential success of our students. Together you can create an effective and holistic learning environment. As part of a community based upon the role of the individual, within the context of a village or tribe, cooperative lifestyles are a core of Californian American Indian values. As a result, many Native students thrive in a collaborative learning environment.

Strong, honest, and unflinching advising is a common tenet of counseling strategies within many California Native groups. I recall being poor, lost, lonely and homesick during my undergraduate years on the east coast. I would call back to my local college, Humboldt State University, to try and transfer closer to home. The Indian teacher and educational personnel program academic advisor would firmly tell me that no, I had lessons to learn from that environment and that I needed to stick it out to completion. Only then could I could return home to share what I had learned from that experience. This was significantly different than the interaction with my European high school counselor, who I can recall telling me that she was "just waiting for my comeuppance." The type of guidance I received from ITEPP has helped shape and mold who I have become both personally and professionally.

In the book *Tasha Goes to University* (Kurtz, 2009), we are introduced to a young Yurok student who is entering her senior year in high school. We see how she works to balance her traditional customs, values, and ceremonies with the responsibilities of a student preparing for college. We are shown this journey and what guidance she receives in the process to help her combine these two seemingly disparate worlds. The story clearly emphasizes the three most critical issues for influencing college success, getting a financial aid package in place, finding a community and peer support system on campus, and staying connected to her home and people. The personal narrative ends with her successfully completing her college career and coming home. She has done this while she has remained grounded in her culture and has become a role model for other students.

Many of the problems in the world are caused by a breakdown in communication: Counseling your students should include helping them to learn how to speak and write clearly and effectively. This includes active listening, which, when bundled with decision-making skills, leadership training, and internal asset development, will get them well on the road to being a student poised to succeed. Helping students develop these skills will give them the abilities and tools to grow and will help motivate them in school. Students who have fewer of these abilities will make poor choices that will negatively impact success in school. Use strong communication skills yourself. Do not leave things unsaid; seek common understanding of the issues at hand. Communication between the family and the school system will help minimize conflict and confusion. Work to achieve clarity and to promote long-term positive relationships based upon mutual respect and cooperation.

One Example of a Culturally Appropriate Counseling Program

The Indian Tribal and Educational Personnel (ITEPP) at Humboldt State University in Arcata, CA is an excellent example of a culturally appropriate model of counseling and advising for Native California students. The following information was taken from their website (Humboldt State University, n.d.):

> The Indian Tribal & Educational Personnel Program's mission is to facilitate and promote academic success and self-efficacy for American Indian students at Humboldt State University that validates tribal cultural values, political status, and promotes the federal Indian policy of Indian self-determination.

> The original Indian Teacher Education Project started in 1969 as a teacher preparation program for 18 American Indian students at Humboldt State University (HSU). In 1979, the renamed Indian Teacher and Educational Personnel Program (ITEPP) expanded to include American Indian students who were preparing for careers in counseling and social work as well as teaching. Since the mid-1980s, ITEPP's annual enrollment has exceeded 30 American Indian students with ever-broadening professional interests. In 2012, the

name was changed yet again to the Indian Tribal and Educational Personnel Program, in a bid to keep students from thinking the program is "Just for Teachers."

Today about 50% of ITEPP's 200+ graduates are employed as teachers, counselors, and administrators in educational settings ranging from preschools, to elementary and high schools, to colleges and universities. Another 25% of ITEPP's graduates serve communities through tribal organizations. The remaining 25% are pursuing graduate degrees or working as business professionals, consultants, and providers of health and human services.

Additionally, Humboldt State University offers a minor in American Indian Education, but the individual classes are sometimes offered in summer-shortened course or occasional as online offerings that can be taken for continuing education credits

The American Indian Education (AIE) minor provides an understanding of the particular educational needs of American Indian students, as well as the skills to apply methodologies and classroom practices conducive to academic success and validation of cultural identity and values. Having a positive self-identity and strong cultural affirmation is key for the success of any student in school and in life, but American Indian students face assaults on their identity and culture on a daily basis. To help ensure success in working with American Indian students and communities, the College of Professional Studies provides a rigorous curriculum designed to heighten awareness of the numerous and complex issues surrounding American Indian education, along with successful educational models and classroom applications.

CONCLUSIONS

The more we can make the education system accessible to all students, the more we will be able to direct our inadequate funds to providing students with additional tools, resources, and programs that will better prepare them for their postsecondary vocational or academic careers. As counselors, it is your job to help shape the experience and skills needed for students or order for them to become confident in their own capabilities to achieve the goals they have set for themselves. In order to promote improved access to the wide range of services and information only available from a school counselor, increased efforts must be made to operate in a manner that is open, inviting, and based upon Native American approaches to counseling and mentoring. This must be done in cooperation with tribes, most easily through their education departments. An analysis must be done to determine what type of employees are needed by the tribe so that students can choose academic and career paths that lead home. Educated young people who desire to live in their home community must have a reasonable expectation of employment, which is often times found with the two largest employers— in California, these are typically the tribe and the school district. To make it a full circle, it would be ideal if some students came back to their high schools to become school board members or credentialed as school counselors, teachers, or administrators so they become the mentors, advisors, and role models for future generations.

In terms of counseling and advisement we, as California Native Americans, must look to our elders, who have shared their wisdom:

- "You got to be smart . . . but be sure to use a little common sense."— Hazel James, Wiyot Elder
- "I believe in my Indian ways. I learned them when I was a small boy; I teach them to my children. I use them when I fish, when I hunt, as I live. They are the way." —Jim Brown, Elem Pomo Elder
- "My family placed much on education. They encouraged me by their interest, love, and enthusiasm. To them, education would open the doors for a more successful life." —Vivian Tye Wintun/ Chimariko school teacher
- "My advice? Why go to school, of course. Learn things; get a good education, for a better life in the future." —Sam Lopez, Tolowa Elder and Indian Cultural Teacher
- "Yes, get a good education. But remember to live in the best of two worlds, don't lose your Indian identity and culture." —Ella Norris, Yurok/Tolowa and Indian Cultural Teacher

The following is a short, informal interview with Mr. Dave Risling—Hoopa/Karuk/Yurok, a long respected educator who has since passed on. He was a founder of many organizations such as DQ University in Davis, California; the California Indian Education Association; California Indian Legal Services; and the Native American Rights Fund:

Job Title: Retired Educational Consultant, Professor Emeritus University of California at Davis, Chairman of the Board of DQ University, Founder California Indian Legal Services and the Native American Rights Fund.

Education Background (degree and colleges attended): Cal Poly, Davis, Sonoma State University, California State–Stanislaus—master's degree in agricultural studies and counseling.

Anything else you want mentioned about you: Be successful in getting Indian people to accomplish things, give them support and resources to help achieve progress. Get support of a broad base of people. I am a lifelong participant in tribal ceremonies.

What is your definition of leadership? To get things done. Know the laws and get support. Deal with congress and the state government and be familiar with the legal process. Before you jump into something make sure you have a plan to get things done. Research the laws and treaties.

How do tribal values influence your perspective of leadership? I meet with tribes from all over the world, you need to be able to work with a diverse group, understand their belief systems and how they think. Talk about success in similar situations; don't push things on people. Study the constitution because the government will try and make laws that go against it. I learned about Indian values from the elders who came to my house when I was a child. Be careful of cultural differences and historic problems so you can work together. Get backing of others. Helping other people is what you need to do.

How do you integrate your traditional values into your work life? The traditional kinds of things get things done. Do not just talk, be active and know the facts to be able to support your efforts with the evidence.

What advice would you give young people about integrating culture into their everyday lives? My dad started high school and wanted us to go to school. He wanted us to be able to live in two worlds. We were raised in the Indian world, but needed to learn about how the white world works so we can start making progress for our people. Know their laws, get educated and work with them as friends to get something done. Teach others; share your culture and values with them.

Can you share with me a leadership/cultural experience or event that helped mold you as an individual? From my father, he took me to the woodshed and asked me if I was going off to college. He said you have already learned about what our needs are but you need to go learn about the white world so we can begin to change things for our people. Give people a chance to learn about their heritage because we can be proud of who we are and also go out in the Western world and be strong in our own identity.

Who were your mentors and what did you learn from them? My father. Also, the 6 Nations people who live by their own cultural institutions, and hold the federal government to the treaties and constitutional principles. When I was teaching I was proud of the doctors and lawyers who I have worked with.

Any last advice? Be able to live in two worlds do not give up anything to succeed, work to get those around you to be supportive for the ideas and values you hold.

Counselors have the potential to have a profound influence of the future of Native students. It is their responsibility to nurture, guide, and ground their students in both their cultural and academic lives so they are best prepared to face the world that awaits them.

REFERENCES

American School Counselor Association. (n.d.a). *The role of the professional school counselor.* Retrieved from http://www.schoolcounselor.org/asca/media/asca/home/rolestatement.pdf

American School Counselor Association. (n.d.b). *What does a school counselor do?* Retrieved from https://www.schoolcounselor.org/press/what-does-a-school-counselor-do

Bransford, J. (1982). To be or not to be: Counseling with American Indian clients. *Journal of American Indian Education, 21*(3), 18–21.

Brave Heart, M. Y. H., & Chase, J. A. (2014, August). *Historical trauma informed clinical intervention research and practice.* Presentation to the AIHEC Behavioral Health Institute. Retrieved from http://www.aihec.org/our-stories/docs/BehavioralHealth/2014/HistoricalTraumaInformedCllinicalIntervention ResearchPractice.pdf

Brave Heart, M. Y. H., & DeBruyn, L. M. (1998). The American Indian holocaust: Healing historical unresolved grief. *American Indian and Alaska Native Mental Health Research, 8*(2), 60–82.

Bruce, M., & Bridgeland, J. (2012). *2012 national survey of school counselors true north: Charting the course to college and career readiness.* New York, NY: College Board Advocacy & Policy Center.

Humboldt State University. (n.d.). *ITEPP: Native American Center for Academic Excellence.* Retrieved from http://www.humboldt.edu/itepp/

Kurtz, V. (2009). *Tasha goes to university.* Humboldt County Office of Education Communication Center. Retrieved from http://www.calstate.edu/CAPP/publications/docs/TashaGoesToUniversity-acc.pdf

Thomason, T. (2011). Recommendations for counseling Native Americans: Results of a survey. *Journal of Indigenous Research, 1*(2), 1–10. Retrieved from http://digitalcommons.usu.edu/kicjir/vol1/iss2/4

Trimble, J. E. (1976). Value Differences among American Indians: Concerns for the Concerned Counselor. In P. Pederson, W. J. Lonner, J. G. Draguns (Eds.), *Counseling Across Cultures* (pp. 65–81). Honolulu, HI: University Press of Hawaii.

Whitset, D. (1999). *Effective counseling with American Indian students.* ERIC document. Retrieved from http://files.eric.ed.gov/fulltext/ED427910.pdf

Additional Resources

Hayes, S. A. (2011). High school counseling: Essential services for reservation-based Native Americans for beginning counselors. *Online Readings in Psychology and Culture, 10*(3). doi: 10.9707/2307-0919.1099

LiteracyNet. (n.d.). *Teaching and learning with Native Americans: A handbook for non-native American adult educators.* Retrieved from http://www.literacynet.org/lp/namericans/strategies.html

Lohse, C. D. (2008). *Striving to achieve: Helping Native American students succeed.* Washington, DC: National Caucus of Native American State Legislators.

Pewewardy, C. (1998). Fluff and feathers: Treatment of American Indians in the literature and the classroom. *Equity & Excellence in Education, 31*(1), 69–76. doi: 10.1080/1066568980310110

Skouras, T. (1998). *Native American Indians and the counseling process: Culture, adaptation, and style.* ERIC document. Retrieved from https://archive.org/stream/ERIC_ED438114/ERIC_ED438114_djvu.txt

http://www2.nau.edu/~jar/AIE/Dropouts.html

CHAPTER 13

MIROMAA

Awakening California Tribal Languages in Digital Spaces

Tomio Endo
California Indian Museum Cultural Center

This work will share insights from our experiences exploring revitalization strategies for Pomo and Coast Miwok languages at the California Indian Museum and Cultural Center (CIMCC) in Santa Rosa, CA. CIMCC's mission is to educate the public about the history, culture, and contemporary life of California Indians and to honor their contributions to civilization. As an intertribal institution, we seek to represent native perspectives of both federally recognized and nonrecognized tribes throughout the state of California. Our work reaches beyond the traditional roles of museums into advocacy, educational reform, youth development, and cultural revitalization. In 2004, CIMCC began working on developing approaches to addressing language revitalization strategies for tribes in our geographic region. We worked on a number of projects assessing the scope of language learning and resources and developing new tools to support tribal communities and individuals in collective strategies for language learning. The following projects were completed from 2004 to 2016:

On Indian Ground: California, pages 181–194
Copyright © 2017 by Information Age Publishing
All rights of reproduction in any form reserved.

- 2004–2005 Pomo Language Repository Planning Program
- 2005–2007 Pomo Language Repository Implementation
- 2007–2008 Pomo Language Distance Learning Curriculum Study
- 2010–2012 Pomo Language Assessment and Documentation Project
- 2013–2016 Pomo Is Happening Now!

Our goal was to foster collaboration and to facilitate sharing of resources. As technologies developed and changed, we applied various strategies for creating tools that could be maintained, accessible, and affordable. Our challenge was to increase Pomo community knowledge of the status of all the Pomo languages currently in use and develop new resources that can be used to spur language growth. We are providing this reflection on our methods and approaches to developing, implementing, and assessing innovative resources that empower Native people to awaken speech communities living in indigenous languages in contemporary California as a means of sharing our journey.

As a project, our key objective is to create and provide tools, resources, and assistance to folks in our community who are interested in learning their native languages. Beyond a doubt, the challenges of our museum being situated in an incredibly diverse linguistic region with more than seven native languages can be difficult, but facilitating the process of developing, creating, managing, and providing these resources in partnership with the community was also be quite rewarding. We see our work as part of a global movement of Indigenous communities to celebrate language as a vehicle of tribal cultures. These special systems of communicating shared meaning and experience remain tied to unique geospatial relationships where language has maintained a unique connection to people, practice, and place. As we begin to use emergent tools and strategies to foster language learning and revitalization, we also are discovering new conceptions of how languages connect communities to a sense of contemporary place. By sharing the story of how we have worked with our community to use these tools and resources, we hope that we can encourage other people working tirelessly to document, preserve, and awaken languages in accessible ways that are both very old and very new.

BACKGROUND

Before we delve into the workings and findings of Miromaa, we must highlight several key factors that have contributed to the historical loss of language within Pomo and other California Indian tribal communities. The vitality of many indigenous languages was destroyed through genocidal practices brought forth during the Spanish mission and gold rush eras (Hinton,

1998). Populations of tribal communities were decimated by disease and violence, and individuals who survived this time period often resorted to active resistance, to hiding, and/or to seeking refuge with neighboring tribes as a means of survival (Castillo, 1978; Cook, 1978). This genocide extended to federal policies that targeted Native peoples and cultures for extermination and contributed to the widespread loss of tribal lands, affecting whole communities and disrupting the continuity of Native languages and cultures throughout many regions of California. During the mid- to late 1800s, federal government officials sought to assimilate Native peoples (see Castillo, 1978, pp. 104–115). Kidnapping of Indian children from their families and tribes was widespread practice in California (Castillo, 1978), and many children were placed in boarding schools where English was the only language permitted to be spoken (Reyhner, 1993). Clearly, federal officials believed that erasure of tribal languages would also erase tribal customs, traditions, cultures, and ways of life (Reyhner, 1993). Towards the ends of the 19th century, many California tribes became landless as the federal government refused to ratify 18 treaties that would have set aside over 7.5 million acres of land for California Indians (Johnston-Dodds 2002). Tribal leaders, having negotiated in good faith, were turned away when they looked back to their ancestral territories because homesteading laws were enacted to further divest them of their lands and resources (Castaneda, 2011). Federal monies were not allocated to begin buying back land for California tribes until 1905, creating many of what are now referred to as California Indian Rancherias. By this point, decades had passed and many people were displaced, and this has had lasting impacts. Contemporary California tribal land bases are small in comparison to tribal territories outside of the state. This failure to recognize tribal stewardship of ancestral lands further complicated the capacity for these communities to maintain and revitalize their languages in a changing society. In the 1950s, the federal government set forth the Termination acts and the Relocation program. Termination was applied to 40 California Indian tribes, essentially erasing their governmental authority and the trust status of their lands. Relocation provided government-sponsored job training and housing assistance off reservations into urban centers such as Oakland, San Francisco, and Los Angeles, and families were encouraged to move away from tribal lands and into the city, where assimilationist policy had a direct negative impact on Native cultural communities (Burt, 1986; Fiske, 1979; Wilkinson & Biggs, 1977).

Yet despite these efforts, Pomo tribal and cultural heritage was not lost. The overwhelming ability of Native people to prevail over the forces of genocide and colonization is a true testament to the Indian community's strength and character. It goes without saying that damage has been done, but by working together, Pomo people are committed to healing and revitalizing the wealth of their cultures. Thus, working across boundaries—both historical and contemporary—is a must in CIMCC's approach to language revitalization. Our communities are connected, our experiences are shared, and while language revitalization happens among dedicated individuals, and various tribes and families, a collective and shared approach is needed to foster learning across a greater segment of the community. Isolated efforts to preserve language have been critical to its survival, yet now we move forward with the challenge of taking a broader collective approach.

MIROMAA: SAVED

In 2011 and 2012, CIMCC conducted a survey on the status of Pomo languages in Sonoma, Lake, and Mendocino Counties. Among the variables assessed in this survey, community outlook on speakership, fluency, barriers to language use, multimedia solutions, and potential language education software design features were measured. CIMCC assessed community member's beliefs and attitudes towards language and language learning. One youth respondent commented, "Our language is part of our culture and we should have some type of tool to pass it on. It is very rare for my generation to speak the language let alone know someone who can" (personal communication, 2012) The 2011 Pomo Language Survey ultimately provided an actionable set of language planning practices to CIMCC that have prioritized the effort to support growth, usage, and performance of Pomoan languages among Native tribes in the ricounty area. These practices included the following priorities:

- Use daily greetings in conversation
- Teach conversational phrases that link and contextualize cultural history and practices
- Support tribal members in obtaining degrees in linguistics
- Create website and audio tools that provide sound and visual of words being spoken
- Create language immersion opportunities and host immersion events
- Teach people that mistakes are part of learning and not to be afraid to make them
- Teach phrases that are applicable to situations to connect words to real life experiences
- Create games that incorporate the Pomo language
- Foster pride in Pomo identity
- Create tools that are applicable to our daily routines and lifestyles
- Let children organize events around language
- Enact stories with song and dance

CIMCC emphasized the need to develop technological tools that bridged the gap between the knowledge of elder speakers and the digital practices that typically engaged tribal youth. However, based upon elder and Pomo speaker feedback, we were cautious and measured in our approach to adopting technological practices. While the Internet created many opportunities to share language resources across time limitations and physical boundaries, it also brought forth questions related to the protection of cultural integrity, accessibility by nonmembers of the community, and copyright/licensing ownership. Over time and successive projects, we worked through many of these issues and ultimately many of the pros began to outweigh the cons. When it came to employing technological strategies the following pros became assets and motivating factors:

- students were regularly and commonly interacting with technology
- new and alternative ways to communicate and interact with language were emerging
- accessibility and convenience were improving
- tools could be available in self-paced formats
- youth were learning through unconscious digestion via game features
- self-publication was suddenly making tools economically feasible

Pursuant to the survey, CIMCC took steps to lead a collaborative approach to reviving Pomo languages by consulting both linguists and tribal members in the process of aggregating existing data intended to produce educational material to support native language learning in the form of the Pomoan Language Repository. This growing repository of interviews, word lists, videos, and audio recordings has been instrumental in supporting collective language learning efforts. Since the development of the Pomo Language Repository, an operational dictionary of Eastern Pomo was developed by speakers, language immersion camps were held at CIMCC, and weekly Southern Pomo language classes were taught by the Western Institute for Endangered Language Documentation and hosted at CIMCC's facilities. In terms of language learning resource development, CIMCC found itself at a crossroads of how to integrate existing resources into user-friendly tools accessible to diverse segments of the tribal community.

Following the growth and development of CIMCC Pomo Language Repository, CIMCC formed an ongoing partnership with the Aboriginal Language and Technology Centre (based in Newcastle, Australia) in order to utilize a software-centered database for the production of a language-learning mobile application that would be intended to introduce and highlight efforts to foster community interest in learning Pomo languages with special focus towards younger consumers of digital technology.

Miromaa—meaning "saved" in the Awabakal language—equipped us with technical resources to materialize data within our existing Pomo Language Repository into an engaging contemporary form of media dedicated to awakening language revitalization efforts for speakers across tribal, political, cultural, academic, linguistic, and geographic boundaries. This was primarily achieved by featuring collaborative data rendered from the Pomo Language Repository shared through mobile software apps that has the capacity to reach the phones, computers, and tablets of a new cohort of potential speakers. Working with Miromaa software, CIMCC'S Miromaa project is ultimately intended to spark collaborative language-learning efforts in Pomo and Coast Miwok country and to generate a sense of community connection to a tribal language.

Developed by Indigenous people for Indigenous people, Miromaa is designed to provide an innovative way of saving and sharing traditional language and cultures and empowering all who wish to awaken language in their contemporary community. Miromaa's stated purpose is "to use technology in order to get the best out of the information you have in front of you" (http://www.miromaa.org.au).

Miromaa was established in 2008 and works in language reclamation, education, and training throughout Australia and the world. The program serves over 100 Indigenous languages. The software program works towards reclaiming, preserving, and disseminating traditional languages. It has full multimedia capabilities, stores all linguistic and cultural materials in one place, builds a huge range of teaching and learning resources, and is provided to Indigenous communities for free or at a low cost. Miromaa's work is integrated into the following four areas:

- Reclamation of the Awabakal language; conducting education in preschools, primary schools and high schools and bringing awareness to the importance that Awabakal language has on cultural identity; creating Awabakal language resources including games, booklets, posters, activities, and much more.
- Providing education and nonaccredited training nationally for the preservation of Indigenous language either in our language and technology training center or into other Indigenous communities. This education program prepares people for employment opportunities and assists with relief of poverty and improving quality of life.
- Puliima is our biennial National Indigenous Language and Technology forum that engages other Indigenous communities from Australia and overseas.
- Miromaa language and education software which is being utilized to preserve more than 100 languages and 24-hour training that is available to all people who have previously been engaged with our orga-

nization. We continue to support Aboriginal people with obtaining the Miromaa software free of charge (http://www.miromaa.org.au/home/about-us.html).

Miromaa software supports communities working with multiple languages. It allows the integration of community and security protocols and fosters immediate training and documentation through a user friendly interface. CIMCC views Miromaa as a technical tool that empowers staff to continue making progress towards awakening language within our communities (Linn, Naranjo, Nicholas, Slaughter, Yamamoto, & Zepeda, 2002). As a digital resource, Miromaa supports our overall collective capacity to:

1. Call for commitment to the practice of language learning
2. Cultivate collective awareness of the reality of our language situation
3. Inspire a commitment to experimentation of new and effective methods
4. Recontextualize language and culture in contemporary society
5. Transform the culture of language learning
6. Create immersive speech communities in daily practice
7. Change community attitudes from loss to collective responsibility and action

Over the course of two year period of using Miromaa to develop introductory language learning mobile apps, we experienced how Miromaa empowers us to facilitate community input, to negotiate the challenges of managing collective intellectual property and meta-data, and to celebrate the creative process of content creation. As we continue to work with Miromaa, we hope that we can contribute to unpack and lay down digital pathways towards community-wide language awakening and collective stewardship of sustainable heritage.

MIROMAA TECH

Miromaa is a program which we have developed to aid in language conservation, reclamation and dissemination work, it is a easy to use, user-friendly database to help you gather, organise, analyse and produce outcomes for your language work. The program enforces good archive practice and helps you gather any and all evidences of language including, text, audio, images and video. You can also use it to store your digitized documents for example pdf and Word documents, Excel spreadsheets plus more. It has a secure environment which can only be accessed by username and password, it can help you work on multiple languages or dialects and it also has a learning area where you can begin learning immediately.

The program can run on either a stand-alone desktop or on a network and you are not just limited to using Miromaa only as the program has the ability to import and export its data in various forms including SIL Shoebox/Toolbox text file format, Lexique Pro text file format, Microsoft Word, tables and more. (Arwarbukarl CRA Incorporated, n.d., paras. 2–3)

CIMCC experienced both opportunities and obstacles in developing and using language-learning technologies such as Miromaa in Pomo and Coast Miwok country. Broadly speaking, a growing corpus of research is demonstrating that the increased availability of digital technologies such as portable recording devices, mobile phone and cloud computing technology, archiving and documentation software, social media at large, and more all present exciting and challenging opportunities and issues surrounding the development and implementation of language-learning resources and programming in Indian country (see Begay, 2013; Thorpe & Galassi, 2014; Vagner, 2014; and Williams, 2013 for examples). While many institutional pathways exist to digital and physical heritage, such as NAGPRA programs in the context of museums, we start with emergent approaches in digital heritage technology at the grassroots level are also continuing to fundamentally shift constituent access to libraries and archives which house indigenous languages and cultures. The Rediscovering Indigenous Language Project based in Australia, for example, reported making use of a website that could be used to increase access to linguistic documentation resources, to consult community stakeholders about appropriate digitized archive access cultural protocols, and to increase active participation in co-creation of new language-learning materials based on what was collected (Thorpe & Galassi, 2014). In this case, Thorpe and Galassi (2014) point to the potential of a digital medium to increase community constituent access to cultural heritage and also demonstrate the importance of community consultation throughout the entire process.

In the same ethos as the Rediscovering Indigenous Language Project, we took similar consultative and cocreative approaches in order to ensure that the Miromaa language archives at CIMCC were built to serve as a living co-created digital archive developed in partnership with our community members. By leveraging these digital archives at CIMCC to organize and manage language and multimedia content in partnership with our community, we were able to produce a range of introductory language learning resources in Southern Pomo, Eastern Pomo, Central Pomo, Northern Pomo, and Coast Miwok. Specifically, our Miromaa archives empowered us to create self-guided language classes, language "kiosks" to be put in public spaces, introductory mobile apps, "talking" dictionaries, online flashcards, and more. In terms of measurable impact incorporating Miromaa into our language revitalization program gave us the ability to increase language learnership, to support and promote language speakership, to increase language public visibility, to increase learning resource accessibility, and to involve our community in the practice of digital heritage stewardship. These cocreated language digital archives at CIMCC equipped us to make resources with our community that did not exist previously; by connecting with our community, we are only just beginning to take our first steps towards awakening these languages together.

MIROMAA: THE TOOL

In sharing our notes on the development, design, function, and interfacing between user and Miromaa software, we hope to illuminate pathways towards increasing and supporting speakership for future users of similar technologies in language revitalization programming. We found that the inclusive design format of the Miromaa software plays an instrumental part in maintaining an inclusive approach to community involvement. Miromaa's focus on presenting a user-friendly user interface environment (UI/UIX) that incorporates "best practice" functions into the UI/UIX mechanics creates a unique opportunity for each community member to interact with linguistic and cultural data. Namely, the UI/UIX system in Miromaa software is structured and designed in such a way that a user can seamlessly use the tool to directly input audio, visual, and linguistic content according admin designated cultural protocols—without the user compromising the documentary integrity of the overall archive. This functionality is achieved through a software design feature; multiple-tiered levels of admin-created usership tied to UI/UIX capabilities that present various formats in which the roles of a learner, user, administrator, editor, and linguist are recognized as valuable contributors to a community-wide effort to language preservation. This design feature is especially significant for use in Pomo/Coast Miwok country because the process of development and dissemination of language learning resources in our area has not always been readily available at high capacity affecting collective ability to offset language loss in our relative speech communities in the tri-county area. From a theoretical perspective, we noticed how effective software design creates new opportunity to address persistent sociocultural barriers in Native American language revitalization efforts (Kroskrity & Field, 2009). The functionality of an inclusive UI/UIX environment covertly erases (Irvine & Gal, 2000) prescriptive beliefs and ideologies about who uses the tool by removing the visibility of access protocol and thereby emphasizing collaborative access and contribution to a shared interest by all—the stewardship of the materials and resources inside the Miromaa environment. Thus, in a pragmatic sense, if everyone has a unique role to offer in awakening language, then the design and functionality of digital tools we use in digital space should respond and function according to the real and imagined cultural and social systems of users involved in the process. We hope that this concept of designing the UI/UIX of digital tools to match community needs and the sociocultural realities of day-to-day experience can serve a powerful methodological signpost for future projects in leveraging digital tools and computer technologies.

This notion of creating synergy between the purpose and design of a digital language learning resource in relation to the daily experiences of the community is being closely evaluated by researchers and tribal communities in many language revitalization projects across North America. In one case, the effectiveness of this synergy was demonstrated in a study on the relative usability of Smart Pen technology—in essence, a "talking pen" in Ojibwe-speaking homes in 2013 (Obonyo, Troy, Baldwin, & Clarke, 2011). In rapid summary, researchers were able to determine that "smartpens and interactive booklets offer promise as a language revitalization tool for communities like the Miami Tribe whose emphasis is on home-based education" (Obonyo et al., 2012, pp. 1–11). There is opportunity here! The targeted use of smartpen technology at home in daily practice can be used to support a more interactive language-learning experience despite having the constraints of learning from a paper document and the lack of immersive opportunities that would be otherwise presented by of a primary speaker. In reversing language shift (RLS) (Fishman, 1991), access to an immersive cultural and linguistic context of primary speakers—where the language is shared in daily practice—is an obstacle that any who work to awaken languages must work with. Therefore, digitally rendered tools, community web archives, computer-mediated communication in social media, and many more methods that align the with daily lives of their users can serve as a part of a collective contextualized pedagogical solution dedicated to empowering the transmission of language in practice (Hinton, 2011). As evidenced by this short example, we must continue to explore the applied advantages presented by the unique capabilities of digital technology that constantly evolve. In developing and adapting new technologies, the potential to support language awakening and the transmission of knowledge RLS by matching the function of the tool to culturally defined protocol and the daily lived experience of the user must be kept at the forefront of cocreative project planning and collaboration.

The ability for the smartpen to "speak" voices of family members and elders who are collectively stewarded by the constituent community is just one small but exciting way to digitally support curious language learners who are awakening language in their community. In comparison to this point, however, we learned that all tools can come with their associated challenges and opportunities. Our Miromaa project required extensive time allocation and communication to overcome challenges in working through the process of content development and content management. While Miromaa software UI/UX mechanics do cater to a wide range of user capabilities, facilitating collaborative data collection and input among a range of project stakeholders was a cocreative process that called for additional time allocation dedicated to communication and troubleshooting. For example, in Miromaa, the process of data input can only be done one word, photo, audio file, and photo at a time (as opposed to batch imports/uploads). We saw this is an opportunity that made the data entry process very accessible to beginners and community members eagerly looking to participate in data input. When we incorporated additional project roles such as tribes, linguists, and community language activists, we needed to spend additional time facilitating communication to ensure that our project stakeholders could collectively review the large amounts of data that were entered into six different Miromaa language archives. Regardless of this, Miromaa's UI/UX mechanics continue to emphasize "best practice" archiving principles while simultaneously facilitating collaborative input and support. Community members can learn to use an effective tool like Miromaa regardless of their relative experience using computer skill sets. For someone beyond "beginner" experience, Miromaa works well in tandem with other tools that can assist in managing meta-data and producing physical learning materials. Various software and computer resources aimed at producing language learning resources from data archived in Miromaa. The functions of software such as Lexique Pro, Photoshop, and Adobe Acrobat all work in synergy with Miromaa to create bingo games, language flashcards, talking dictionaries, and much more using local, meaningful content. Keeping in mind the need to allocate time and resources to facilitating a collective effort using computer technology, Miromaa and other software can serve as part of a community-centered effort to support people learning native languages in daily practice.

DIGITAL DOMAINS

At CIMCC we continued to ask ourselves, how will access to these new tools shift the ways in which Indigenous languages are being awakened? How does access to Internet and computer technology shift existing methods of language revitalization programming in daily community practice? There is much to learn, but we cannot overemphasize the importance of allocating time and resources dedicated to empowering community to create and manage content creation using digital tools like Miromaa archives.

The opportunities presented by these constantly emerging forms of human communication must be continuously shared and adapted to fit the existing needs and priorities in contemporary tribal cultural contexts. We look forward to building on our work at CIMCC developing immersive and innovative language learning resources dedicated to empowering our community in awakening their tribal languages. Using Miromaa taught us that this creative process requires focus on our core mission and a willingness to try new tools with optimism guided by community directive. In working through the process of making mobile apps and in creating Miromaa digital language archives with our partners at the ALTC, we have learned that we must diligently work to navigate the challenge of creating digital resources and educational materials that remain closely tied to our cultural contexts, while simultaneously generating exciting, new, and innovative approaches to educating the public at large. While our focus was largely on creating resources for tribal communities, we realized that our strategies had to include information sharing with the larger community. While we are sensitive to cultural protocols and tribal community perspectives on who should engage in language learning, we realized that awakening tribal languages among members of tribal communities included a broader context. Education and outreach among non-Indians fosters appreciation and respect for tribal cultures. Not only are we saying, "We are still here," but we are generating support and recognition for our need to take language learning to a new level.

In closing, we have recognized the need of an online indigenous space at CIMCC, where our cultural context defines the ways in which we share our stories, teach our languages, and communicate our values. For us, this digital space currently exists in Internet, blogs, websites, Instagrams, social media groups, and even in apps—all centered around the key concept of sharing, communicating, and reflecting culturally meaningful content to participants who share situated knowledge in a community of practice. Situated in this context, CIMCC has engaged several approaches to leveraging digital places to create a cultural space for people from all backgrounds to visit and become familiar with the rich history of Native language and cultures of our region. Through introductory language learning apps, a free self-guided language class online, and interactive kiosks and makerspaces, we've taken an inclusive digital approach to language revitalization by involving our people in the process of content creation for educational resources. We have especially worked to offer tools, experiences, and approaches that are all grounded by the focus on meeting the cultural needs and educational goals of people in our community.

So we must now ask: What cultural contexts exist in your community digital space? How will you make those digital connections between people, practice, and place work in ways that increase the capacity of our community members to participate within as social actors? We are optimistic we when we look towards developing more language learning resources and educational opportunities using digital tools like Miromaa in Pomo and Coast Miwok languages. For many years we believed these tools were outside of our grasp and that we did not possess the infrastructure or resources to adapt these resources for our own purposes. Fortunately, the climate of many of these technologies has changed and the hopes for new platforms are on the horizon. Indigenous activists around the globe are working in concert to improve, adapt, and transform technologies to serve their context. Sharing these experiences has inspired creative pursuits and collaborations, and for us in Pomo and Coast Miwok country, we continue on, facilitating the emergence of cultural context in digital space, and on Indian ground.

For more information about CIMCC language resources visit http:// cimcc.org/education-center/cimcc-aboriginal-language-apps/. For more information about Miromaa visit www.miromaa.org.au.

REFERENCES

Arwarbukarl CRA Incorporated. (n.d.). Miromaa ALTC. Retrieved from http:// www.miromaa.org.au/miromaa.html

Begay, W. (2013). *Mobile apps and indigenous language learning: New developments in the field of indigenous language revitalization* (Master's Thesis). Retrieved from ProQuest Dissertations and Theses database. (1537553) .

Burt, L. W. (1986). Roots of the Native American urban experience: Relocation policy in the 1950s. *American Indian Quarterly, 10*(2), 85–99. doi:10.2307/1183982

Castaneda, T. A. (2011). California Indian land claims activism and urban Indian place-making. *Proceedings of the Southwestern Anthropological Association, 4*, 1–7.

Castillo, E. (1978). The impact of Euro-American exploration and settlement In W. C. Sturtevant & R. Heizer (Eds.), *Handbook of North American Indians* (vol. 8, pp. 99–127). Washington, DC: Smithsonian Institution.

Cook, S. F. (1978) Historical demography. In W. C. Sturtevant & R. Heizer (Eds.), *Handbook of North American Indians* (vol. 8, pp. 91–99). Washington, DC: Smithsonian Institution.

Fishman, J. A. (1991). *Reversing language shift: Theory and practice of assistance to threatened languages* (2nd ed.). Tonawanda, NY: Multilingual Matters.

Fiske, S. J. (1979). Urban Indian institutions: A reappraisal from Los Angeles. *Urban Anthropology, 8*(2), 149–171.

Greenwood, J. (2011). Performance, language revitalisation, and digital technology. *New Zealand Journal of the Sociology of Language*. Retrieved from http://www.drama.org.nz/publications/new-zealand-journal-of-research -in-performing-arts-and-education-2011/

Hinton, L. (1998). Language loss and revitalization in California: Overview. *International Journal of the Sociology of Language, 132*, 83–93).

Hinton, L. (2011). Language revitalization and language pedagogy: New teaching and learning strategies. *Language and Education, 25*(4), 307–318.

Irvine, J. T., & Gal, S. (2000). Language ideology and linguistic differentiation. In P. V. Kroskrity (Ed.), *Regimes of language: Ideologies, polities, and identities.* Santa Fe, NM: School for Advanced Research Press.

Johnston-Dodds, K. (2002). *Early California laws and policies related to California Indians.* Sacramento, CA: California Research Bureau, California State Library.

Kroskrity, P. V., & Field, M. C. (2009). *Native American language ideologies: Beliefs, practices, and struggles in Indian country.* Tucson, AZ: University of Arizona Press.

Linn, M. S., Naranjo, T., Nicholas, S., Slaughter, I., Yamamoto, A., & Zepeda, O. (2002). Awakening the languages: Challenges of enduring language programs; field reports from fifteen programs from Arizona, New Mexico, and Oklahoma. In B. Burnaby & J. A. Reyhner (Eds.), *Indigenous languages across the community* (pp. 105–126). Flagstaff, AZ: Northern Arizona University. Retrieved from http://www2.nau.edu/~jar/ILAC/index.html

Obonyo, V., Troy, D., Baldwin, D., & Clarke, J. (2011). Digital smartpen technology and revitalization of the myaamia language. *Journal on Computing and Cultural Heritage, 4*(4), 1–11.

Reyhner, J. (1993). American Indian language policy and school success. *Journal of Educational Issues of Language Minority Students, 12*(Special Issue), 35–59.

Thorpe, K., & Galassi, M. (2014). Rediscovering indigenous languages: The role and impact of libraries and archives in cultural revitalisation. *Australian Academic and Research Libraries, 45*(2), 81–100.

Vagner, I. (2014). *Language revitalization on the web: Technologies and ideologies among the northern Arapaho* (Master's Thesis). Retrieved from ProQuest Dissertations and Theses database (1558776).

Williams, B. (2013). *Social media: Facilitating language revitalization in endangered Midwestern Native American languages.* Northridge, CA: California State University.

Wilkinson, C. F., & Biggs, E. R. (1977). The evolution of the termination policy. *American Indian Law Review, 5*(1), 139–184. doi:10.2307/20068014

CHAPTER 14

FUNDING, FINANCE, AND SCHOOL ACCOUNTABILITY

Rodney Beaulieu
California State University, San Marcos

The largest American Indian student population is in California. According to the California Department of Education, there were 34,704 California Indian students during the 2015–2016 academic year (California Department of Education, 2017b). The 2010 U.S. Census Bureau indicates that American Indians are only 1% of the entire California population.

There continues to be a misunderstanding about California Indian educational funding and general resources. A common stereotype is that casinos made California tribes wealthy, but what is perhaps forgotten is that casinos are relatively new tribal resources. Gambling on California tribal lands was legalized in 2000 following a constitutional amendment, Proposition 1A, which authorized "compacts" with the state. Revenue from the casinos is only now trickling down to tribal communities, mostly for basic infrastructure, such as schools, clinics, fire-fighting stations, roads, streetlights, telecommunication equipment, improved sanitation and water sources, playgrounds, and so on. These amenities have been absent in tribal communities, and anyone who has visited reservations over the last generation would know that.

On Indian Ground: California, pages 195–207
Copyright © 2017 by Information Age Publishing

This report provides a brief history of major funding for California Indian public schools, followed by an illustration to dispel the myth that California Indians are getting disproportionately more state funding than other racial/ethnic groups. It ends with questions about oversight responsibility and calls for more input from tribal representatives on the direction of public schooling.

A BRIEF HISTORY OF REGIONAL FUNDING

Until 1972, the funding for school districts was almost exclusively sourced from local property taxes, and local officials set the tax rates without voter approval. In impoverished communities where the property tax base was low, schools suffered from underfunding, and this was especially true for American Indian communities in California. Conversely, wealthy communities with high property values were successful at providing state-of-the-art schools. In effect, this model of school funding resembled the "separate and unequal" arguments from the Jim Crow era and perpetuated structural inequality for American Indians. This model of funding K–12 schools was eventually challenged by a series of California Supreme Court cases, but only relatively recently. See *Serrano v. Priest, 5 Cal.3d 584 (1971) (Serrano I); Serrano v. Priest, 18 Cal.3d 728 (1976) (Serrano II); Serrano v. Priest, 20 Cal.3d 25 (1977) (Serrano III)*. The first case, a class action case, initiated by public-interest attorneys on behalf of all California public school students, focused on unequal opportunities and the battle against discrimination. The second case struck down California's funding structure as a violation of equal protection under the state constitution because the per-pupil expenditures varied greatly and depended on the school district's tax base. From *Serrano I*, the California Legislature enacted SB90 to begin a process for leveling the income base for school districts based on an average daily attendance (ADA) revenue limit, a step toward address disparities in education by restructuring county funding. Counties were required to levy property taxes in each school district at a rate to meet the district's annual budget, yet substantial disparities in per-pupil revenues continued to be a problem. In a follow-up case, *Serrano II*, the court held that California's school financial system failed to provide equitable treatment of all public school students, violating equal protection rights. Today, the amount of unrestricted funding per district is guaranteed by the State of California using a formula that is calculated by multiplying the district's revenue limit per student by the district's daily attendance average (ADA). Because revenue from local property taxes varies from district to district, the ratio of funding from California is unique to each district. Communities with a rich tax base continue to fare better than those overshadowed by low property values and tax abatements.

BUREAU OF INDIAN AFFAIRS (BIA) AND BUREAU OF INDIAN EDUCATION (BIE)

A substantial source of funding for California Indian education comes from the U.S. Government through the Bureau of Indian Affairs and the Bureau of Indian Education, both under the Assistant Secretary of Indian Affairs. The overall budget is proposed to increase to $2.9 billion, which is almost $137.6 million more than 2016 (Office of the Budget of the U.S. Department of the Interior, 2017). This includes creating opportunities for American Indian youth with an allocation of $1.1 billion in programs, and allocating $49.3 million to improve opportunities and outcomes in the classroom, expand multigenerational programs for early childhood development, improve instructional services and teaching quality, promote enhanced language and cultural programs, and support broadband and digital access. The budget also provides $138.8 million for constructing and repairing school facilities. A 2017 goal for BIA and BIE is to increase the percentage of tribal students in colleges and universities. BIE is working with the Tribal Colleges and Universities to develop programs that increase awareness of Indian students' culture and history and support recruitment and retention.

American Indian boarding schools were established in the U.S. during the late 19th century, and two still exist in California under the rule of the U.S. Department of the Interior, Bureau of Indian Education (BIE). Sherman Indian High School in Riverside supports grades 9–12, and Noli School in San Jacinto supports grades 6– 12. Both schools are funded through grants supported by the Indian School Equalization Program (ISEP) to comply with part B of the Individuals with Disabilities Education Act (IDEA).

IMPACT AID

The mission of the Impact Aid Program is to provide financial support to local educational agencies that are burdened by federal activities and to provide support services for staff and other interested parties. It has been providing assistance to American Indians/Alaska Natives since the 1950s and was reauthorized under Title VII of the Every Student Succeeds Act of 2015. It compensates for lost property tax revenue where communities are exempt from property taxes, such as Indian reservations. The nationwide budget for Impact Aid remained the same for several years ($1.28 billion) and increased to $.13 billion for the 2017 fiscal year. To be eligible for an Impact Aid grant, the school district must serve at least 400 children in average daily attendance (known as "federally connected children") or at least 3% of the total number of children in average daily attendance. Parents are also required to review the school's Impact Aid application, educational plans, and existing evaluations; discuss views with school personnel regularly; assess and provide feedback on their child's participation; make recommendations; and provide assessment input. The government webpage that hosts information about Impact Act has not provided details about California awards. For more information, see U.S. Department of Education (n.d.b).

INDIAN EDUCATION FORMULA GRANTS

Established in 1972 and reauthorized in the 2001 No Child Left Behind Act (NCLB) and again in 2015 under Title VI of the Every Student Succeeds Act (ESSA), the Indian Education Formula Grant Program is designed to serve the unique cultural, language and educational needs of American Indian and Alaska Native students, including preschoolers. Through the Office of Indian Education, grants supplement regular school programs where enrichment programs such as culturally-responsive after-school programs, indigenous language classes, early childhood education, tutoring, and dropout prevention programs. The most recent reported funding for California was in 2007 for the amount of $5.78 million to 93 grantees to support 29,823 Indian students at the equivalent of $194 per student (retrieved March 20, 2016 from U.S. Department of Education, n.d.a). To be eligible for a grant, school districts are required to have a minimum of 10 students (or have at least 25% of the total number enrolled) but some states, including California have an exception to this rule (U.S. Department of Education, n.d.b).

JOHNSON O'MALLEY

The federal government recognized the need to supplement school district programs that serve American Indian/Alaska Native students back in 1934 and passed the Johnson-O'Malley Act. This program supplements local school districts through a wide variety of programmatic interventions, including programs to promote culture and language, enhance academics, and prevent dropouts. To be eligible, school districts must have an established Indian Education Committee (IEC) that reviews programs and advises on the budget. Eligible students range from ages 3 years of age to grade 12 and must be members of federally recognized tribe. In recent years, the Indian Education Committee's (IEC) responsibilities have broadened, and they now have legislative authority to recommend teaching curricula, methods, and texts. They approve budgets for the program and can provide recommendations for hiring and removal. School district employees are prohibited from serving on IECs to avoid a conflict of interest. For more information, see U.S. Department of the Interior, Bureau of Indian Education (2015a).

TRIBAL EDUCATION DEPARTMENT (TED)
GRANT PROGRAM

TED grants are awarded to tribes for developing and operating their own educational programs. Funds up to $150,000 are intended to improve educational outcomes and improve the effectiveness of schools that qualify for Bureau of Indian Education funding. Areas of capacity building include developing and enforcing tribal educational codes, facilitating tribal control over all educational matters related to Indian students on reservations, and developing and coordinating educational programs. By the end of 2016, 11 tribes had been awarded a grant, but none were from California (U.S. Department of the Interior, Bureau of Indian Education, 2015b).

EDUCATION INNOVATION
AND RESEARCH PROGRAM GRANTS

A series of grants are offered through the Office of Innovation and Improvement (OII) in collaboration with the Bureau of Indian Education. Awards are for school districts or local educational agencies that serve urban schools that serve high-need students, such as American Indians. Priority is given to low-performing schools that focus on early learning social-behavioral competencies and evidence-based practices. Early-phase awards are between $7 and 8 million, mid-phase awards are $1.4–1.6 million, and expansion grants are $2.7–3 million. For more information, see U.S. Government Printing Office (2016).

U.S. DEPARTMENT OF EDUCATION, OFFICE
OF ELEMENTARY AND SECONDARY EDUCATION

Several competitive grants have been available through the Office of Elementary and Secondary Education (OESE): Native American Language Program Grant, Indian Demonstration Grant, and Indian Professional Development Grant. The Native American Language Program Grant is authorized under Title VI, Part A, of the Elementary and Secondary Education Act and was amended to the Every Student Succeeds Act (ESSA), Section 6133. Grant awards for 2016 has not been provided on the government websites. Nationwide, only about 25 competitive grant applications are expected for 2017 (U.S. Government Publishing Office, 2017).

The Indian Demonstration Program Grant is designed to serve preschool and K–12 American Indian students through local educational agencies or school districts that develop and demonstrate effective services and programs. In 2016 only three programs in California received grants

(Pinoleville Pomo Nation, San Diego County Superintendent of Schools, and Karuk Tribe), together totaling $1.2 which is about 6.8% of the nation-wide $18.2 million allocation (U.S. Department of Education, 2016). No demonstration grants are planned for 2017.

Indian Professional Development Grants are intended to increase the number of American Indian professions in schools by funding the training of teachers, teaching aides, administrators, social workers, and ancillary educational personnel. Grants are also available for American Indians who already serve in these roles and want additional training. Awardees must perform work related to their training and service must benefit American Indian education. In 2016, only one award was granted in California: $335,247 to California State University–Chico, to support 20 American Indian students pursuing teaching careers. That is less than 5% of the $6.7 million budget (U.S. Department of Education, n.d.d).

U.S. DEPARTMENT OF EDUCATION, OFFICE
OF INNOVATION AND IMPROVEMENT (OII)

In collaboration with the Bureau of Indian Education, the Office of Innovation and Improvement offers grants for the Teacher and School Leadership (TSL) Incentive Program (CFDA). The 2017 estimated funding is $1.5 billion with no award ceiling. Available for American Indian education programs, the goal is to provide funds for developing, implementing, improving or expanding school management systems for teachers, principals, and other school leaders in high-need schools. First awards will be granted in September 2017. For more information, see U.S. Department of Education (2017).

CALIFORNIA DEPARTMENT OF EDUCATION

Like the U.S. Government, the California Department of Education has an Internet-based portal to search for available grants. See http://www.cde.ca.gov/fg/fo/af/. A recent search for funding opportunities related to California Indian education, using variations of the term "Indian" as a search criteria produced this repeated response: "No funding profiles found! Please try different search criteria." Eight grants were currently advertised, one for implementing K-12 high-speed network and one for migrant education: three related to food or nutrition programs, one for K-12 high-speed network, one for migrant education, one for special education, one for child care, and one for mental health services. California Indians qualify to apply for at least seven of these grants, assuming applications fit grant specifications. A search on the CA.GOV website (California Department of Education, n.d.c) for grant programs revealed only one program for facilities construction, repairs, and maintenance with priority to schools. All the 17 schools have low American Indian enrollment.

Starting in 2013, the Local Control Funding Formula (LCFF) was implemented to improve funding to public K–12 schools in low-income communities, and it gives more authority on how school systems spend their revenue. The new model is based on per-student expense allocations and the number of students and school personnel. Schools that are necessarily small, such as rural schools, can potentially get more funding, but because the funding formula is evolving, projections for per-student allocations is different each year and depends on school demographics. The average statewide allocation for 2015–2016 was $10,795 per student.

AMERICAN INDIAN EDUCATION CENTERS (AIEC)

Authorized by California Education Code, Section 33384, the AIEC program was established in 1974 by Senate Bill 2264 to strengthen the delivery of instructional services to American Indian students in public schools through the administration of educational resource centers. In the California Department of Education's Report to the Governor and the Legislature Executive Summary of 2016 (California Department of Education 2016), in 2013–2014, about 4% of California Indian students received services from 24 AIECs. While information about other years of service are missing from the report, key services included programs on reading and math, improving self-concept of participants, summer recreational and academic experiences, and employment preparation. Twenty-four American Indian education centers were funded at a total of $4,002,741 for the grant year 2013–2014 and served 1,559 students during the school year and 892 students during summer program services. Two centers have closed since that time, and information about current grant opportunities or current awards is not provided on the California Department of Education website.

AMERICAN INDIAN EARLY CHILDHOOD EDUCATION

Begun in the 1970s, the American Indian Early Childhood Education (AIECE) program is designed to help California Indian children develop reading and mathematics skills and promote self-esteem. It serves children prekindergarten children through grade 4. Competitive grants are designated to schools with at least 10% American Indian students for three-year cycles and administered through seven county offices. Total funding for fiscal year 2015–2016 was $550,000 for all AIECE programs (California Department of Education, n.d.e).

ILLUSTRATION OF CALIFORNIA
INDIAN PER-STUDENT FUNDING

There are two main sources at the California Department of Education website (California Department of Education, n.d.d) that provides data on how funds are allocated to school districts and both are organized with "Current Expense Per Average Daily Attendance (ADA)" information. One source is a spreadsheet with allocations for each of the 949 districts. Figures for individual schools within those districts can be found at a second source (http://dq.cde.ca.gov/dataquest/) where database information can be sorted along student demographics with DataQuest (California Department of Education, 2017a). In a recent search (March 2017) of the database, one school district is shown to have 34 American Indian students, representing 42.5% of the school population at Alpine County Unified, yet that same district is listed again (on another line) as having five American Indian students, representing 100% of the school population. The ADA expense for each of these two data entries appear as the same figure ($32,361), suggesting an apparent mistake in government tracking and reporting.

The California Department of Education database shows there are 1024 publicly funded schools and 18 of them have an Indian student population that is greater than 15%. Including the earlier-mentioned school (Alpine County) that was misreported in the database with 34 American Indian students, the Indian count at 17 schools ranges from 7 to 866, and ADA expense ranged between $12,028 and $37,852. The school with the highest ADA expense was $37,852, though it only had 65 students, most of whom were not American Indian (45% White, 25% Indian, 17% Hispanic, 1.5% African American and 1.5% Asian). At $48,711, the highest ADA expense in the database, Indian Springs Elementary, had 60% White students and no American Indian students. The next highest, Bolinas-Stinson, was $38,809 and had 67.6% White students and no American Indians. If the data are correct, each of these two schools tripled the California average per-student expense of $10,795, and the main beneficiaries were not American Indian students or other minority groups.

Those who have never visited an American Indian reservation might not be familiar with the struggle that Indians still experience in having equal access to educational opportunities. Reservations exist because American Indians were forced from their larger territories to make way for the dominant population, usually through illegal means and broken agreements. In California, reservations have a long history of poverty because sustainability on small plots of land is impossible, internal resources are limited, and outside employment is limited by discrimination. Moreover, schools have been underfunded because tribes do not impose a property tax on reservations to generate income. Even if they did, property values are not usually assessed on reservations and, if they were, many families could not afford the cost.

Many rural schools, regardless of racial/ethnic demographics, require more non-local funding because they are at a disadvantage with generating their own funds from property taxes. That is why *Serrano v. Priest* was needed—to level funding at a statewide level rather than the local level. For illustration purposes, consider the following ADA expense comparison between the smallest American Indian schools and the smallest predominantly White schools from the California Department of Education database for the academic year 2015–2016. For this illustration, because the number of American Indians students is very small relative to other racial groups, the comparison group includes all schools that had more than 15% Indian population, regardless of the remaining balance of students, and all schools had 866 or fewer students. As Table 14.1 shows, only a few of the 18

TABLE 14.1 Percent of California Indian Students at Rural Schools (2015–2016)

County	District	American Indian	% of School Population	ADA Expense
49	Kashia Elementary	14	100.00	21,451
12	Klamath-Trinity Joint Unified	866	80.71	16,795
23	Round Valley Unified	260	60.89	18,354
47	Junction Elementary	18	58.06	15,507
14	Big Pine Unified	78	45.35	21,046
13	San Pasqual Valley Unified	319	44.00	19,865
11	Stony Creek Joint Unified	43	43.88	19,994
2	Alpine County Unified	34	42.50	32,361
47	Happy Camp Union Elementary	38	31.67	12,028
53	Burnt Ranch Elementary	28	28.87	14,994
4	Feather Falls Union Elementary	16	24.62	37,852
36	Needles Unified	176	18.78	12,810
12	Loleta Union Elementary	54	18.56	15,696
45	Mountain Union Elementary	13	18.31	15,682
47	Yreka Union Elementary	169	17.57	14,176
47	Gazelle Union Elementary	7	17.07	12,065
25	Surprise Valley Joint Unified	23	16.79	13,959
47	Little Shasta Elementary	1	16.67	25,682
	n = 18		Total:	340,317
			Mean:	18,907
			SD:	6,985

schools had a proportionally high percentage of Indian students compared to other student groups.

Criteria for White schools is that White students comprised at least 66% of the population (the majority), Hispanics were no more than 33% of the school population, African Americans did not exceed 10% in population, and there were no American Indians. Like the American Indian sample, all schools with 866 students or less were added the White sample, although the largest had 532 students; there were no schools that fit the criteria between 532 and 866. Table 14.2 outlines the demographics.

TABLE 14.2 Percent of White Students at Smallest California Rural Schools (2015–2016)

County	District	White	% of School	Hispanic	% of School	ADA Expense
21	Union Joint Elementary	4	66.67	2	33.33	29,547
21	Lincoln Elementary	10	90.91	1	9.09	16,956
53	Trinity County	15	100.00	0	0.00	26,624
9	Silver Fork Elementary	15	93.75	1	6.25	31,748
12	Orick Elementary	16	100.00	0	0.00	27,274
47	Bogus Elementary	14	87.50	0	0.00	16,540
47	Forks of Salmon Elementary	15	88.24	1	5.88	16,471
12	Peninsula Union	31	91.18	1	2.94	20,173
49	Montgomery Elementary	30	85.71	3	8.57	20,319
10	Pine Ridge Elementary	78	91.76	5	5.88	24,573
50	Knights Ferry Elementary	65	71.43	13	14.29	9,828
15	Midway Elementary	78	82.98	16	17.02	21,133
21	Bolinas-Stinson Union	71	67.62	21	20.00	38,809
42	Ballard Elementary	105	84.68	16	12.90	15,630
44	Mountain Elementary	105	84.68	8	6.45	12,593
49	Kenwood	105	74.47	15	10.64	16,310
42	Cold Spring Elementary	127	84.11	11	7.28	23,735
53	Douglas City Elementary	136	75.56	21	11.67	9,792
47	Butteville Union Elementary	146	66.36	35	15.91	9,013
21	Lagunitas Elementary	224	81.16	26	9.42	13,091
41	Woodside Elementary	293	71.64	48	11.74	25,901
41	Portola Valley Elementary	427	68.10	84	13.40	22,318
37	Cardiff Elementary	532	72.88	136	18.63	13,286
	n = 23				Total:	461,664
					Mean:	20,072
					SD:	7,682

While there were no significant differences between the two groups around ADA expenses ($t = 0.50$, $p > .05$), this illustration confirms that rural schools require proportionally more funding because they have few students. But more importantly, it illustrates the fact that California Indians in public schools are not getting proportionately more ADA expense allocations than other students.

NEXT STEPS FOR ADVANCING CALIFORNIA INDIAN EDUCATION

At the state level, California needs to do more to address the educational needs of California Indians. For example, the American Indian Education Oversight Committee (AIEOC) at the California Department of Education appears to be inactive. It is charged to "provide input and advice to the State Superintendent of Public Instruction on all aspects of American Indian education programs established by the state" (see www.cde.ca.gov/sp/ai/re/aiecommittee.asp) yet annual reports stopped being posted since 2012 (California Department of Education, n.d.a), meetings have been infrequent (and without a quorum), and the last meeting was over a year ago (California Department of Education, n.d.b). This inadequate oversight and lack of communication draws numerous questions about state-level responsibilities.

Having access to updated educational data would be helpful for targeting services for California Indian students across the state. DataQuest allows users to access an array of information by county, district, and school, and by school performance, test scores, school staffing, and student demographics. It would be helpful if the database also contained financial details from the annual Current Expense of Education report (California Department of Education, n.d.d) provided by the California Department of Education. In this way, information about funding disparities across communities, student demographics, and ADA expenses would be more transparent.

Finally, and most urgent, the State of California must do more to provide funding for California Indian communities to educate children, and they should actively publicize grant opportunities. While grants are available through an array of programs, the California Department of Education does not have a consolidated system for communicating information that serves California Indian educational interests.

REFERENCES

California Department of Education. (2016). The American Indian Education Center Program: Report to the Governor and the Legislature executive summary. Retrieved from http://www.cde.ca.gov/sp/ai/re/lraiec2016.asp

California Department of Education. (2017a). *DataQuest Reports for Accountability.* Retrieved from http://www.cde.ca.gov/ds/sd/cb/dataquest.asp

California Department of Education. (2017b). *Selected statewide date for 2015–2016: American Indian or Alaska Native students.* Retrieved from http://dq.cde. ca.gov/dataquest/Cbeds1.asp?PctAm=on&cChoice=StatProf1&cYear =2015-16&cLevel=State&cTopic=Profile&myTimeFrame=S&submit1=Submit

California Department of Education. (n.d.a). *American Indian Education Oversight Committee.* Retrieved from http://www.cde.ca.gov/sp/ai/re/aiecommittee.asp

California Department of Education. (n.d.b). *American Indian Education Oversight Committee, Public meeting agendas & minutes.* Retrieved from http://www.cde. ca.gov/sp/ai/re/aieocmtgnotices.asp

California Department of Education. (n.d.c). *Available funding.* Retrieved from http://www.cde.ca.gov/fg/fo/af/

California Department of Education. (n.d.d). *Current expense of education.* Retrieved from http://www.cde.ca.gov/ds/fd/ec/currentexpense.asp

California Department of Education. (n.d.e). *Early childhood education (ECE): AIECE program directory.* Retrieved from http://www.cde.ca.gov/sp/ai/ec/

Every Student Succeeds Act, Pub. L. No. 114-95 § 114 Stat. 1177 (2015–2016).

Individuals with Disability Education Act , Pub.L. No. 101-476, 20 U.S.C. §1400 (2004).

Office of the Budget of the U.S. Department of the Interior. (2017). *Budget justifications and performance information fiscal year 2017.* Retrieved from https://www. doi.gov/sites/doi.gov/files/uploads/FY2017_IA_Budget_Justification.pdf

Serrano v. Priest, 5 Cal.3d 584. (1971). California Supreme Court.

Serrano v. Priest, 18 Cal.3d 728. (1976). California Supreme Court.

Serrano v. Priest, 20 Cal.3d 25. (1977). California Supreme Court.

U.S. Department of Education. (2016). Programs, Indian education—Demonstration grants for Indian children. Retrieved from https://www2.ed.gov/programs/indiandemo/awards.html

U.S. Department of Education. (2017). *Office of Innovation & Improvement, Teacher and School Leader Incentive Program.* Retrieved from https://innovation.ed.gov/ what-we-do/teacher-quality/teacher-and-school-leader-incentive-program/

U.S. Department of Education. (n.d.a). *Indian Education: Formula grants to local education agencies.* Retrieved from https://www2.ed.gov/programs/indianformula/ index.html

U.S. Department of Education. (n.d.b). *Indian education: Formula grants to local education agencies.* Retrieved from https://www2.ed.gov/programs/indianformula/ index.html

U.S. Department of Education. (n.d.c). *Office of Elementary and Secondary Education, Impact Aid Programs.* Retrieved from https://www2.ed.gov/about/offices/ list/oese/impactaid/whatisia.html

U.S. Department of Education. (n.d.d). *Programs, Indian education—Professional development grants.* Retrieved from https://www2.ed.gov/programs/indian-profdev/awards.html

U.S. Department of the Interior, Bureau of Indian Education. (2015a). *Johnson-O'Malley program.* Retrieved from https://www.bie.edu/JOM/

U.S. Department of the Interior, Bureau of Indian Education. (2015b). *Tribal Education Department Grant Program*. Retrieved from https://www.bie.edu/Programs/TribalEduDeptGrantProgram/index.htm

U.S. Government Publishing Office. (2016, December 15). Applications for new awards; Education Innovation and Research Program—Early-phase grants. *Federal Register, 81*(241). Retrieved from https://www.gpo.gov/fdsys/pkg/FR-2016-12-15/html/2016-30085.htm

U.S. Government Publishing Office. (2017, March 9). Authenticated U.S. Government Information, 13100. Notices. *Federal Register, 82*(45). Retrieved from https://www.gpo.gov/fdsys/pkg/FR-2017-03-09/pdf/2017-04630.pdf

CHAPTER 15

PARENTS AND TRIBAL COMMUNITY EFFORTS

Tishmall Turner
Tribal Liaison, California State University San Marcos

Hunwut Turner
Rincon Indian Education Center

This chapter provides examples of the new era of the reclamation of American Indian education by parents and the tribal community, which leads to maintaining sovereignty and preserving tribal culture for future generations. Tribal community involvement and the vital parental participation lost during years of historical trauma in Indian education policies and practices are reformed through tribally run education programs, through the higher attainment of education by Native parents, and by the entire community's participation and investment in education. This chapter highlights educational programs in Southern California and the promising practices that are sustain and make them successful.

On Indian Ground: California, pages 209–221
Copyright © 2017 by Information Age Publishing
All rights of reproduction in any form reserved.

PECHANGA CHÁMMAKILAWISH SCHOOL

California Indian education is steeped in relation to cultural loss caused by one major factor: the missions. Education was once scorned because many American Indians thought that if you became educated, you would lose your culture. In *The State of the Native Nations* (Cornell, Kalt, & Begay, 2008), the authors explain that the "outcomes of tribal operation of schools and other related curricular developments will take time to appear" despite reports from tribal communities that "local control has a positive impact" (p. 207) on American Indian student achievement. The case studies in this chapter demonstrate the impact, improvement, and success of tribally operated education programs in Southern California and their impact in reshaping attitudes and beliefs about education from a negative history to one in which education is seen as the road to cultural and economic prosperity. The Native pride movements that began in the 1960s combined with the casino revenues ushered in during the 1990s brought a flurry of educational and cultural initiatives that have strengthened many tribes throughout the state. These initiatives now work together to assure that the Indian youth and older descendants learn both cultural pride and how to succeed in mainstream society (Gelles, 2013). Several tribal communities throughout the state have developed and funded their own private tribal schools and are beginning to see the positive impact from these schools and programs on the community.

The Pechanga Chámmakilawish School is located on the Pechanga Indian reservation in Riverside County and was founded in 2002. *Chámmakilawish* means "our future" in the Luiseño language. The school's mission is to ensure that each child develops a foundation for success through the development of a healthy self-esteem by participating in a rich learning environment.

Andrew Masiel, Jr., director of education, has been the principal for the last 9 years. Masiel is a Pechanga tribal member who always saw himself as "working for the kids." Masiel pursued his higher education in order to gain support in his role as principal. "I always felt like I was going to school for everybody," he said (personal communication, April 12, 2017). The school serves approximately 100 students per year, from infant to 5th grade, and each grade includes a Luiseño language immersion component. The students live both on and off the reservation. The average student-to-teacher ratio is about 7:1. Students receive more individual attention compared to the national ratio of 16:1. According to the National Center for Education Statistics also listed California as having the highest student–teacher ratio in the country for the academic year of 2011–12 at 23.4:1 (The Hechinger Report, n.d.). The school has united the tribal community and ended generations of divisions among families. The school voluntarily participated in the Western Association of Schools and Colleges (WASC) accreditation and received a 6-year term (the highest you can achieve), which reaffirms for the community that their tribal school is on par with other public schools. The school is the most highly regarded Pechanga tribal program from their tribal membership. Most tribal programs have some type of political struggle and difference of opinions, but, Mr. Maisel explains, "Education has always been a priority at Pechanga and one that everyone can agree on common ground" (A. Masiel, personal communication, June 19, 2015).

Parent participation at all levels in the school is highly encouraged, and the roles for parents are defined in the school policies. The school board is comprised of elected members from the tribal community, usually parents and relatives of the students, who follow the school's bylaws to govern the school. "The school board has staggered terms and they come and go," says Masiel. The reporting line for the principal is directly to the governing board. Parents are required to report any issues about the school directly to the principal.

Students at some of the local high schools are required to perform community service and many return to the Pechanga Chámmakilawish School to complete their hours. The students often say, "This is our home." Students continue to be involved in the school after 5th grade by returning to teach, volunteer, and be involved with the language program. School staff reinforce positive cultural habits to students who "keep returning even after leaving the 5th grade," says Masiel.

The school's transforming impact on the students and on the entire community was hardly imaginable with its humble beginning. The school began in a small wing of the tribal government building by first operating a preschool. The program continued to grow one grade at a time each year until it reached the goal in providing services up to the 5th grade. The school continues to use a wing of the government building and some outlying buildings, but Masiel hopes to have one building for the school in the future when funding allows. Needless to say, the school is completely funded through tribal economic development from the Pechanga Band of Luiseño Indians. School administrators, parents, and the tribe are searching for other avenues to support the school through federal and private grant contributions. The Pechanga School developed in part because the public school system was not able to meet the tribe's educational, academic, and physical needs for students to be successful. American Indian students have special cultural needs in order to be more successful academically. American Indian students tend to be more visual and tactile learners; they learn more easily by hands-on, experiential methods—for example, through the oral history of the tribal people in which students are immersed in an activity that demonstrates the history. Many Native students realize they live in two worlds: tribal and nontribal (Luiseño and American). To bridge these worlds, signs of praise, motivation, and encouragement are posted through-out the school in both languages.

One of the key contributing factors to the issues in education that American Indian communities face is due to the lack of native language speakers. The loss of language negatively impacted and eroded important cultural knowledge and practices. To meet this challenge, all teachers at the Pechanga School are required to participate in language classes during the traditional school year before the school day starts and during a boot camp in summer. The Pechanga Cultural Committee then approves and validates all cultural teachers that the school employs. Because all teachers learn and practice the language, the students are able to participate in Luiseño language and cultural lessons in every class. As a result, Masiel says, "I feel the language will never die with these kids."

Working together, the school and the tribe provide a comprehensive educational program that is academically, culturally, and socially appropriate for each student. The Luiseño culture is present in every classroom, cultural projects are weaved into the curriculum, and all lessons are appropriately designed for mastery in each grade level. The younger children learn about the alphabet, shapes, and animals from pictures that are significant in Luiseño culture. Older students learn from hands-on projects to gather various plant materials on field trips in order to make traditional clothing, tools, and baskets. These culturally conscious and tribally centered practices are the key ingredients to building a successful program for American Indian students. These practices nurture American Indian youth to become independent thinkers while providing them with social skills that will enable the Pechanga children to become productive members of the tribe and the outside community.

ALL TRIBES AMERICAN INDIAN CHARTER SCHOOL

The All Tribes American Indian Charter School, located on the Rincon Indian Reservation, is a public charter school that opened its doors to 17 students in grades 6-8 on September 10, 2001 with Michelle Parada and Maryann Donahue as the head teacher and administrator. The school's mission was to reduce the dropout rate on the local reservations (M. Parada, interview, July 31, 2015). In the *State of American Indian and Alaska Native Education in California*, Proudfit and Gregor (2014) identify that the graduation rate for American Indians is 67% statewide; however, less than 25% of these high school graduates complete the requirements to enter one of the state's public 4-year universities. All Tribes School set out to redress these issues by providing American Indian students with a wraparound curriculum that is culturally relevant and socially responsive to community needs.

All Tribes Charter began with students from the Rincon Band of Luiseño Indians, La Jolla Band of Luiseño Indians, Pala Band of Mission Indians, and San Pasqual Band of Mission Indians. All Tribes has continued to grow, and the school now offers transition kindergarten–12th grades as well as an adult education program. Their current enrollment has grown to 92 students and includes students from the Barona Band of Mission Indians, Mesa Grade Band of Mission Indians, Los Coyotes Band of Cahuilla and Cupeño Indians, Pechanga Band of Luiseño Indians, and nonnative students living in neighboring communities. They also have 24 adults participating in their adult education program at various levels. The student-to-teacher ratio at All Tribes is 12:1, which is well below national and state averages and demonstrates the individual attention that each student receives.

The All Tribes American Indian Charter School strives overall to create a foundation that will promote higher learning standards and achievement through exploring diverse experiences, opportunities, and interests while adjusting to the learning needs of the students. The school is quick to offer the flexibility for the students to be involved in various programs, such as transitioning from high school to college or directly into the workforce. This has been a hard lesson for the administrators to learn that not every student wants to pursue college. They have learned to adapt their programs to meet the needs of all students.

The school graduated 86 high school students from 2006–2015—which is a major accomplishment because many of the school's students were in perilous situations academically and disciplinarily before they came to All Tribes. The school evaluates the students' perceptions and attitudes about education in important pre- and postgraduation surveys. The school surveys the high school graduates in their senior year, and 95% respond that they never expected to graduate while 27% of young men report never expecting to be alive at the age of 18 years old (All Tribes American Indian Charter School, 2010). The school's success in changing these statistics is due to its philosophy of "teaching the way that the students learn," says Michelle Parada. Their mission has evolved to provide students with a quality education that inspires the students to complete work, enhance vocabulary, and develop a strong math background, all of which improve student success to get into college or to successfully enter the workforce after high school graduation.

The All Tribes School designed programs to achieve their mission by meeting the educational *and* social needs of their students. The school did this by diversifying the curriculum for students who want to pursue a successful college transition with no remediation and by establishing a career track for students who do not want to pursue higher education. The career track aims at making every graduate self-sufficient after high school.

Providing place-based education that fits the needs of its students takes creativity and community involvement. Cultural leaders from local tribal communities provide language and cultural classes on campus two days a week. The school uses the Future Farmers of America curriculum to fulfill a leadership development course. Classes are small and every student receives one-on-one attention when they need it. Indian Health Council, Inc., is a partner organization that provides onsite counseling services with parental consent. The governance council is made up of a representative from each of the initial reservations that have students attending. This provides an avenue of community and parental input that was not present in the public school system. The school would not have developed and grown without the parental input and demand to expand from their original program.

RINCON INDIAN EDUCATION CENTER

The Rincon Indian Education Center, Inc. (RIEC) a nonprofit 501(c) 3. The RIEC is located on the Rincon Indian Reservation in Valley Center, California in north San Diego County. The RIEC provides services to American Indian families on each of the surrounding Indian reservations of La Jolla, Pala, Pauma, and San Pasqual. The RIEC was established in January 1974 as an intertribal organization promoting Indian self-determination and education. The RIEC recently celebrated 40 years of providing services as one of the first education centers funded by the California Department of Education.

The RIEC provides services to students grades K–12 attending the Valley Center–Pauma Unified School District and Warner Springs School District. The school districts combined have a population of over 6,000 students. The American Indian population represents roughly 20% of the student body. Three hundred AI students and community members from prenatal through adult education attend the RIEC for services. The RIEC is committed to supporting Native American individuals in excelling their knowledge to meet the demanding challenges of the future. There is a strong need for the RIEC to increase the level of education and employment of American Indians in the community.

Although American Indians are the only group with guaranteed healthcare, education, and welfare through treaty rights, many sadly have the worst health, education, and poverty rates of any population in the U.S. Over 50% of American Indians meet the federal poverty guidelines and approximately 50% of the children live with relatives other than their biological parent(s). Single-parent homes are common, and the frequency of domestic violence against Indian women is the highest in the nation. Low levels of literacy have a direct correlation to these statistics environments

(Cornell, Kalt, & Begay, 2008). Limited access to educational assistance has prohibited change in these conditions.

The RIEC works locally to intervene and change these negative impacts by providing a wealth of services and resources to the tribal community. The REIC collaborates with many educational entities, such as the California Department of Education, the U.S. Department of Education, the San Diego County Office of Education, the Bureau of Indian Affairs, British Petroleum, University of California San Diego, California State University San Marcos, San Diego State University, University of California Riverside, Palomar Community College, Southern California Tribal Chairmen's Association, Indian Health Services, and local fire and sheriff departments.

The RIEC has administered a multitude of grants and contracts that have provided successful programs to the surrounding reservations. The REIC administered the following grant programs:

- Johnson O'Malley
- Federal Even Start program that was established in 2004
- 21st Century Community Learning Center grant from 2005–2009
- A+ for Science, a California Arts Department Grant
- Carol M. White Physical Education grant
- CSUSM Language Grant
- Hewlett Packard grant in 2001; provides continuous services to the eighteen San Diego County reservations to present.

Through its extended network of partnerships, the RIEC provides after-school tutoring, culture classes, Luiseño language classes, adult education classes, professional development workshops, GED classes, guidance counseling, high school equivalency programs, remedial academic classes, career development guidance, computer and Internet classes, TANF services, and CPR and first aid training. The RIEC is also a site for classes with local community colleges and provides support to successful youth programs such as Young Explorers' Club, Young Native Scholars, UNITY, Inter-Tribal Sports, Tukwut Scholars, and American Indian Recruitment program. The RIEC is involved in many community outreach programs such as Upward Bound, annual Sovereignty Conferences, drug prevention conferences, college career days, and an annual Southern California Tribal Chairmen's Association high school graduation celebration. The RIEC staff participates in community meetings to assess the community needs, as well as to provide surveys to the community and share direct services as a result of these assessments.

The REIC provides services to students to model healthy lifestyles, behaviors, and attitudes needed to be successful in life. Many of the REIC's programs facilitate 30 minutes of physical exercise before tutoring sessions and advocate for a healthy lifestyle by providing nutritional snacks that incorporate fresh fruit and vegetables for students. Students are encouraged to participate in "talking circles" to share and address their social or emotional concerns. As a result of participating in the talking circles, students become more confident in themselves and in their ability to cope with stressful situations, which leads them be more involved in the community. They are more likely to participate in other cultural and athletic after participating in the RIEC.

In addition to successful grant programs, the REIC contracts with outside entities to provide tutorial services to nine reservations in North San Diego County for over 8 years. The overlapping of best practices implemented through these grant programs has changed attitudes, behaviors, and the conditions in the community in regards to educational attainment.

RINCON STORY TELLERS

The Rincon Youth Storytellers (RYS) help students build skills through language acquisition and traditional singing/storytelling in the oral tradition. RYS is creating a culturally rich identity for youth. RYS is an after school program comprised of 20 3rd–12th grade students from Rincon and surrounding reservations. Director Ami Admire founded the organization in 2004. Soon after the storytellers began travelling to local schools, colleges, and conferences performing traditional Luiseño and other tribal songs, stories, and games. Utilizing several mediums of mixed visual art including photographs, original artwork, language, technology, and performance the Rincon Youth Storytellers express to their audiences that "Indian culture and heritage is not something that used to be practiced, but is continuing to be practiced" (A. Admire, interview, July 31, 2015).

Ami Admire has a BA in liberal arts, has taught cultural art classes at the Rincon Education Center Inc. (RIEC) since 1999, and is the great granddaughter of first-language Luiseño speakers. Rincon Elders Patricia Duro, Lorraine Hyde, and other community members support her work with the RYS. Further, she has been a colleague and student of linguist and Luiseño dictionary author Eric Elliott, PhD, and a student of traditional language classes held on her reservation. Admire is implementing grassroots language revitalization through the RYS in order to increase Luiseño language use and restore the connection between language and culture. Linguist Leanne Hinton (2008) explains:

> Language and culture are closely intertwined. One important reason many people want to learn their ancestral language is that they want to regain access to traditional cultural practices and traditional values. It is often said that language is the key to and the heart of a culture. (Hinton & Hale, 2008, p. 9)

As the Rincon Youth Storytellers sing songs, narrate, and perform stories, they hear the sounds of and speak their almost extinct ancestral language. They begin to develop an understanding of their cultural and historical background. This is done by acting out the stories that their ancestors preserved, singing the songs they sang, and playing the games they played. From this background, the youth develop public speaking and literacy skills as they perform in front of various sized and often diverse audiences. The acquisition of such a knowledge base is a powerful tool that can be accessed when engaging in classes, socializing in groups, and when making plans for how they will maintain a professional and culturally rich identity for themselves in the future.

The RYS Introductory Language Program combines curriculum taken from two sources: (a) traditional Luiseño from local Elders and community members and (b) formal academic Luiseño as offered by Dr. Eric Elliott. RYS director Ami Admire has studied with Dr. Elliott and regards him as a source of support as he fortifies her language goals by allowing her access to his Luiseño curriculum and texts, which she uses to supplement her lessons.

Southern California Tribal Chairmen's Association (SCTCA) provides support to RYS in the form of a technical advisor, facilities, and access to media devices. The current media program includes but is not limited to the rerecording of nontraditional children's songs in Luiseño and the preservation of storytelling events by teaching students how to record and document performances.

The combined Luiseño storytelling and community outreach program has a series of interdependent goals. First, the program strives to teach local tribal youth stories approved by the Rincon Culture Committee and recognized by their community. Second, the program seeks to create a bridge of cultural sharing between Rincon elders and RYS students as several community elders participate in the creation of costumes, props, and guidance. Third, the group's off-reservation performances offer members of the nontribal community exposure to local tribal culture.

The RYS director is confident the Rincon Youth Storytellers can grow into a larger organization that will continue to perform regularly. Each year, the Valley Center Pauma School District recognizes the RYS by inviting the group to perform a four-day 'tour' at their school sites for California Indian Day. Since 2005, RYS's yearly performance schedule has grown from 5 performances a year to 13. In addition, the students repeatedly ask if they could increase their commitment from one to two or more days a week. Parents assist with production of the plays by helping make costumes and driving youth to practice and performances.

From 2006 to 2010, the Rincon Youth Storytellers program has been funded by local elder donations and limited resources provided by the senior committee and the Rincon Indian Education Center, Inc., which continues to furnish the RYS with a classroom; provide, an office for director, Ami Admire; and continues a fiscal line item to house their donations from elders, private citizens, and fundraising. Since 2010, the director, Ami Admire, has been volunteering her time. The development of additional funding will ensure the continued success of these current and future projects and enable the support of new and existing storytellers as they cultivate skills that will prepare them for the 2015–2016 seasons and beyond.

The RYS fill a role in the community that was missing—active storytelling. People play *peon* (a traditional gambling game) and sing songs, but nobody tells traditional stories. The youth are learning more than how to tell or perform a story. They are learning the purpose and function of the storyteller's role in the community. To enact a story properly, the youth must seek permission from elders who guide them in determining what is appropriate to share with the community. There are some stories and songs taught to the students, but the students do not share these because they are meant only for the tribal community to hear and see. The students learn respect and how to be mindful of cultural traditions, their value, and their meaning.

Luiseño people use storytelling as a way to pass down their beginnings, customs, history, and heritage. It was and is a way to pass down how to live in our environment, how to explain everyday natural occurrences, and how to survive in our homelands. As Luiseños explored their land, storytelling became an important tool. Storytelling provides an oral map or guide to religion, customs, and beliefs. Through storytelling, Luiseño tribes shared, preserved, and paid tribute to their early beginnings, so future generations could continue their legacy.

RYS is strengthening cultural identity and self-esteem through story telling.

> People become the stories they hear and the stories they tell. By telling our Luiseño stories we become stronger in our mind, body, and spirit. People will ask who you are and you will answer, "I am the story of myself." You must know the story of the people before you. (Patricia Duro, Luiseño elder, personal interview, May 15, 2017)

SOUTHERN CALIFORNIA TRIBAL CHAIRMEN'S ASSOCIATION RESOURCE PROGRAM AND HIGH SCHOOL GRADUATION CELEBRATION

Southern California Tribal Chairmen's Association (SCTCA) operates numerous programs to benefit their 18 member tribes in the region. Their programs are mostly focused on social economic development.

The annual SCTCA high school graduation celebration is one of the most successful intertribal events in the Southern California region. The resource center program and a committee of tribal leaders from the consortium organize it. The event provides the tribal leadership of each community an opportunity to recognize their high school graduates with an eagle feather. The feather is a symbol of a life achievement and is provided in a public forum for the entire community to recognize the individual student. The feather is for the students to remember their hard work, to be proud of their culture, and know that they have the many more years to continue their success. Students and their family are invited to attend the event. Each tribal leader presents the graduates with an eagle feather from their tribe. This event has been held continuously for the last 20 years and is highly anticipated by the youth and tribal leaders. The first celebration had 12 graduates in 1995, and the event has grown to an average of 110 graduates from the SCTCA member tribes. It is an event that is highly anticipated by the graduates and their families to attend and celebrate their milestone achievement. SCTCA and other tribal organizations provide competitive education awards and scholarships at the event to students that choose to continue their education after high school. This event is sponsored by tribal donations.

INTERTRIBAL YOUNG MEN'S CAMP

The Intertribal Young Men's Camp was started in 2014 by a group of invested community members both men and women. Members represent the Indian Health Clinic, Inc., Southern California Tribal Chairmen's Association, Palomar Community College, the Rincon Indian Education Center, the Pala Band of Mission Indians, the Pauma Band of Luiseño Indians, the San Pasqual Band of Mission Indians, La Jolla Band of Luiseño Indians, and the Rincon Band of Luiseño Indians.

The first annual Intertribal Young Men's Camp was completed with much success in the summer of 2015 at Del Mar beach on the Camp Pendleton military base. The camp focused on young men's health and wellness, future careers, and cultural knowledge and awareness, along with promoting healthy and positive interaction between tribal communities. The youth were chaperoned by 10 positive adult male role models and mentors from our local tribal communities. The goal of the programs is to have the youth collaborate as a team and to have an educational and memorable experience.

The program was a two-night interactive oceanfront campout. The activities included male bonding by traditional ways of coming of age through stories and songs as well as mental, physical, and spiritual balance to lead a productive and healthy life with all native male speakers. The youth took ownership of the camp by preparing their own meals, setting up the campsite, and maintaining it for the weekend. One speaker spoke about physical fitness, and his speech was followed by an obstacle course that was overseen by active Marines. Another speaker shared his personal experience about drugs and gang life and how he has changed his life around and now teaches native youth to make good choices and how to avoid negative obstacles. Fun mentoring activities included learning how to read the tides, observe currents, and learn how to surf. The young men learned about the traditional areas on the base and their traditional names and places.

All of the youth completed evaluations at the end of the camp, and all reported that they had a very enjoyable time and would return again. One sixteen-year-old student was quoted as saying, "The best time I ever had during a summer trip" (H. Turner, interview, August 7, 2015). The camp provided the first opportunity for many of the youth to explore the cultural life and activities offered. This program was financially supported by private donations from tribes and tribal agencies. The committee is excited about the success of the camp and hope it will become annual and larger event. They hope to include more neighboring tribes in the next year's camp.

CONCLUSION

The educational and cultural programs in Southern California tribal communities are successful because they integrate culturally responsive course materials and resources that link traditional knowledge into the curriculum and into the life skill development for the students. The use of tribal art, history, language, geography, literature, and science infuses the educational experience to meet the needs of American Indian students. The students are learning how to navigate among other Indigenous nations and in the larger non-Indian world. All of the program examples provided in this chapter are cross-cultural and collaborative efforts among multiple tribal organizations and intergenerational community members. The programs aim to support the student to become whole and to balance life in two worlds while they are living in contemporary homes, having access to media and technology, and living with new information about traditional life that was taught in earlier generations. These programs are working to combine these two worlds by incorporating technology into their programs with culture and language.

Parents play an important role in the programs by providing input that they did not feel comfortable voicing outside of their community before. The programs allow parents to be involved in their children's education and become educational leaders in their communities. All of the programs in this chapter view parents as partners in providing an education to their students; they are their children's first teachers. This advocacy has also encouraged many parents to return to school and learn more about their language and culture.

These programs have been structured through innovative tribal people who incorporate tribal views, values, heritage, and culture through building pride in education, cultural teachings, and maintaining tribal sovereignty for generations to come.

The authors of this chapter are siblings who were raised on the Rincon Indian Reservation in San Diego County by parents who were activists for Indian self-determination and education beginning in the early 1970s. Their children carry on this activist legacy today as leaders in Indian education in their own tribal community, in the state, and in the nation.

REFERENCES

All Tribes American Indian Charter School (2010). *High school senior exit survey.* Rincon Reservation, CA: Author.

Cornell, S., Kalt, J. P., Begay, M. A., Jr. (2008). The state of Native nations: Conditions under U.S. policies of self-determination. New York, NY: Oxford University Press.

Gelles, P. (2013). *Chumash renaissance: Indian casinos, education, and cultural politics in rural California.* Santa Barbara, CA: Solitude Canyon Press.

The Hechinger Report. (n.d.). Education By the Numbers. Retrieved from http://educationbythenumbers.org/content/california-student-teacher-ratio-highest-country_572/D

Hinton, L., & Hale, K. (Ed.). (2008). *The green book of language revitalization in practice.* Bingley, England: Emerald Group.

National Center for Education Statistics. (2016). Elementary and secondary education: School characteristics and climate. In International Center for Education Statistics (Eds.), *The condition of education 2016* (pp. 126–128). Retrieved from https://nces.ed.gov/programs/coe/pdf/coe_clr.pdf

Proudfit, J., & Gregor, T. (2014). *The state of American Indian and Alaska Native education in California.* San Marcos, CA: California Indian Culture and Sovereignty Center, CSUSM: Creative Commons Attribution Non-Commercial-ShareAlike 4.0 International License.

CHAPTER 16

EDUCATIONAL RESEARCH

Using a Health-Based Model

Deborah J. Morton
Departments of Public Health and American Indian Studies,
California State University San Marcos

Tribal groups work tirelessly to maintain sovereignty rights, preserving and upholding tribal authority and protection over their land, people, businesses, cultures, and services, such as healthcare and education. Research conducted by individuals or groups without tribal oversight has produced unethical or misguided findings that have the potential for negative impact in Indian country. In California, the efforts of a tribally based institutional review board (IRB), particularly in the field of health sciences, has had a dramatic effect on the research agenda, building capacity for new research collaborations, methodologies, application of beneficial results, and protection of tribal communities in the world of peer-reviewed published papers and their dissemination.

On Indian Ground: California, pages 223–231
Copyright © 2017 by Information Age Publishing
All rights of reproduction in any form reserved.

INSTITUTIONAL REVIEW BOARDS (IRBS)

The use of a tribally based IRB for research in education has not been widely used, if at all, as these studies are typically created and governed by research protocols from institutions of higher education. While these institutions have policies and procedures that reflect an awareness of the need to protect human subjects, these same offices rarely have specific protocols for American Indians/Alaska Natives (AI/AN). In California, there are no state institutions with tribally specific protocols. The University of Arizona has been at the forefront of the development and inclusion of tribally specific IRBs for state institutions (Firebaugh, Fox, & Williams, 2016). These efforts are likely the result of the State's response to the lawsuit by the Havasupai Tribe against Arizona State University and the misuse of health research in the Grand Canyon (NCAI, 2016).

In the world of health and medical research in California, it is not only wise but prudent to create and to locate a tribally based IRB at a health clinic. As sovereign nations, tribal communities have the responsibility to regulate research on their lands. Clinics in the state are all tribally owned and operated by tribal consortiums without much interference from governmental institutions as there are no Indian health service clinics or hospitals. Tribal clinics are models of the repositioning of healthcare practices that incorporate traditional healing alongside Western medical practices—examples of tribal sovereignty at its best.

Clinic administrators are anxious to secure extramural funding for various medical and health-related research that can benefit their patient population as well as bring in needed revenue. Clinic professional staff are knowledgeable regarding the overlap of tribally specific health issues and behavioral correlates and can provide invaluable input for any health-related research protocols and interpretation of results. Clinics serve as tribal gathering and activity centers for the community, thus naturally facilitating recruitment for research subjects. The success of research projects that have traditionally been avoided by the community due to shared historical knowledge of past abuses by academic health and medical scientists is expanded. Trust is enhanced. Members of the IRB committee itself are clinic administrators, professional staff, or active members of the tribal communities that own the clinic and serve as knowledgeable research ambassadors for all projects. These IRB members create legitimacy for the larger community due to their IRB education and experience and, once again, foster recruitment to meet project goals.

Tribal health IRBs are more easily facilitated if there is collaboration with local academic and health research institutions. At least one tribal IRB member needs to be an academic scientist and an Indian or, if not, a nontribal academic scientist with Indian country experience. These scientists foster the exchange of tribal versus institutional research methodologies, making it possible for the movement of Western academic institutionalized research pedagogy towards a more integrated and tribally empowered model of health research.

Modifications of traditional academic IRB policies and procedures for tribal IRBs must be made. The Navajo IRB requires researchers to spend one year visiting the various chapter houses of the Navajo Nation before they can conceive or design a project, let alone submit an IRB application (ACI, 2008). Time-wise, this is a long commitment prior to initiating a proposal, but this requirement leaves no doubt the Navajo Nation will not permit research that is not fully respectful, appropriate, and needed from an insider's perspective.

CULTURALLY RESPECTFUL RESEARCH

Research in Indian country must be held accountable and must be respectful of tribal belief systems. In keeping with this concept, the California tribal IRB previously discussed has several unique requirements that are not present in academic institutional IRBs. First and most importantly, the tribal IRB supports clinic decisions regarding strategic planning and thus the board of the tribal health consortium regarding the present and future research agenda. Scientific researchers coming from various sources may or may not be sensitive to inherent tribal ways of knowing and believing and their ideas regarding the focus of specific research projects may not be of benefit or interest from a tribal lens. The IRB has the power to say no to any research project not discussed with clinic administrators prior to securing funding, or when funding has been secured, that is not deemed relevant by the IRB.

Secondly, methodological flaws that may be tribally inappropriate in research proposals can also be avoided as the IRB committee is made up of cultural experts who have the power to suggest modifications. A mechanism for direct interaction of the IRB committee and the investigator is provided. Again, this does not happen in the traditional scientific academic IRB arena. These exchanges further more than confidence in the specific project; they serve to promote real conversation, collaboration, and resolution across both academic and tribal misconceptions.

The issue of data access and ownership is of major concern for tribal communities. When data are shared with researchers outside of the original research project investigators, it is difficult to control how those data are used and interpreted. The California tribal IRB requires that all datasets produced in a research project must be returned to the clinic after completion. This requirement allows the clinic to maintain control over all future uses of the dataset. Datasets returned must be in the form of a clean, aggregate, de-identified file ready for analysis. Scientific researchers agree to support this policy before final IRB approval is initially given and are allowed to retain a copy of the research dataset as long as a copy is also given to the tribal clinic. Such a requirement allows for future use of the dataset, such as making new comparisons and trend analyses through time as well as possible new applications. Such capacity can only serve the long-term benefit of the clinic and its health service delivery.

Another policy of the California IRB reflects the importance of notice for informed consent documents. Informed consent allow subjects to know their role, their rights, and how their personal, private health-related information will be used along with how confidentiality and anonymity will be maintained. Small tribes with small datasets are at higher risk of breaches in confidentiality than larger tribes with larger datasets or aggregate data from many tribes when final results are disseminated. The IRB policy requires that all informed consent documents must be read aloud to the participants before they sign their names. Moreover, in many instances, the informed consent documents, already approved by a university/institution IRB before application to the tribal IRB, require editing by the tribal IRB. Language needs to be less technical and readily comprehensible as well as condensed enough so the informed consent can be read aloud in a reasonable timeframe. This requirement, which has become well accepted by researchers, promotes trust and confidence among hesitant participants as well as members of the tribal IRB in their job to protect their people.

The California clinic IRB aids in the prevention of helicopter research, the practice of using minority communities as resources for data for personal gain, but never giving anything back—basically flying over, hovering, extracting what is personally needed, then flying off, never to return. The California IRB researchers are required to present progress reports and findings on a yearly basis back to the local tribal community for representatives from the tribal consortium board of directors to view, to interact, and to ask questions of the researchers. This venue of communication is another opportunity for academic scientists to exchange ideas and findings with the tribal community thus creating more trust and allowing tribal members to get to individually know and experience the minds and hearts of academic scientists—and vice versa.

IRB committee members are a subset of the local tribes; therefore, they have a personal and community stake in the project and are able to direct their opinions concerning any research project through the mechanism of the tribal IRB. IRB members represent the tribal health board and rule on behalf of that body regarding any research conducted in their tribes. They stand as the legitimate authority, thus purveying a level of trust in the project that is passed to the tribal community at large.

A tribal IRB may be thought of as its own distinctive focus group. Backed with cultural authority, IRB members are the first to encounter a fully developed research proposal and can give their opinions/concerns back to the investigator, similar to a focus group. Furthermore, they significantly increase their knowledge of survey construction and scientific methods and learn the creative expertise needed to write useful and appropriate questions needed to elicit the information being sought. IRB members themselves may decide to become volunteer subjects and support recruitment and legitimization when asked by family and friends about a research project being discussed through the tribal grapevine.

Finally, an extremely important requirement placed on researchers by the California tribal IRB is that all draft manuscripts must be reviewed prior to submission for possible publication in a peer reviewed journal, a chapter in a book, a published interview about the research, or any other print material created about the research project. Again, this policy does not exist in traditional academic institutions. No tribal names or Indian clinic names are allowed in the manuscript. However, pseudonyms can be created for tribal clinics or any other organization. Any statements that may cause potential harm or cast a negative light on the tribal community, regardless of what part of the research results are being discussed, cannot be reported in the manuscript. This practice may seem akin to censorship of results, but in practice it prevents again what happened in Havasupai where the tribe was damaged by published papers reporting schizophrenic gene rates and new ideas regarding origin stories in their population (Andrews, 2004). The IRB has legitimate tribal power, authority, and credibility to ensure published research does not weaken or hurt their tribe in any way, thus protecting future appropriate research and associated benefits for the entire tribe. If this power did not exist, it would defeat the purpose of an IRB in the first place.

Based upon the federal requirements of the office of human research protection, a tribally based, managed, and operated IRB can be a valuable asset delivering long-term comprehensive benefits. Federal registration and adherence to federal rules and regulations associated with ethical research practices has no set-up costs and can be managed with limited administrative costs and dedicated tribal advocates. Members of other tribal governing boards or committees can be assigned to the IRB for either long or short terms. Training can be handled with minimal costs by academically prepared tribal members or outside scientific collaborators. New open attitudes and exchanges of understanding and collaboration between scientists and tribes promote trust and benefit from new and innovative research in many arenas. New tribal IRBs forging new levels of trust and commitment with academic partners can only lead to pioneering projects in every field of research as they provide the ethical compass for decision making.

EDUCATIONAL RESEARCH NEXT STEPS

Educational research, in communities that value intersecting relationships, often means that health, education, and economics intersect, creating perspectives framed by individual tribal cultures and languages. As tribes become more sophisticated about governance and relationships with outside agencies, several questions arise that need careful consideration for your community.

Would it make sense to establish a tribally based IRB for educational research alone in Indian country? Yes, of course. But where could it be located? Who would serve as IRB members? What IRB protocol would be need modification to make it more relevant for educational topics and simultaneously tribally sound? Is there an existing relationship with an academic institution to create the impetus, the collaborative agenda, and the new personal relationships needed? Research in education investigates an absolute plethora of topics, behaviors, learning theories, the latest developments in neurologic development and cognitive knowing as well as traditional/indigenous ways of acquiring knowledge, storytelling, oral traditions, and culturally based ways of teaching outside of the mainstream classic classrooms of Western education. All of these considerations require thoughtful decision-making.

And it is equally important that we work with those tribal communities who wish to engage in research to ensure that the "best practices," such as the health model, are reviewed and revised appropriately.

CALIFORNIA AMERICAN INDIAN/ALASKA NATIVE RESEARCH

A review of research on American Indians/Alaska Natives in California reveals that minimal data on this population are available to educators. The most significant research recent reports are issued by the California Indian Culture and Sovereignty Center. These reports, listed below, provide the following data:

- 2012: *State of American Indian/Alaska Native Education in California*. This report compiled data on American Indians and Alaska Native in K–12, community college, California State University and University of California systems. The data include enrollment, graduation rates, dropout rates, degrees conferred, and personnel.
- 2014: *State of American Indian/Alaska Native Education in California*. This report determines where enrollment and transfer numbers are decreasing or increasing to determine what best practices are

available in postsecondary institutions to attract, to retain, and to graduate AI/AN students. Enrollment rates are declining across the California systems. This report highlights American Indian Centers across the state.

- 2016: *State of American Indian/Alaska Native Education in California*: This report provides a case study for the creation of a 21st century model for public universities. The report also mapped the K–12 data for high school graduation rates, dropout rates, and student completion of A-G requirements for college entry. This report is linked interactively on the web using GIS.

These three reports comprise the most comprehensive review of educational data on American Indians/Alaska Natives in California currently available (California Indian Culture and Sovereignty Center, 2016).

Research at the doctoral level in education that specifically focuses on American Indians/Alaska Natives is representative of the following:

- Sandoval's (2007) *Bridging Generations: American Indian Family Perceptions of Home/School Partnerships* examines families on a California Indian reservation.
- Medina's (2007) *Selling Indians at Sherman Institute, 1902–1922* is a historical look at California's Bureau of Indian Affairs boarding school.
- Berry's (2008) *Hearing Their Voices: College Experiences of Urban American Indian Women* describes community college participation.
- Lentis' (2011) *Art Education in American Indian Boarding Schools: Tool of Assimilation, Tool of Resistance* again looks at Sherman Indian School.
- Williams' (2012) *Schooling Experiences of Central California Indian People Across Generations* documents educational practices among American Indians California's Central Valley across generations.
- Casper-Denman's (2013) *California Indian Education Association: Working Towards Educational Sovereignty* discusses the push to educational sovereignty and the creation of this association.
- Lorimer's (2013) *Reconstructing the Past: Historical Interpretations and Native Experiences at Contemporary California Missions* examines "revisionist" history and the role of missions in indigenous education.
- Blalock's (2013) dissertation *Culturally Sustaining Pedagogies: Understanding School Practices and the Academic Achievement of American Indian and Alaska Native Students through a Multidisciplinary Lens* analyzes the relationship between culture and schooling.

- Mendoza's (2014) *Influences and Life Circumstances Guiding Native American Students to Pursue Higher Education* uses semistructured interviews to explore persistence.
- Whalen's (2014) *Beyond School Walls: Race, Labor and Indian Education in Southern California, 1902–1940* documents the "outing system" or the work program sponsored by federal boarding schools.
- Stahl-Kovell's (2014) *Reimagining Red Power: Native American Community, Activism, and Academics in Postwar America* is a historical analysis of the Red Power Movement and its connection to Native American studies in higher education throughout California.

These studies reflect recent analyses of educational practices over a wide range of subjects and tribal perspectives.

DISSEMINATION OF RESEARCH

The final caution is one that is reflected in Warner's (2013) essay "Research as Activism." Without wide distribution of research findings, the work, the effort, the findings may sit on shelves. The incorporation of Indigenous research methodologies and the publication of studies using these need to impact mainstream venues for research. Tribal needs and goals are best met if we share our research widely so that tribal communities can change. The ability to publish in academic and scientific journals is important, but we also have access to wide distribution on the Internet. Tribes are well positioned to own their own research agenda and to make relevant decisions about dissemination of those findings.

REFERENCES

Andrews, L. (2004, Winter). *Havasupai tribe sues genetic researchers.* Louisville, KY: University of Louisville School of Medicine.

Arizona Cooperative Extension. (2008). *Process of conducting research on the Navajo Nation.* Retrieved from http://extension.arizona.edu/sites/extension.arizona.edu/files/pubs/az1472.pdf

Berry, L. C. (2008). *Hearing their voices: College experiences of urban American Indian women* (Doctoral Dissertation). Retrieved from ProQuest Dissertations and Theses.

Blalock, N. R. (2013). *Culturally sustaining pedagogies: Understanding school practices and the academic achievement of American Indian and Alaska Native students through a multidisciplinary lens* (Doctoral dissertation). Retrieved from ProQuest Dissertations and Theses.

California Indian Culture and Sovereignty Center. (2016). State of American Indian/Alaska Native Education Reports. Retrieved from http://www.csusm.edu/cicsc/projects/education-report.html

Casper-Denman, K. (2013). *California Indian Education Association: Working towards educational sovereignty* (Doctoral dissertation). Retrieved from ProQuest Dissertations and Theses.

Firebaugh, E. L., Fox, M. J., & Williams, C. (2016). Responsible and ethical research in Indian Country. Retrieved from http://courses.ais.arizona.edu/content/responsible-and-ethical-research-indian-country

Lentis, M. (2011). *Art education in American Indian boarding schools: Tools of assimilation, tool of resistance* (Doctoral dissertation). Retrieved from ProQuest Dissertations and Theses.

Lorimer, M. M. (2013). *Reconstructing the past: Historical interpretations and native experiences at contemporary California missions* (Doctoral dissertation). Retrieved from ProQuest Dissertations and Theses.

Medina, W. O. (2007). Selling *Indians at Sherman Institute, 1902–1922* (Doctoral dissertation). Retrieved from ProQuest Dissertations and Theses.

Mendoza, M. (2014). Influences *and life circumstances guiding Native American students to pursue higher education.* (Doctoral dissertation) Retrieved from ProQuest Dissertations and Theses.

National Congress of American Indians. (n.d.). Havasupai Tribe and the lawsuit settlement aftermath. Retrieved from http://genetics.ncai.org/case-study/havasupai-Tribe.cfm

Sandoval, N. I. (2007). *Bridging generations: American Indian family perceptions of home/school partnerships* (Doctoral dissertation). Retrieved from ProQuest Dissertations and Theses.

Stahl-Kovell, D. W. (2014). *Reimagining red power: Native American community, activism, and academics in postwar America* (Doctoral dissertation). Retrieved from ProQuest Dissertations and Theses.

Warner, L. S. (2013). Research as activism. In P. Boyer & D. Davis (Eds.), Social justice and racism in the college classroom: Perspectives from different voices (pp. 133–150). Dulles, VA: Emerald Group.

Whalen, K. P. (2014). *Beyond school walls: Race, labor, and Indian education in Southern California, 1902, 1940* (Doctoral dissertation). Retrieved from ProQuest Dissertations and Theses.

Williams, T. (2012). *Schooling experiences of Central California Indian people across generations* (Doctoral dissertation). Retrieved from ProQuest Dissertations and Theses.

CHAPTER 17

CALIFORNIA URBAN INDIAN EDUCATION

Linda Sue Warner
California Indian Culture and Sovereignty Center

URBAN INDIANS

Somlai (2004, p. 16) noted that it "is of no value to maintain a definition of urban Indian culture as an involuntary melting of Indian and Western worldviews, as this at once denies the conscious actions of individuals, as well as continues to contrast Indian vs. Western, traditional vs. modern, backwards vs. assimilated." In large urban areas, where American Indians were relocated post-World War II, the tribal community is typically physically located in one region, as ethnic groups tend to live and work within segregated areas. Within these regions, traditions, relationships, and lifestyles are specific to the culture/s which, for American Indians, are similar and yet quite different. Intertribal marriages contribute to the creation of an "urban" Indian community that has layers of nuanced behaviors, including those of the majority community within which they live. Fixico (2000) defines urban Indians as "Native Americans who moved to cities and to border towns, and who experienced urban life" (p. x). The definition must also include the children and grandchildren of those who were relocated from Indian country.

On Indian Ground: California, pages 233–241
Copyright © 2017 by Information Age Publishing
All rights of reproduction in any form reserved.

Lucero (2010) uses two criteria for defining the urban Indian. First, the respondent must "identify as an American Indian adult who had lived since childhood in an urban area, away from the reservation or a tribal community" (p. 329). The participant must also "self-identify as having a strong and positive cultural identity" (p. 329). These definitions, often overlapping, serve to highlight the diversity in identity, in a population that struggles with identity issues surrounding who is American Indian.

In 1961, a low budget docudrama chronicled the lives of three American Indians over a period of twelve hours in a downtown Los Angeles neighborhood. *The Exiles,* representing a 1950s perspective from American Indians who had recently migrated from their reservations to Los Angeles, reflected a major shift in the city's evolution at the end of World War II (Winchell & Zonn, 2012). Los Angeles was the more important relocation destination, and by 1960 it had the largest urban concentration of American Indians in the country (Nabokov, 1992). The BIA's Voluntary Relocation Program encouraged reservation Indians to move to urban areas; California Indians were relocated to the Midwest and East, and California became home to approximately 70,000 Indians from other states (UCLA American Indian Studies Center, n.d.). Education programs suffered extensively with this policy change.

Blackhawk's (1995) depictions of early removal stresses "disparate communities with unique historical conditions and societal organization" often with vastly divergent "cultural systems and community experiences" (p. 16) as they sought to navigate a new identity amid the country's policies of American Indian urbanization and migration to Los Angeles specifically. Blackhawk notes that his research indicates that Los Angeles urbanization linked well over 100 tribes. This relocation effort is an early urban education experiment as it was part of the Bureau of Indian Affairs Adult Vocational Training program (AVT)—the second iteration of the BIA relocation program whose specific intent was cultural assimilation. The relocation program began in the 1950s and continued through AVT until the mid 1970s.

By the late 1970s, one of California's largest Indian education projects provided services to exceptional education students in Ventura United School District. This district had more than 20 tribes represented in the 20 elementary schools, four junior highs, and three senior high schools. Ventura United School District leadership, forty miles north of Los Angeles, supported the Indian Self-Determination Education Assistance Act (1975) by beginning a K–12 program designed to provide special activities in language arts, speech therapy, reading, cultural enrichment, and counseling. In addition, the district included summer school, which focused on enrichment rather than academics. The active involvement of the Indian parent committee assured that the intent of self-determination was met (Fendrick, 2001).

AMERICAN INDIAN IDENTITY

Pewewardy (1998) asserted that Indian people can "define ourselves in our own terms and our tribal languages" (p. 70) and linked identity to a process, specifically, *becoming*. Personal identity is one's self-perceived central, or distinguishing, characteristics. Characteristics associated with personal identity might include gender, religion, race/ethnicity, as long as the individual perceives these characteristics as variables that are important in defining him or her. Even the nomenclature for identifying those who call themselves American Indian or Native American is debated often. Pewewardy (1998) cautioned that tribal identity is a personalized process that is influenced by legal and political considerations, psychosocial factors, proximity or access to a given culture, socialization, and one's own sensibility.

American Indian identity is perhaps more complex than that of other groups, comprising the following:

- A political/legal status (federal statutes, enrollment, state requirements)
- Social/cultural (ethnicity)
- Psychological/developmental (Indian heart, self-concept, sense of "I")
- Biological/ancestry (heritage, lineage)[1]

The transformation of Indian identity can be found in each of these domains. In 2001, Liebeler's work on multiracial identification examined the "fringes" of American Indian identity asserting that many individual may legitimately claim more than one race. Typically, the predictors of a child's racial identification involved the identity characteristics of the American Indian parent. Such identifiers include tribe, ancestry, and language use and physical location of the household. Dis/incentives for claiming to be American Indian often fluctuate, perhaps as resources change. Recent census growth in self-identified American Indians has broadened identity boundaries for determining "Indianness" (Table 17.1).

There is a broad range of descriptors for the definition of the American Indian. For purposes of the census, the U.S. Census Bureau counts anyone an Indian who declares himself or herself to be such. Census data since 1960 highlights the complexity of identity self-designation for American Indians that is particularly pronounced in multitribal urban areas. Gonzales (1998) notes that a substantial definition of American Indian is the result of early anthropologists who portrayed American Indians as static, rigidly bound, and identifiable entities based on "observable characteristics of physiognomy, language, religion, customs, behaviors, and material culture" (p. 201)— essentially a model that has no relevance to contemporary urban Indians. To be eligible for Bureau of Indian Affairs (BIA) services, an Indian must (1) be a member of a tribe recognized by the federal government and (2) must, for

TABLE 17.1 Conceptual Framework for Defining the Definition of American Indian

Scientific/Biological	Political/Legal	Social/Cultural	Psychological
Blood, blood quantum, descendency, lineage, ancestors	Tribal enrollment, enrolled, enrollable, tribal member, registered	Culture, knowing the ways, values/beliefs, language, living on the reservation, family ties, ceremonies	Indian heart, my identity, knowing I am Indian, feel(ing) Indian

some purposes, be of one-fourth or more Indian ancestry. By legislative and administrative decision, the Aleuts, Eskimos, and Indians of Alaska are eligible for BIA services. The need for specific definitions of American Indian identity are the historical baggage of treaty negotiation and land acquisition in the United States. Today the federal government recognizes Indian tribes as groups that Congress or the executive branch have created a reservation for by treaty, agreement, statute, executive order or valid administrative action. Since the 1960s, the American Indian population has been increasingly made up of mixed-blood Indians. Urban Indians, with continued high rates of intermarriage, will result in larger numbers of self-identified in the 21st century. But regardless of who determines legal tribal membership, the American Indian holds two distinct places in American iconography. First, they represent the only minority group that nonminority people want to identify with, going so far as to claim relationships based on a story of tribal heritage that is only marred by the fact that someone in their lineage refused to be counted by the government. Second, they are the only minority group in the United States with sovereign status—members of nations within a nation, governed by federal laws and regulations. The issues of Indian identity are complicated by more than society perspectives and personal needs; legitimate identity issues affect jurisdictions, resource allocations, including Indian health benefits, and taxation for a start. For urban Indians, removed from traditional homelands, these issues only get more complex.

BIE PROGRAMS IN CALIFORNIA

The Bureau of Indian Education (BIE) operates an off-reservation boarding high school in Riverside, CA, and funds Noli School in San Jacinto, CA. The University of California–Los Angeles reports that the United States Department of Interior funds California education at $4,589,488, an estimate of $100.72 per capita. Sherman Indian High School (SIHS, n.d.) is the only urban Indian school funded by the BIE in California.

The mission of the SIHS has changed since its inception early the last century. Founded as an agricultural and trade school, Sherman evolved into a comprehensive high school in order to better meet the needs of all Native American youth. In 1970, Sherman was accredited as a secondary school accepting student from across the nation. Sherman was initially accredited as a comprehensive high school in 1995 by the Western Association for Schools and Colleges (WASC). The school enrollment has steadily declined and currently is between 400 and 500 students from the Western United States.

Urban American Indian student survival is grounded in education and, as such, needs to be reflected in current practice. Through illustrations of urban Indian culture, Shinahora (2014) broadens the definition of education and moves it outside of the typical institutional setting to include participation in all things considered cultural or traditional to American Indians. With this wider definition, the education of urban Indians moves to local community groups where cultural protocols and perspectives are taught by parents and community members. Education, in this manner, reflects the historical context where American Indians were taught by elders and for urban Indians, this is as close an approximation as can be found. Shinahora notes that this is actively supported by tutoring and counseling for students who wish to continue their education.

The vision and mission of the Southern California Indian Center (SCIC) is "There is Future in Tradition." The SCIC provides education and socioeconomic services to over 230,000 Native Americans representing more than 250 tribes in Los Angeles County, Orange County, Riverside County, and Kern County (Southern California Indian Center, n.d.). The SCIC is typical of the types of services provided by an urban Indian center that often include education services. Urban school districts with larger enrollments of American Indian/Alaska Native students rely on federally set-aside funding for programming. The services provided by programs, such as Johnson–O'Malley or impact aid, are minimal and often do not impact the day-to-day delivery of services in the classroom.

JOHNSON–O'MALLEY IN CALIFORNIA

California was the first state to receive funds under the Johnson–O'Malley (JOM) act of 1934. In the 1950s, The BIA began to phase out California JOM support. This support lapsed until 1969. Support for JOM in California remains hampered by eligibility and tribal jurisdictional statistical areas, primarily as a result of the urbanization of tribal people in California, in contrast with other states where school districts are primarily rural or reservation.

The Johnson–O'Malley Act of 1934 was passed to subsidize education to American Indians living within their borders. Today, the program's purpose is primarily to assist in efforts designed to meet the specialized and unique educational needs of American Indian students (Northern California Indian Development Council, n.d.). School districts must establish an Indian Education Committee (IEC), primarily parents or guardians of American Indian students enrolled in the district; the committee will have authority to participate fully in the planning, development, implementation, and evaluation of supplemental and operational programs in the district. In addition, the IEC has specific authority to "recommend:

- Curricula, texts, materials, and teaching methods
- Criteria for employment in the program
- Qualified prospective educational programmatic staff members
- Appropriate action to the contractor
- Cancellation or suspension of a contract, if the contractor fails to permit such Committee to exercise its powers and duties.

Parent committees have the authority to approve and disapprove all programs to be contracted, including approval of the budget, and these actions are required to be part of the official minutes of the parent committee. These limited safeguards are in place because of the historical misuse of monies allocated to school districts for American Indian/Alaska Native students.

The Indian education committee or parent organization may establish additional safeguards that include position descriptions and detailed descriptions of duties in the bylaws of their organization. Any additional responsibilities are negotiated with the local school district. The types of additional services that are often included are:

- Making an annual assessment of the learning needs of Indian children in the community affected
- Having access to all reports, evaluations, surveys, and other documents to carry out its responsibilities
- Requesting periodic reports and evaluations
- Meeting regularly with school district administration
- Holding regular committee meetings, open to the public

Second, in conjunction with the Indian education committee, the school must formulate an educational plan that outlines the programmatic and fiscal services and includes:

- Educational goals and objectives that adequately address the educational needs

- State standards and requirements and how standards will be met and maintained
- Provisions that education facilities be open to visits and consultations by the IEC, Indian parents, and federal government representatives
- Include budget estimates and financial information needed to determine program costs
- Procedures and methods to be used in achieving program objectives
- Overall program implementation: staff practices, parental and community involvement, evaluation of program results and dissemination
- Determination of staff and program effectiveness in meeting stated needs of target students

AN URBAN INDIAN SCHOOL MODEL FOR REFORM

The model for urban Indian education in public schools in the United States has been that of a magnet school. Schools in Buffalo, NY and St. Paul, Minneapolis made great progress using these models under the leadership of capable, qualified American Indian administrators in the 1970s and 1980s. By the turn of the century, the retirement or replacement of most of these administrators interrupted the pace of urban Indian education. Regardless of the success or failures of past initiatives, it is clear that there is a need for a clearly articulated vision for urban schools with students of American Indian/Alaska Native/Native Hawaiian descent. In spite of these efforts, there is no hallmark for urban Indian education in California. If we value the culture, language, and traditions these students represent, and if we expect these urban students to be able to reflect on their knowledge as positive learning experiences, it is vital that we rethink the current models and assess their impact as well as their potential.

An overview of the scholarly work on curriculum and instruction since 1970 indicates a real advocacy for incorporation of culture, language, tradition, and spirituality in schools serving American Indian students. This is seen most in the writings of American Indian educators whose scholarship has increased significantly in these 30 years. This advocacy parallels the writings and philosophy of mainstream scholars who testify to the benefits of teaching children using what they already know.

Introducing traditional values in an urban school environment may not be an option to a classroom teacher who serves in an institution with multiple races and ethnicities yet also serves a high population of American Indian students. The strategies for lesson building can begin with a cultural value, however, regardless of the classroom situation. Core values are essentially that—core to the well-being of the community. One example of how an urban Indian school has been successful in doing this is the work in a predominately

Northern Woodland region. We used core values that link closely to Ojibwe tribal values. Traditional values are holistic and form a rich framework within which to view native ways of knowing. Taken as a whole, traditional values and beliefs create high expectations and supportive, caring relationships between the student, as learner, and the teacher. These values create a safe and secure place to share cultural practices and tribal knowledge that will support the continued resilience of tribal peoples. Creating such a place in an urban setting required that our energy be directed at the roots of the culture, which meant we had to talk to those culture bearers who knew and understood not only the languages, but the practices.

This strategy is replicated in an urban postsecondary institution in California. In Southern California, the California Indian Culture and Sovereignty Center (CICSC) uses tribal core values from the regional tribes (there are 28 within San Diego County) and 110 throughout the state to create programs and support American Indian students at California State University–San Marcos, a public university. Based on the regional core values, they are have incorporated policies and practices from the following framework. The mission of the center is as follows:

> The CICSC fosters collaborative research and community service relationships between the faculty, staff and students of CCUSM and members of local tribal communities for the purpose of developing and conducting research projects that support the maintenance of sovereignty and culture within those communities. (CICSC, n.d.

This mission is grounded in the core values (Table 17.2) that are reflective of the tribes in this region. Educators who respect and incorporate tribal core values, culture, language, and history in courses delivered to American Indian/Alaska Native students can connect students to their histories and lifestyles using contemporary standards for excellence.

TABLE 17.2 Core Values	
Responsibility (Individual projects supported by extra-mural funding)	To support political and economic development, education, health and wellness, media and film, language preservation, and natural resource management
Reciprocity (presentations/training)	To reinforce collaborative research fostering indigenous research methods
Respect (Original research)	To champion sovereignty and cultural preservation
Relationships (Community Outreach)	To create and sustain communication between tribes and scholars

NOTE

1. This format was derived from Research Focus Group conference call, October 19, 2005.

REFERENCES

Alexie, S., & Burnett, C. (Producer), & Mackenzie, K. (Director). 1961. *The Exiles.* [Motion Picture]. United States: Milestone Films.

Blackhawk, N. (1995). I can carry on from here: The relocation of American Indians to Los Angeles. *Wicazo Sa Review, 11*(2), 16–30.

California Indian Culture and Sovereignty Center (CICSC). (n.d.). Mission. Retrieved from http://www.csusm.edu/cicsc/

Fendrick, M. (2001). Indian education in California: One school district's program. *Education, 102*(1), 43–46.

Fixico, D. L. (2000). *The urban Indian experience in America.* Albuquerque, NM: UNM Press.

Gonzales, A. (1998). The (re) articulation of American Indian identity: Maintaining boundaries and regulating access to ethnically tied resources. *American Indian Culture and Research Journal, 22*(4), 199–225.

Indian Self-Determination Education Assistance Act, 25 U.S.C. § 450b (1975).

Lucero, N. M. (2010). Making meaning of urban American Indian identity: A multistage integrative process. *Social Work, 55*(4), 327–336.

Nabokov, P. (1992). *Reservation to city: Indian migration and federal relocation.* Department of Geography, Research Paper No. 131. Chicago, IL: University of Chicago.

Northern California Indian Development Council. (n.d.). Johnson-O'Malley Program Fact Sheet. Retrieved from http://ncidc.org/education/jomfactsheet

Pewewardy, C. (1998). Fluff and feathers: Treatment of American Indians in the literature and the classroom. *Equity & Excellence, 31*(1), 69–76.

Sherman Indian High School. (n.d.). About us. http://www.sihs.bie.edu/index_files/Page388.htm

Shinohara, A. (2004). *The world of urban Native Americans: People, community and challenges for cultural survival in contemporary Southern California* (Unpublished Master's Thesis). California State University, Fullerton, CA.

Somlai, M. (2004). *Cultural sovereignty: The maintenance and performance of urban community among American Indians* (Unpublished doctoral dissertation). University of Wisconsin, Milwaukee, WI.

Southern California Indian Center. (n.d.). Home page. Retrieved from http://www.indiancenter.org/

UCLA American Indian Studies Center. (n.d.). *Case study in funding inequity: Education.* Retrieved from http://www.aisc.ucla.edu/ca/Tribes9.htm

Winchell, D. G., & Zonn, L. (2012). Urban spaces of American Indians in the exiles. *Geographical Review, 102*(2), 149–165.

CHAPTER 18

ADDRESSING "ANTI-INDIAN" HISTORICAL BIAS IN CALIFORNIA PUBLIC SCHOOLS THROUGH BETTER PRACTICES

Sabine Nicole Talaugon
Iwex Consulting

MOTIVATIONS AND METHODS

In the state of California, K–12 public school curricula often misrepresent and/or underrepresent American Indians history, culture, and governance. These misconceptions perpetuate prejudices about American Indians and Alaskan Natives (AIAN) such as stereotypes and idea that AIAN people are extinct. When society perpetuates stereotypes and misconceptions about a minority population over an extended time, the group often believes the prejudice or stereotype, so when stereotypes about AIAN people are consistently validated through public school curricula, AIAN students begin to accept these negative images (American Indian Education Handbook

On Indian Ground: California, pages 243–261
Copyright © 2017 by Information Age Publishing
All rights of reproduction in any form reserved.

Committee, 1991). For AIAN students, exposure and internalization of these negative images can contribute to a feeling of alienation in the classroom, leading to lower educational attainment (Freng, Freng, & Moore, 2007).

AIAN people are not only an ethnic/racial group, but they have a political and legal status different than other minority groups. The United States government has a fiduciary duty to work with AIAN tribes as sovereign nations and provide services that are responsive to their needs (Getches, Wilkinson, Williams, & Fletcher, 2011). In the past, the United States has systematically sought to assimilate AIAN people into mainstream culture; therefore, changing public school curriculum to accurately portray AIAN people rather than degrade them to prove that American identity is superior is a fundamental change that challenges the patriotic and assimilationist roots of American education.

Currently, much of the material in K–12 public school social science and history curriculum is historically biased. Anti-Indian historical bias occurs because authors of materials want to justify current society and place it in a positive light. This bias is inherited from materials in the past that sought to justify the genocide, indentured servitude, forced relocation and forced educational assimilation of AIAN people. Historical bias has improved over the years, but often persists in the way that materials depict or omit AIAN people's role in United States history and contemporary existence.

Historical bias is one of the reasons that many AIAN students get caught in a cycle of educational failure because they are taught that "Indians" historically were impediments to civilization (Locke & Lindley 2007). Teachers are often not given the resources in their training to teach history and social studies in a way that affirms AIAN contributions to history and society (Freng et al., 2007). Stereotypes about American Indian people have developed in response to the goals and actions of the United States government. The notion that Indigenous people of the land that is now America were inferior and even "childish" compared to European settlers justified the "doctrine of discovery" and "Manifest Destiny" concepts that led to forced and otherwise coerced relocation through treaties and among other destructive policies (Getches et al., 2011). Some of the most degrading stereotypes were created during the Gold Rush and "westward expansion," including the idea that Indians were violent and warlike. Other than attempts to protect their land, homes, and communities, there is no evidence that Indians made unprovoked war upon settlers (Costo & Henry, 1970). This stereotype justified genocidal policies, such as federal troops and agents killing Indians to make land available to settlers, and created the public sentiment that it was honorable for pioneers to kill Indians (Aguirre & Turner, 2010). After most American Indian people were isolated to reservations and other Indian lands, American sentiments towards AIANs retreated back towards the idea of the "noble savage" (American Indian Education Handbook

Committee, 1991). This stereotype serves to dignify AIAN people by discontinuing blatantly genocidal policies, acknowledging that they deserve small portions of land, but that they remain "savages" who need to erase their culture and assimilate into the dominant one.

Historical bias exists because of the way that history and social science texts inherit the sentiments of previous texts. For example, the majority of 19th-century journalists wrote with strong anti-Indian sentiments, using Indian stereotypes. These accounts are often the basis for history research, so the anti-Indian imagery continues in many textbooks (American Indian Education Handbook Committee, 1991). Additionally, materials often present Indigenous people as inferior because social science and history curricula often seeks to justify current society, focus on success, and instill a sense of patriotism (Supahan, 1999). Studies of literature on AIAN representation in textbooks have found that although blatant racist language has been removed, depictions of American Indians still promote stereotypes through omission, misrepresentation, and simplification of information regarding American Indians (Marquez, 2011). Studies of textbooks have found that representation often perpetuates the ideas of inferiority, the "noble savage," and more recently the privileged "casino Indian" (Hawkins, 2005).

For example, many textbooks say that the purpose of Spanish missionaries was to "improve" the lives of native people. This motivation requires that California Indian people's lives needed to be improved, or further, that Indian religions, cultural values, economies, and governing structures needed to be "civilized" by European people. The primary motive of missionaries was not to improve Indians' lives, but to control the natural resources and human capital to build the Spanish empire in America. Life for California Indians was not improved by the mission system; it was jeopardized (Nunez & the California Indian Museum and Cultural Center, 2010). Historical bias is also demonstrated in social science and history curriculum by the invisibility of AIAN experience after the mission era. This omission keeps AIAN people "stuck in time," validating old stereotypes of inferiority and extinction. Historical bias can also lead to tokenization in the classroom. For example, AIAN students may be asked to self-identify during discussion of history involving AIAN people. On these occasions, students who assert their identities may be called into question for "not being a real Indian" and may be expected to know information about all AIAN people under the assumption of a homogeneous Indian culture and history, or may be asked to "perform" or otherwise demonstrate their culture.

By entirely eliminating a history of disenfranchisement, cultural genocide, and assimilation, the status quo limits all students' ability to connect history with current racial stereotypes and prejudices (Locke & Lindley, 2007). Educational communities perform best when students can honor the experiences and contributions of their members, so when a historically biased curriculum is taught, students miss the opportunity to develop common understandings and respect. Furthermore, historical bias can alienate AIAN students, leading to psychological withdrawal from their education and cultural dislocation, thereby lowering their ability to perform to their best capacity and negatively affecting overall AIAN educational attainment (American Indian Education Handbook Committee, 1991).

As we address historical bias, we must recognize that it is a fundamental and somewhat radical change because AIAN people have been historically targeted by explicit and implicit assimilation policies, including forced boarding school attendance (Freng et al., 2007). When educators and advocates of accurate AIAN information consider addressing historical bias, they do not merely seek to replace old curriculum with new curriculum. These advocates seek to "balance" out the bias with supplemental curriculum and provide information that is relevant to performance standards and improving understanding for a better society.

Teachers need the resources to recognize and balance historical bias because solely addressing the socioeconomic status of AIAN students in classrooms does not adequately provide the cultural responsiveness required for AIAN students to excel (Beaulieu, 2006). Multicultural education theory provides a framework for critical reflection.

> *"In order to endorse the national culture, people must see themselves reflected and valued within that culture. We must make all children feel included in our national identity."*
>
> —James Banks (Carjuzaa et al., 2010, p. 193)

Multicultural education theory recognizes that the dominant groups create the social narrative taught in school and argues that teachers should develop a critical lens to teach material (Howard, 2003). It contends that students should learn about the diversity of the world in order to participate in a democratic society. If future citizens are not taught to understand each other, ignorance and misapprehension will negatively affect their economic, political, and social relationships (Carjuzza, Jetty, Munson, & Veltkamp, 2010).

Race-based school achievement data consistently show that African American, Latino, and American Indian and Alaska Native students do not fare well within the current school system. These achievement gaps may persist because of a cultural gap between the curriculum and needs of students of color. By 2020, almost half of the school age children will be students of color (Freng et al., 2007), so it is pertinent that for school systems to embrace multicultural education as a frame for inclusivity in education, which our society touts as the "great equalizer." Multicultural education calls for teachers to construct their lessons in culturally relevant and socially meaningful ways to improve education for these disadvantaged groups (Howard, 2003).

Teachers should learn multicultural education and critical reflection because some may construe building mission diagrams or dressing as pilgrims and Indians for Thanksgiving as "cultural inclusion," when in fact these activities can be degrading to AIAN students. Multicultural education and critical reflection helps teachers realize that there are more appropriate ways to include AIAN experiences in their lessons.

American Indian and Alaskan Native tribes retain sovereignty, or government-to-government status with the U.S. government. The U.S. government also has a fiduciary trust responsibility to tribes. This unique relationship is critical to this analysis because it provides the rationale to change education practices. Through legal and political evolution, tribal government status now means that tribes should be consulted upon matters having to do with Indian lands, sacred sites, and services provided to tribal people by the government. Because the vast majority of AIAN students now attend public schools, the sovereign status should allow tribes to influence the way that their children are taught. Tribes want their children to receive an education that helps them perpetuate self-governance, culture, and history.

Although AIAN people only make up 1.9% of California's population, California has the largest AIAN population compared to all other states, totaling 723,225 people. In the 2011–2012 school year, AIAN enrollment in K–12 public schools in California was 43,552 or about 0.7% of the overall student body. According to a report using publicly available data by the California Indian Culture and Sovereignty Center, AIAN students have higher high school dropout rates, lower high school graduation rates compared to the average rates of most other ethnic/racial groups. These statistics are similar to the trends of national AIAN academic achievement. In California, 21% of all AIAN people have less than a high school diploma, which is higher than every group outside of Latinos. Of the 2007 cohort who graduated in 2011, only 68% of the AIAN cohort graduated, compared with 76.3% in California overall. Also in 2011, California's overall dropout rate was 14.4%, while the AIAN dropout rate was 20.7% (Proudfit & San Juan, 2012). These educational achievement gaps not only present a social justice problem, but also pose a threat to AIAN tribes' abilities to exercise their sovereign rights to self-determination.

In a 2011 survey of teachers, parents, and leaders of native-focused organizations, 83% said that the state education standards are not adequate in relation to the representation of California Indians in history and social science (Myers-Lim, 2011). The majority of the sample also reported that they felt the current 4th-grade texts representing California Indians pre-European contact, during the mission era, and the gold rush era are not historically accurate nor culturally sensitive. In a 2012 survey of California teachers conducted by the CIMCC, most teachers cited lack of time and funding for materials that are accurate and relevant as their primary challenges to teaching about California tribal history and culture (Myers-Lim, 2012). Teachers also reported other challenges faced in trying to learn about California tribal history and culture, including:

- Lack of hands-on activities
- Restrictions (funding or otherwise) on transportation for field trips
- Lack of access to accurate, updated, and culturally sensitive information
- Difficulty of teaching information that teacher is unfamiliar with
- Outdated material, lack of age-appropriate websites
- Few historical novels that integrate tribal life in a meaningful way
- Large number of tribes
- Generalizing by region
- Presenting the truth without exacerbating ethnic/racial tension

These are common themes among teachers and advocates for addressing historical bias. These themes indicate that we need a holistic approach to this issue. Increasing the sense of belonging by addressing biases can improve academic disparities.

BETTER PRACTICES IN CALIFORNIA

The San Manuel Band of Serrano Mission Indians (hereafter San Manuel) is a federally recognized tribe located in Southern California near the city of Highland. San Manuel, in partnership with Cal State San Bernardino, San Bernardino City Unified School District, and San Bernardino County superintendent of public instruction, facilitates an annual California Indian Cultural Awareness Conference for 3rd- and 4th-grade elementary students in their area. The weeklong conference is held the fourth week of September, at the time of California Native American Day, which was established as an official state holiday in 1998 through AB 1953. It provides information on California Indian culture, with a focus on the culture of the region. Since 1999, nearly 45,000 students, teachers, and community members have attended the conference at California State University San Bernardino (San Manuel, 2012). The week before the conference, San Manuel holds a teachers' workshop to familiarize teachers with the materials that will be presented to their students and provide teachers with resources to integrate California Indian information into their curriculum. The overall theme of the workshop is to help teachers become more analytical and critical of the potential misinformation and omission of Native culture and history in education. San Manuel believes that teachers will be more inclined to include true historical and cultural knowledge with exposure, which creates an ability to make connections.

In 1966, Humboldt State University (HSU) established its commitment to AIAN communities by establishing the Center for Indian Community Development (CICD) to provide services and outreach to tribal communities. In 1969, the Office of Indian Education granted HSU with funds for a program that trained 20 teachers in Indian education. The purpose of the program was to increase the number of AIAN teachers in classrooms, thereby making classrooms better for AIAN students and influencing them to go to college. This was a 4-year program, in which they earned their bachelors and teaching credential including courses in Native American Experience, Native American Education History and Social Historical Implications. They later expanded the program to include other educational personnel because they felt that teachers were too isolated and did not have enough leadership influence (Laura Lee George, personal communication, January 2013). The Title VII funding for this particular program continued until the late 1980s.

Today, Humboldt houses a support program for AIAN students, providing outreach, academic advising, and advocacy for students. Additionally, the Center for Indian Community Development continues to work to improve educational experiences for K–12 AIAN students.

The California Indian Museum and Cultural Center (CIMCC) in Santa Rosa, California, is a resource for the educators in the State of California. The purpose of the CIMCC is to "culturally enrich and benefit the people of California and the general public." . CIMCC goals are "to educate the public about California Indian history and cultures" (https://cimcc.org/about-cimcc/about-us/; para. 2). One of CIMCC's important projects is the Tribal Youth Ambassadors program, which is an intergenerational collaboration engaging Native youth with the wider community of local Native people to share their traditions and celebrate cultural diversity. The program serves two dozen Native youth, empowering them with informed facts and confidence to address bias in school through mentoring from AIAN educators and professionals. CIMCC has many resources for teachers. They have teaching enrichment kits about California Indian history, Native American history, and native language resources. CIMCC also developed a website on California Indians and Spanish missions for K–12 teachers. The website is a clearinghouse of connected and comprehensive California Indian generated information. The site includes storytelling videos, lesson plans, alternative class project ideas, and other resources. Tribal museums and cultural centers such as CIMCC can be important sources for developing social and cultural understanding for local areas.

BEST PRACTICES FROM MONTANA

Montana's commitment to accurate representation began with a constitutional amendment, which was not codified until 30 years after it was enacted. Since the enactment of the Indian Education for All Act in 1999, Montana has created many state codes that prioritize accurate and balanced representation of American Indian history, culture, and governance and the educational experience of AIAN students.

In 1972, by a vote of 99–1, the Montana State Legislature amended Article X of the Montana State Constitution to include a commitment to preserve cultural integrity of American Indians in Montana's definition of "quality education" (Magone & Elser, 2009). Representative Carol Juneau (Hidatsa-Mandan) sponsored House Bill 528, the 1999 Indian Education for All Act, which codified the constitutional amendment, but the bill did not allocate funds for implementation, so the promise remained unfulfilled. The legislature rejected the Office of Public Instruction's (OPI) requests for funding in legislative sessions 2001 and 2003. In response to denial for funding, American Indian elementary students raised more than $7,000 to support programs under the act. Without funding from the state, the Indian Education for All Act would remain an empty promise.

In 2004, eleven school districts, six citizens, and four education groups sued the state of Montana for failing to administer and fund Montana's constitutionally mandated public school system. The Montana Indian Education Association, six tribes, and tribally related public interest groups submitted an amicus brief explaining how the state and local officials mostly ignored the constitutional commitment to preserve cultural integrity of Montana Indian tribes.

In 2005, the legislature allocated $3 million for the OPI and $7 million directly to school districts to implement IEFA. Tribal colleges received $1 million to write tribal historical curriculum. OPI established a Division for Indian Education in 2005 to implement IEFA, expanding the team of people working on IEFA from one person to seven specialists (Magone & Elser, 2009). IEFA offers professional development opportunities to all school personnel, including administrators, support staff, and school board trustees. IEFA requires all school personnel to understand the "Seven Essential Understandings Regarding Montana Indians," which are stated in this text because they are ideal, adaptable standards that can improve teachers' ability to incorporate multiculturalism and to be critical of historical bias:

1. There is great diversity among the 12 tribal Nations of Montana in their languages, cultures, histories and governments. Each Nation has a distinct and unique cultural heritage that contributes to modern Montana.
2. There is great diversity among individual American Indians as identity is developed, defined and redefined by entities, organizations and people. A continuum of Indian identity, unique to each individual, ranges from assimilated to traditional. There is no generic American Indian.

3. The ideologies of Native traditional beliefs and spirituality persist into modern day life as tribal cultures, traditions, and languages are still practiced by many American Indian people and are incorporated into how tribes govern and manage their affairs. Additionally, each tribe has its own oral histories, which are as valid as written histories. These histories pre-date the "discovery" of North America.
4. Reservations are lands that have been reserved by the tribes for their own use through treaties, statutes, and executive orders and were not "given" to them. The principle that land should be acquired from the Indians only through their consent with treaties involved three assumptions:
   a. Both parties to treaties were sovereign powers.
   b. Indian tribes had some form of transferable title to the land.
   c. Acquisition of Indian lands
5. There were many federal policies put into place throughout American history that have affected Indian people and still shape who they are today. Many of these policies conflicted with one another. Much of Indian history can be related through several major federal policy periods:
   – Colonization/Colonial Period 1492–1800s
   – Treaty Period 1789–1871
   – Assimilation Period—Allotment and Boarding School 1879–1934
   – Tribal Reorganization Period 1934-1958
   – Termination and Relocation Period 1953-1971
   – Self-determination Period 1968–Present
6. History is a story most often related through the subjective experience of the teller. With the inclusion of more and varied voices, histories are being rediscovered and revised. History told from an Indian perspective frequently conflicts with the stories mainstream historians tell.
7. Under the American legal system, Indian tribes have sovereign powers, separate and independent from the federal and state governments. However, the extent and breadth of tribal sovereignty is not the same for each tribe (Montana Office of Public Instruction, 2001).

By 2010, approximately 600 AIAN education workshops were delivered to thousands of Montana educators (Carjuzza, et al., 2010). OPI assessed needs continuously through surveys, written responses collected at educational conferences, and evaluation of on-site trainings (Carjuzza et al., 2010). OPI also supplies schools with lesson plans, tribally produced histories, and grants to school districts for developing curriculum in collaboration with tribal personnel. IEFA focuses on authentic literature, so curricula about tribal histories and culture rely on participation from the states 12 tribes, 8 tribal governments, and 7 tribal colleges. In addition to social science and history curricula, curriculum specialists and educators who revise content and performance standards in other subjects work with the OPI Indian Education division to include IEFA content and perspectives.

One of the challenges to IEFA is that teachers feel intimidated by integrating Indian Education material in their curricula because they feel that their Indian education was inadequate. To solve these insecurities OPI does trainings and conferences and has created online resources. For example, since 2005, OPI has been collaborating with University of Montana's (UM) continuing education department and tribal leaders ona graduate course called Indian Education Leadership Training. This project was funded by Montana School districts' grants for materials and personnel development. IEFA's focus on critical literacy rather than "blame, shame, and guilt" improves the program's palatability for Montana educators (Magone & Elser, 2009). Additionally, many educators do not view IEFA simply as a state mandate, but also a funded opportunity to address ethical concerns in a curricular area (Magone & Elser, 2009).

Montana State Code requires the state to provide an IEFA payment to public school districts as part of the BASE (base amount for school equity) budget. These funds may only be used for IEFA purposes. Last year Montana received multiple grants from the Office of Indian Education: Little Big Horn Tribal College, Salish Kootenai College, and Stone Child College received Indian education professional development grant funds (Office of Indian Education, 2015).

CONSTITUTIONAL AMENDMENT AND COMPREHENSIVE REFORM IN CALIFORNIA

Montana provides the most comprehensive model to address the problem of historical bias and the consequential related problems. If California were to follow Montana's model, it would:

1. Amend the state constitution to include preservation of American Indian cultural integrity in the definition of "quality education."
2. Codify the amendment to ensure implementation and funding. In Montana this was called the "Indian Education for All Act." The codes should include:
   – Create an office to coordinate, plan, facilitate, and evaluate better educational resources and professional development for California history, culture and governance.
   – Require all teachers to recognize important elements about AIAN people similar to the "Essential Understanding of Montana Indians."

- Provide grants so that school districts can develop curriculum in collaborations with tribal personnel.
- Provide funding directly to schools for professional development and curriculum planning.
- The activities of the relevant office should consult with a coalition of tribal representatives to ensure adequate cultural authenticity and that the tribes' right are not unintentionally infringed upon.
3. Provide upfront funding to a university to create AIAN history curricula. In Montana, the state funded tribal colleges to develop curriculum. Currently, California does not have any tribal colleges, but the California State University system has shown its commitments to AIAN education in collaboration with tribes and tribal organizations, so they would be ideal candidates for this project.

Comprehensive reform similar to IEFA, which consistently promotes respect, relevance, reciprocity, and responsibility, could be highly effective in California. The programs promote the tenets of multiculturalism and focus on building and sustaining relationships, creating valuable social capital over time. Multiculturalism scholars argue that successful implementation of multicultural education involves the entire school system, so true effectiveness may not occur until the program is fully adopted in every school (Carjuzza et al., 2010).

A constitutional amendment will demonstrate the state's commitment to sustaining and restoring the political and cultural integrity of California Indians. By way of being a state-level entity, the Indian education office will help coordinate the efforts of local tribes and organization in California. Additionally, materials distributed by this office will have authority, ensuring that more teachers will respect tribal perspectives.

Requiring teachers to have a grasp of essential understandings of California Indians will help them integrate lessons and curriculum and cultivate compassion and practical understanding of California Indians. The provision of grants for schools to collaborate with tribes will also create avenues of communication and new opportunities for understanding for educators as well as students. This provision will help tribes exercise their sovereign rights to influence their children's education.

While the other steps in this alternative are the responsibility of the state, tribes rather than the state, should work towards getting the constitutional amendment on the ballot as a proposition. To place a proposition on the ballot, advocates must obtain a two-thirds vote in the California State Legislature to propose it, or initiate it with signatures equivalent to 8% of the votes cast in the last gubernatorial election. The proposition would then have to win by a majority of the votes. All California tribes and many urban AIAN people care strongly about this issue. Casino tribes can leverage their economic resources and political power to campaign California voters. This will also increase the visibility of the problems caused by historical bias.

According to census data, AIAN people are the largest racial/ethnic minority group in Montana, composing of nearly 6.5% of the population. AIAN students comprise 11.6% of Montana's public school population (Montana Office of Public Instruction, 2012). These numbers are important for the prioritization of this education policy issue in Montana. Census data says that AIAN people only comprise 1.7% of California's population. This significantly lower proportion of AIAN people will make the political success of this proposal more difficult. Additionally, California is significantly more diverse compared to Montana. As a smaller part of the population, the ability of comprehensive reform to get passed in California is limited.

This alternative will be very expensive. Montana initially spent $10 million for the first 2 years, including curriculum development and the beginnings of professional development. For the next 2 years, the state appropriated only $3 million for implementation, and there is evidence that tribal colleges acquired federal funding for related activities. The population in California is much larger, so the budget would have to be significantly bigger, but we can learn from Montana by reaching out the federal Office of Indian Education for grant funding. Additionally, we can leverage our resources rather than starting from scratch. Many tribes and organizations such as the Indian Land Tenure Foundation (www.iltf.org) have created valuable curriculum models for California Indian education, and these models can be used to develop an overarching curriculum.

BEST PRACTICES FROM WASHINGTON

Washington State House Bill 1495 strongly encourages school districts to adopt and teach tribal sovereignty and history in the common schools. HB 1495 established the Office of Native Education (ONE), which developed, promotes, and evaluates curricula about tribal sovereignty and the history of federal policy towards federally recognized tribes. ONE also helps districts collaborate with local tribes to incorporate history, culture and government into the curricula. ONE collaborates with Washington State School Directors Association and tribal councils to convene about funding and implementing programs to close achievement gaps. ONE is also responsible for an annual report on Native education. For the purposes of this analysis, we will focus on ONE's online curriculum for grades 4 through 12, "Since Time Immemorial" (STI).

In 2005, Washington passed House Bill 1495, upon realizing the state's failure to meet Washington's 1999 Millennial Accord of "educating the citizens of our state, particularly the youth who are our future leaders, about tribal history, culture, treaty rights, contemporary tribal and state government institutions and relations and the contribution of Indian nations to the state of Washington" (Governor's Office of Indian Affairs, n.d.). STI strives to provide everything that teachers need to confidently teach tribal sovereignty history including materials, lesson plans, support, research, and resources for further study and collaboration. It revolves around the idea that sovereignty is best exercised when tribes are involved in the educational governing affairs of the school systems that education AIAN children (Washington Superintendent of Public Instruction, 2015).

Washington's Office of Public Instruction recommends units about tribal sovereignty for grades 4 through 12. There are three levels of material for teachers to choose from, based on curricular needs and teaching time constraints. The teacher decides how much, in what depth, and how often to include the units. Each level builds upon the last. The curriculum is designed for regular updates, based on frequent collaboration and input from all stakeholders including tribal leaders, school boards, administrators, and educators. It is designed to be easily accessible and low cost for teachers. Figure 18.1 models the way that the curriculum is set up for teachers.

The key to STI materials is their ability to allow tribes to tell their stories in their own words, with the help from educational entities such as the Washington State School Directors Association. The STI materials are available online so that they can be regularly modified, updated, and refined. The meaning of sovereignty shifts as tribal treaty challenges make their way through the court system. A textbook format would make it difficult for the materials to continually change, especially as Washington focuses on teaching about local tribes' histories. These materials are also valuable because they include visual, kinesthetic, and auditory materials for diverse learners.

In 2008, three districts and one tribal school started a pilot program. Since then, ONE has continued developing the curriculum and classroom based assessments. They have also continued their outreach, bringing the curriculum to more schools. ONE has made 45 presentations on the curriculum. In 2009, an additional 18 schools piloted the curriculum. Since 2008, they have held three regional cultural education exchanges annually. From 2009 to 2010, ten inservice training workshops were held. In 2011, Washington received a grant from the Bill and Melinda Gates Foundation for $75,000 to support teacher training, four pilot schools, and the alignment of the curriculum with the newly adopted Common Core Standards.

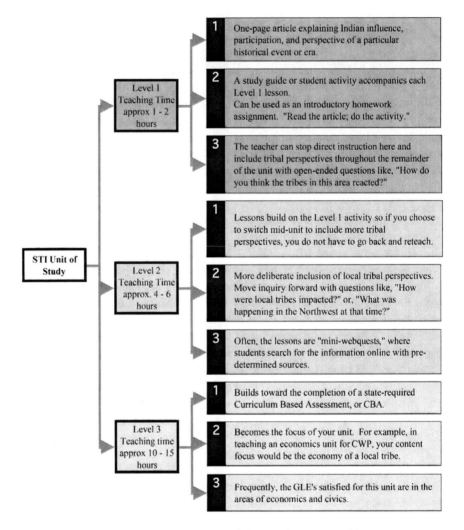

Figure 18.1 Since Time Immemorial: Tribal sovereignty in Washington state (STI) curriculum flow chart.

VOLUNTARY TRIBAL SOVEREIGNTY-BASED CURRICULUM IN CALIFORNIA

Washington provides an approach to challenging historical bias in which the state created a tribal sovereignty focused curriculum and offers it as an option for teachers. If California were to adopt this approach it would:

1. Establish legislation (house bill or senate bill) that expresses the state's intention to improve tribal sovereignty through education representation.
2. Create an office to deal with planning, facilitating, coordinating, and evaluating better curriculum for California Indian history, culture, and governance, but focuses on tribal sovereignty and political/legal history and contemporary relationships of tribes and the government in partnership with tribes. This curriculum should be flexible so that teachers can choose how much time and depth to devote to it. Additionally, this office will:
   - Reach out to school districts, based on needs assessment, to promote this curriculum and the goals of the legislative intention
   - Assist districts in collaborating with local tribes to tailor lesson to local experiences
   - Provide professional development to teach teachers who volunteer to use this curriculum how to integrate it into their lessons
3. Contract with an independent agency or have the relevant office create an annual report on AIAN education.

This would be more effective that the status quo, but the voluntary nature of the alternative will challenge effectiveness. This will provide teachers with education and resources for teaching about AIAN contributions to U.S. history and the relationship between tribes and the government in the past and present. The curriculum development, outreach, and professional development will improve resource accessibility, teachers' confidence in their ability to teach the information, and assurance that the information is relevant to content and performance because it will be sanctioned by the state. Additionally, teachers will appreciate the aspect of flexibility in the curriculum.

Perhaps because of the optional nature of Washington's approach, the majority of Washington school districts have not taken the steps to build a collaborative relationship, this would be a similar challenge in California. Where districts and teachers do decide to use these resources, AIAN students will experience a sense of inclusion. Even if a student experiences some school years with inclusion of the curriculum and some without, they will understand that allies exist within the school system, giving them a sense of hope and inspiration for their academic achievement.

This program will be less costly than comprehensive reform. In Washington, the state provided $20,000 the first year and $50,000 the second (the third year is unclear), and they acquired a grant from the Bill and Melinda Gates Foundation the fourth year. California is much more populous and diverse (i.e., stronger need for ESL curriculum), so the cost will be significantly higher. The initial cost will be a burden, but this will be an investment for the future. California should plan to spend at least $1 million in the first year and decide on the following budget based on curriculum progress and needs assessment (including the variability in participation of tribes and other organizations).

RECOMMENDATION

Because each of the individual state policies does not prove to be effective, equitable, and politically and financially feasible in California, the recommendation is a hybrid model of Montana and Washington. I scale down Montana's comprehensive reform and use Washington's curriculum model to allow for flexibility and possibility of "true native education" in some areas in California. To implement this hybrid model California should:

1. Establish legislation expressing the state's intention to improve representation of AIAN history, culture and governance, following the bill process described in previous sections. This legislation should include:
   - Creation and provision of funding for an office to deal with the planning, facilitation, coordination and evaluation of curricular resources and professional development. This office will also assist tribal and school collaboration.
   - Provision of funding for curriculum development, perhaps through partnership with a university.
   - Formulation of a tribal coalition that can provide input in the curriculum development.
   - Development of a database for educators that provide information on who to contact for more local information, resources and support.
2. Begin to require teaching credential programs to include essential understandings of California Indians.
3. California Indian tribes should work towards a constitutional amendment to include the preservation of the cultural integrity of California Indian tribes.

The legislation will finally demonstrate that state's commitment to alleviating academic achievement gaps, tribal sovereignty, and fulfillment of the trust responsibility. This legislation will build a foundation for adequate resources, relationships, and structures. Tribes will help lobby legislators to get this bill to pass as described in the above sections.

The curriculum should be modeled after Washington's for grades 4 through 12 with three integration levels, but with some differences (Washington Superintendent of Public Instruction, 2015). The Department of

Education should require at least the first level of information for all grades that discuss history, social science, government, and economies as these subjects relate to the United States. Where AIAN history, culture, and governance are not represented, this curriculum will supplement the lessons. In curriculum, lessons, and texts where AIAN information already exists, this curriculum will replace it. This would not require immediately reprinting textbooks, because it will be available online, but this information should be integrated into textbooks as new ones are integrated into the system. With this model, equity concerns still exist but are significantly mitigated. For example, districts in areas where AIAN students have advocates will more likely experience the higher levels of curriculum, but all districts will require at least the first level where it is relevant.

These improved lessons will help AIAN student feel included and stop the cycle of internalizing inferiority. Nonnative students will gain an improved sense of multicultural learning, a practical knowledge of AIAN history, culture, and governance, and respect for their fellow students. This curriculum will stop the perpetuation of improve stereotypes in education.

The office's duties to assist tribal and school collaboration and the development of the database will help tribes exercise their sovereignty. The database will improve equity of implementation, because a primary barrier to collaboration is lack of relationships between educators and tribes and tribal organizations. Creating a new office will take some of the burden of implementation off of school districts and teachers because they will provide training and support. This overarching organization will improve information to all stakeholders and create a stronger collaboration.

Both Washington and Montana require that teachers take an educational unit in American Indian history, culture, and governance while they complete their credentials. By requiring teaching credential programs to include essential understandings of California Indians, new teachers will have a foundation for implementing the curriculum and to teach through a critical lens.

The last recommendation, the constitutional amendment, would go through the same political requirements as discussed in the Montana section. This will demonstrate the state's commitment to AIAN sovereignty and the trust responsibility. The campaign will increase awareness of AIAN people in California, potentially improving the stereotype that AIAN people are extinct or no longer relevant to contemporary realities. California tribes can learn from Montana's experience by maintaining a cohesive political front and invoking the importance of adequate education for the youth. If possible, California tribes should also consider trying to elect at least one of their own to a state legislator office. These actions should follow a more thorough survey of the necessary political barriers to develop a political strategy and implementation phasing.

By implementing this alternative, California AIAN students will experience an improved sense of inclusion in public school classrooms, and teachers will gain knowledge and a critical lens to teach about AIAN history, culture and governance.

Over time this will improve educational achievement for AIAN people, and improve relations between AIAN tribes and nonnative people and governing bodies through increased awareness and understanding. This fundamental change can even help ameliorate AIAN people's feelings of institutional distrust, caused by traumas past and present and educational and governmental experiences.

DEDICATION

This chapter is dedicated to my grandfather, Joe *"Askishiniwish"* Talaugon.

Kiy xutinana'n net 'atiš.
Our struggle is an act of love.

REFERENCES

Aguirre, A., & Turner, J. (2010). *American ethnicity: The dynamics and consequences of discrimination.* New York, NY: McGraw-Hill.

American Indian Education Handbook Committee. (1991). *The American Indian: Yesterday, today, and tomorrow: A handbook for educators.* Sacramento, CA: California Department of Education.

Assembly Bill 1953, California State Assembly, Chaptered September 21, 1998.

Beaulieu, D. (2006). A survey and assessment of culturally based education programs for Native American students in the United States. *Journal of American Indian Education, 45*(2), 50–61.

Carjuzaa, J., Jetty, M., Munson, M., & Veltkamp, T. (2010). Montana's Indian Education for All: Applying multicultural education theory. *Multicultural Perspectives, 12*(4), 192–198.

Columbia Falls Elementary School District et al. v. Montana, no. 04-390 Supreme Court of Montana, 2005 MT 69, 326 Mont. 304, 109 P.3d 257.

Costo, R., & Henry, J. (1970). *Textbooks and the American Indian.* San Francisco, CA: The Indian Historian Press.

Freng, S., Freng, A., & Moore, H. (2007). Examining American Indians' recall of cultural inclusion in school. *Journal of American Indian Education, 46*(2), 42–57.

Getches, D. H., Wilkinson, C. F., Williams, R. A., & Fletcher, M. L. M. (2011). *Cases and materials on Federal Indian law* (6th ed.). St. Paul, MN: West Academic.

Governor's Office of Indian Affairs (n.d.). Institutionalizing the Government-to-Government Relationship in Preparation for the New Millennium. Retrieved from http://www.goia.wa.gov/government-to-government/data/agreement.htm

Hawkins, J. (2005). Smoke signals, Sitting Bulls, and slot machines: A new stereotype of Native Americans? *Multicultural Perspectives, 7*(3), 51–54.

Howard, T. C. (2003). Culturally relevant pedagogy: Ingredients for critical teacher reflection. *Theory into Practice, 42*(3), 195–202.

Locke, S., & Lindley, L. (2007). Rethinking social studies for a critical democracy in American/Alaska Native Education. *Journal of American Indian Education, 46*(2), 1–19.

Magone, M., & Elser, T. (2009). Indian education for all: A change of heart and mind. *International Journal of Educational Management 23*(4), 314–325.

Marquez, B. (2011). *Who's left out? Representations of American Indians in social studies textbooks, 1959–2010.* Stanford, CA: Stanford University School of Education.

MN Statute § 122A.63 (2007), §124D.78 (2001) Minnesota Department of Education, Indian Education. Retrieved from http://education.state.mn.us/MDE/StuSuc/IndianEd/

Montana Office of Public Instruction. (2001). *Essential Understandings Regarding Montana Indians.* Retrieved from http://opi.mt.gov/pdf/indianed/resources/essentialunderstandings.pdf

Montana Office of Public Instruction. (2012). *Montana Public School Enrollment Data.* Retrieved from http://opi.mt.gov/pdf/Measurement/EnrollBook2012.pdf

Myers-Lim, N. (2011). *California Indigenous needs assessment.* Santa Rosa, CA: California Indian Museum and Cultural Center.

Myers-Lim, N. (2012, March). *Mission Education Survey.* Santa Rosa, CA: California Indian Museum and Cultural Center.

Nunez, J., & the California Indian Museum and Cultural Center. (2010). *California Indian enrichment kits: A teacher's guide.* Santa Rosa, CA: Author.

Office of Indian Education. (2015). Announcements and Highlights. Retrieved from https://www2.ed.gov/about/offices/list/oese/oie/index.html

Proudfit, J., & San Juan, S. (2012). *The state of American Indian and Alaskan Native (AIAN) education in California.* San Marcos, CA: California Indian Culture and Sovereignty Center.

San Manuel. (2012). *California Native American Day* [Press release]. Retrieved from https://www.sanmanuel-nsn.gov/Portals/1/News/CNAD%20press%20release_FINAL.pdf

Indian Country Media Network. (2008, April 2). Innovative online course trains Montana teachers in Indian education. Retrieved from https://indiancountrymedianetwork.com/news/innovative-online-course-trains-montana-teachers-in-indian-education-2/

Supahan, S. (1999). *Points of view vs. historical bias: Recognizing bias in texts about Native Americans.* Hoopa, CA: Klamath–Trinity Joint Unified School District's Indian Education Program.

Washington Superintendent of Public Instruction. (2015). Since time immemorial. Retrieved from http://www.k12.wa.us/IndianEd/TribalSovereignty/

ABOUT THE CONTRIBUTORS

Tamara Alexander is a proud member of the Karuk Tribe. She has been involved in the early childhood education field for nine years and has taught in the Tribal Head Start program for six years. She attended her tribe's head start program when she was three years old and now is able to say she works for that very same head start program. Tamara finds it to be a joy to be part of the first school setting children are exposed to. Being able to work within tribal communities is such a rewarding experience for her—allowing her to give back to her community.

Dr. Kishan Lara-Cooper, PhD, is a member of the Yurok Tribe and a descendant of the Hoopa Valley and Karuk tribes of northern California. She is an assistant professor of middle childhood development and language development in the department of child development at Humboldt State University. She coordinates the minor of American Indian education program and teaches courses in history, social and cultural considerations, and instructional practices in American Indian education.

Ayukîi. Nani aaréek **íimshaapaneech**. Naa káruk **áraara**, káru vúra má'su'araara. Naa káru nani'áraaras kah'tim'îin káru uutim'îin nu'aramsîiprivti. Naa káru nani'áraaras Bootlers. **André Cramblit** is an enrolled member of the Karuk Tribe from the Klamath and Salmon Rivers in far NW California on the Oregon border. He is from the villages of Katimiin (upper falls) and Utimiin (lower falls). He comes from a family of Dance Makers whose allotment is at Butlers Flat on the Salmon River. He has danced in the Brush Dance, Flower Dance, War Dance, and the Pikiyavish (World Renewal) Dance, and

On Indian Ground: California, pages 263–269
Copyright © 2017 by Information Age Publishing
All rights of reproduction in any form reserved.

he participated in a Jump Dance to reclaim tribal land during the GO Road Supreme Court Case. He is a traditional storyteller, gambler, and singer/ drummer.

For 30 years he has been involved in American Indian Education at all levels (teacher's aid, bus driver, K–12 teacher, Head Start teacher and director, college instructor, principal, and tribal education director). In addition to his baccalaureate in sociology/education from Dartmouth College he has earned a teaching credential from Humboldt State University. André has served as the chair of the Karuk Language Restoration Committee since 1990. He became a founding member of the California American Indian Education Oversight Committee in 2007 and still is a member of that committee. He serves as a trustee of the California Indian Legal Services. He has written a policy briefing on implementing Common Core State Standards with American Indian students and is currently the operations director for the Northern California Indian Development Council (http://www.ncidc. org). He lives in Arcata, CA with wife Wendy and son Kyle and continues to be counseled by traditional leaders as well as academics.

Rodney Beaulieu is from Acadian Mi'kmaq heritage from Canada and the United States. His undergraduate training is in Human Services and Psychology, and his PhD is in Educational Psychology from the University of California, Santa Barbara. He teaches in the College of Education, Health, and Human Services at California State University San Marcos, and his professional history includes educational administration and healthcare administration. Rodney helped to develop educational programs in Canada, the United States, Mexico, China, and Saudi Arabia. He was awarded "Best Dissertation" from the Amercian Sociological Association, raised funds for educational programs and the Food Bank, and volunteered for several nonprofit organizations. His research interests are action oriented, focusing on ways to improve personal development, organizations, and communities.

Tomio Endo is a project coordinator at the California Indian Museum and Cultural Center in Santa Rosa, CA. As a linguistic anthropologist, Tomio's research interests include researching processes of cultural transmission and emergence within sustainable systems within local, global, and digital lingua-cultural communities; understanding the impacts of linguistic ideology in Native American linguistic communities; providing technical support for language and cultural revitalization efforts in Native Californian speech communities; developing participatory research approaches in language revitalization and documentation utilizing software and digital technology; and examining current ethics, theory, and practice of anthropological research in indigenous contexts.

Dr. Theresa Lynn Gregor, PhD, is a descendant of the Iipay Nation of Santa Ysabel (Kumeyaay). She grew up on the Santa Ysabel Indian Reservation in Northern San Diego County and she maintains close connection with her tribal community.

Theresa is an adjunct professor in the American Indian studies department at Cal State University–San Marcos and she is the associate researcher for the California Indian Culture and Sovereignty Center, where she researched and wrote the annual State of American Indian and Alaska Native Education report (2014–2016). She is also the executive director for the Inter-Tribal Long Term Recovery Foundation (ITLTRF), which has a mission to strengthen and enhance the coordination of emergency preparedness and disaster recovery services for tribes in Southern California.

Kristy Harmon is a proud wife and mother of four. She has been involved in the early childhood education field for eight years and teaching in Tribal Head Start program for five years. Working with children and families is not only her chosen career, but also her passion.

Mikela Jones is a member of the Little River Band of Pomo Indians located in Northern California. Though he is not a member, he is also a relative of the Paiute Shoshone Tribe in Owyhee Nevada. Mikela has received his Bachelors of Arts from CSU–Sacramento in philosophy with an emphasis on ethics and applied law. He was the first male from his tribe to earn a four-year degree. Mikela has also earned a Master's of Science from San Diego State University in school counseling and became the first person from his tribe to earn a Master's degree. As of now, Mikela works as principal for the United Auburn Indian Community Tribal School outside of Sacramento, CA. In his spare time he does his own consulting, providing trainings on youth leadership, wellness, and motivation. He has been doing community wellness and leadership trainings for over 10 years. Mikela has lived by these words: "Success is not by chance, but by choice." Therefore, he is making the decision to succeed and promotes this philosophy to Indian Country.

Melissa Leal, PhD, is Esselen and Ohlone and grew up in Sacramento, CA. She earned her PhD in Native American Studies from the University of California–Davis in 2012. Her research includes the reciprocal relationship between hip hop culture and Indigenous youth with an emphasis on performance, education, and film. She has worked with American Indian youth in the education field for more than 15 years. She is the lead researcher and advisory board coordinator for *Rebel Music: Native America*, an MTV World documentary. She teaches culture, language, and dance for various tribal communities in Northern California. She is a poet, dancer, and author. She believes in the power and necessity of revitalizing indigenous languages. She has taught Native American Film and Cinema at California State University–Sonoma and currently teaches Ethnic Images in Film at Sierra College. She is the executive director of education for Wilton Rancheria.

Gerald A. Lieberman, PhD, is an internationally recognized authority on school improvement using natural and community surroundings as interdisciplinary contexts. Over the past 30 years, he has created and conducted professional development programs for more than 10,000 educators and other professionals, working with formal education systems at local, state, national, and international levels. Dr. Lieberman's newest book, *Education and the Environment: Creating Standards-Based Programs for Schools and Districts*, was recently published by Harvard Education Press. From 2003 to 2010, Dr. Lieberman served as the educational leader for the State of California's Education and the Environment Initiative, a cooperative endeavor of the California Environmental Protection Agency, the California Department of Education, the State Board of Education, the governor's secretary of education, the Integrated Waste Management Board, and the California Natural Resources Agency.

Dr. Lieberman received his PhD and MA from Princeton University and his BA from UCLA. He is a past chair of the Commission on Education and Communication of IUCN, the International Union for Conservation of Nature. He lives in Poway, California.

Nicole Lim is Pomo from Northern California. She received her Bachelor of Arts Degree from the University of California at Berkeley and a Juris Doctorate from the University of San Francisco School of Law. She has worked for the National Indian Justice Center and the California Indian Museum and Cultural Center over the past 15 years. During the summer of 1998, she interned at the U.S. EPA Region IX Indian Programs Office, and she has taught undergraduate courses on U.S. law and American Indians at San Francisco State University. She also served as an assistant professor of ethnic studies, Native American program at Sacramento State University. She is the director of community relations for Naqmayam Communications, an Indian-owned and -operated public relations firm that handles accounts with tribes, tribal organizations and corporations that seek visibility in Indian Country. Ms. Lim conducts training for NIJC's regional and on-site training programs in the subject matter of fetal alcohol syndrome and its impact on justice systems, juvenile delinquency and gang violence, and federal Indian law. She also is the executive director of the California Indian Museum and Cultural Center. She directs programs for education/curricular reform, exhibition development, native language revitalization, and tribal youth enrichment. In 2014 she was appointed to the 4th District Agricultural Association's Sonoma-Marin Fair Board, and she serves as the co-chair of the government relations committee for the California Association of Museums.

Deborah J. Morton, PhD, is an assistant professor in the master of public health program at CSUSM and associate professor emeritus from the department of family and preventive medicine, division of epidemiology at University of California, San Diego. As an epidemiologist, Dr. Morton has a long history of varied research experience in many areas of public health/medicine such as diabetes, osteoporosis, arthritis, cardiovascular disease, obesity, and tobacco use, primarily in ethnic and sexual minority populations, and has authored or coauthored over 70 publications in scientific journals. In 2005, she was given the UCSD Chancellor's Diversity Award for her work in the LGBT community. Dr. Morton is also currently affiliated faculty with the department of American Indian studies and the California Indian Culture and Sovereignty Center (CICSC) at CSUSM.

In the tribal/reservation community in San Diego County, Dr. Morton has a long collaboration with Indian Health Council, an American Indian health clinic owned and operated by nine tribes. Dr. Morton is Founder and current chair of the clinic's own tribally based institutional review board (IRB) created in 2004. This tribal IRB has reviewed and supported many research projects whose results have had direct benefits for the Indian clinic and their tribal community patient population. This tribally based IRB has established a positive bridge between tribal people and academic researchers, not an easy task due to many historical abuses in Indian Country by unethical scientists and health researchers.

Joely Proudfit, PhD, is a descendant of the Pechanga band of Luiseño Mission Indians. Dr. Proudfit holds an MA and PhD in political science with emphasis in public policy and American Indian studies from Northern Arizona University and a BA in political science with emphasis in public law from California State University Long Beach. As the first member of her family to complete a high school diploma, she serves as a role model for Native youth and encourages self-determination through knowledge and education. In fall 2008, she joined the faculty at CSU San Marcos as program coordinator for Native Studies. She now serves as department chair of the newly established American Indian Studies department. Dr. Proudfit is also the director of the California Indian Culture and Sovereignty Center (CICSC) at CSUSM.

Dr. Proudfit is the owner of Naqmayam Communications, an independent, full-service, California Indian-owned and -operated public relations agency. Dr. Proudfit is also the founder and executive director of the California's American Indian & Indigenous Film Festival. Dr. Proudfit, Chris Eyre (director/producer) and Heather Rae (producer) recently formed Native Networkers, an alliance to promote American Indian representation throughout the film industry. Additionally, President Barack Obama appointed Dr. Proudfit in February 2016 to the National Advisory Council on Indian Education.

Stanley Ralph Rodriguez is a member of the Santa Ysabel Band of the Iipay Nation. Stan holds the office as legislator for the band. Stan is a board member for California Indian Storytellers Association and for Advocates for Indigenous California Language Survival and has participated in the master apprentice program. Stan is a proponent for language immersion and developing oral situational fluency as a primary goal for language instruction. Stan was the prior chairman of the board of trustees for D-Q University and is on the board of trustees for Kumeyaay Community College. He has taught the iipay/Kumeyaay language on the following reservations: Manzanita, Santa Ysabel, San Pasqual, Barona, Viejas, Sycuan La Posta, and Mesa Grande. He also teaches at Kumeyaay Community College and Cuyamuca Community College. Stan has also assisted in developing lesson plans and instruction for Kumeyaay communities in Baja California and for communities throughout California. He has conducted language training for ILI in New Mexico ALDI at the University of Arizona in Tucson, and NWILI at the University of Oregon. Stan has also conducted language training in Canada and Australia and worked with the Seneca nation in New York and the Aleut nation in Kodiak Alaska. Stan teaches traditional tool making and participated in various documentaries, one that received an Emmy for best documentary 2014 and another that was nominated for an Emmy for best documentary 2015. Stan has done presentations for the University of Southern Denmark and participated in the folk life festival for the Smithsonian Institute in Washington, DC and has worked with the Audrey Museum in Los Angeles, CA. Stan has a master's degree in human behavior and at the present time is a doctoral student at UCSD. Stan is a Navy Desert Storm veteran with 9 years honorable active service. Stan currently teaches counseling techniques at the Navy Drug and Alcohol Counselors School in San Diego, CA and has taught various courses for the department of defense in the following regions: Japan, Korea, Singapore, Australia, Diego Garcia, Guam, Okinawa, Bahrain, Sicily, Canada, and Papua New Guinea.

Nicolasa I. Sandoval, PhD, is education director for the Santa Ynez Band of Chumash Indians and a lecturer in the education department at the University of California at Santa Barbara. In 2013, Governor Edmund G. Brown appointed her to the California State Board of Education, which sets K–12 education policy in the areas of standards, curriculum, instructional materials, assessment, and accountability. Sandoval serves on the boards of the Santa Barbara Foundation and UCSB Alumni Association. Sandoval holds a PhD in education from UCSB, an MA in museum studies from the George Washington University, and a BA in public relations from Pepperdine University.

Sabine Nicole Talaugon is a descendant of the Santa Ynez Band of Chumash Indians, and received her bachelor's degree from Mills College in 2012 and her Master's in Public Policy in 2013. During her undergraduate and graduate work, she had the opportunity to work in the fields of education and health. Her master's thesis about addressing anti-Indian bias in California public schools, written for the California Indian Museum and Cultural Center, received a Public Policy Outstanding Thesis Award in 2013. After graduate school, she pursued health policy, serving as the Director of Programs & Evaluation at the California Consortium for Urban Indian Health. She currently consults under Iwex Consulting and serves on the Board of Intertribal Friendship House in Oakland, CA. Through Iwex Consulting, she practices policy analysis and program evaluation. In the Samala Chumash language, "iwex" means to grind in a mortar, a word chosen to represent a piece of the work done to build resiliency and self-determination for our communities.

Hunwut Temet Michael Turner is an enrolled member of the Rincon Band of Luiseno Indians, who was raised his whole life on the Rincon Indian Reservation. Turner has a bachelor's degree in political science with a minor in public administration. Turner taught high school at Under the Oaks high school located on the Rincon Indian Reservation, for two years. Turner has, for the past 18 years, worked for the Rincon Indian Education Center, a not-for-profit organization established in 1974.

Mr. Turner has worked on numerous language and educational projects with Southern California tribes. He has produced six children's books in the Luiseno language. He wrote and ran the Rincon Even Start program, the Carol M. White Physical Education program, and the American Indian Education program.

Tishmall Turner is a Rincon Band of Luiseño Indians tribal member. Ms. Turner is the first full-time appointed California Indian tribal liaison in the California State University System. As a tribal liaison for California State University–San Marcos, she provides guidance to the university president, other campus administrators, and faculty to improve institutional relationships with California tribal communities. In addition to her responsibilities as a liaison, she regularly mentors American Indian students and conducts outreach to tribal youth about higher education. Ms. Turner serves on numerous boards and committees, such as the Rincon Economic Development Corporation board of directors, Palomar Health Foundation board, and the National Museum of American Indian National advisory council. Her professional memberships include the National Indian Education Association and Leadership North County Alumni Association, and she is an honorary member of the All Tribes American Indian Charter School Future Farmers of America. She has assisted in publishing children's books and annual calendars in the Luiseño language among other cultural projects.

CPSIA information can be obtained
at www.ICGtesting.com
Printed in the USA
LVOW08s2236130917
548674LV00001B/1/P